Memoirs of an Agent for Change in International Development

Memoirs and Occasional Papers
Association for Diplomatic Studies and Training

In 2003, the Association for Diplomatic Studies and Training (ADST) created the Memoirs and Occasional Papers Series to preserve firsthand accounts and other informed observations on foreign affairs for scholars, journalists, and the general public. Sponsoring publication of book series is one of the ways in which ADST, a nonprofit organization founded in 1986, seeks to promote understanding of American diplomacy and those who conduct it. Together with the Foreign Affairs Oral History program and ADST's support for the training at the State Department's Foreign Service Institute, these efforts constitute the Association's fundamental purposes. Ludwig Rudel's account of his origins, government service in USAID, and post-government development efforts comprise the 28th volume in the series.

SELECTED SERIES TITLES

- Claudia Anyaso, ed., *FIFTY YEARS OF U.S. AFRICA POLICY*
- Janet Ballantyne and Maureen Dugan, eds., *50 YEARS IN USAID: Stories from the Front Lines*
- Thompson Buchanan, *MOSSY MEMOIR OF A ROLLING STONE*
- J. Chapman Chester, *FROM FOGGY BOTTOM TO CAPITOL HILL Exploits of a G.I., Diplomat, and Congressional Aide*
- John Gunther Dean, *DANGER ZONES: A Diplomat's Fight for America's Interests*
- Robert E. Gribbin, *IN THE AFTERMATH OF GENOCIDE: The U.S. Role in Rwanda*
- Allen C. Hansen, *NINE LIVES, A FOREIGN SERVICE ODYSSEY*
- John G. Kormann, *ECHOES OF A DISTANT CLARION: Recollections of a Diplomat and Soldier*
- Armin Meyer, *QUIET DIPLOMACY: From Cairo to Tokyo in the Twilight of Imperialism*
- William Morgan and Charles Stuart Kennedy, eds., *AMERICAN DIPLOMATS: The Foreign Service at Work*
- Howard L. Steele, *BUSHELS AND BALES: A Food Soldier in the Cold War*
- Daniel Whitman, *A HAITI CHRONICLE: The Undoing of a Latent Democracy*
- Susan Clough Wyatt, *ARABIAN NIGHTS AND DAZE: Living in Yemen with the Foreign Service*

For a complete list of series titles, visit <adst.org/publications>

For John:

THE VERY JOHN McDONALD CITED IN THE "ACKNOWLEDGEMENTS" OF THIS BOOK, WITH GRATITUDE AND RESPECT.

11/12/15

Memoirs of an Agent for Change in International Development

My Flight Path into the 21st Century

Ludwig "Lu" Rudel

Memoirs and Occasional Papers Series
Association for Diplomatic Studies and Training

Arlington Hall Press
Arlington, Virginia

Arlington Hall Press is an imprint of the Association for Diplomatic Studies and Training <www.adst.org>.

   Excerpts from "Le West End," "Heil Wien! Heil Berlin," "Literally Zero," and "An Ideal Spot for Mass Marches" are from The Hare with Amber Eyes by Edmund de Waal. Copyright 2010 by Edmund de Waal. Reprinted by permission of Farrar, Straus and Giroux, LLC

   The six photos appearing on the book cover, all photographed by the author, are, from top left to right: Topkapi on the Bosphorus; statue of Atatürk in Ankara; Taj Mahal in India; Pink Palace in Jaipur; Belly Dancer in Ankara; and flight by author over the Giza pyramids in Egypt.
   The photograph of the author, appearing on the back cover, is provided by courtesy of the photographer, Joan M. Rudel.
   Additional photos corresponding to the events described in the following chapters may be accessed through the website: www.rudel.net.

ISBN: 0965394948
ISBN 13: 9780965394949
Library of Congress Control Number: 2014909689
LCCN Imprint Name: Arlington Hall Press, Arlington, VA

**These writings are dedicated to my adopted and beloved country,
The United States of America**

It is said that an eastern monarch once charged his wise men to invent for him a sentence, to be ever in view, and which should be true and appropriate in all times and situations. They presented him the words: *'And this too, shall pass away.'* How much it expresses! How chastening in the hour of pride! How consoling in the depths of affliction! *'And this, too, shall pass away.*

And yet, let us hope it is not quite true. Let us hope, rather, that by the best cultivation of the physical world beneath and around us, and the best intellectual and moral world within us, we shall secure an individual, social and political prosperity and happiness, whose course shall be onward and upward, and which, while the earth endures, shall not pass away.

—ABRAHAM LINCOLN, Speech delivered on
September 30, 1859, Milwaukee, Wisconsin

CONTENTS

Photos that accompany the text may be accessed at the website: www. rudel.net

ANNEXES

PREFACE

THE QUEST FOR IMMORTALITY runs deep in the human spirit. We want to leave something behind to mark our short visit to this planet. At a minimum, one may erect a tombstone. Others manage a park bench with a plaque. Those who are lucky in life, or accomplished––or both––may have the wing of a hospital, or a museum, named after them. Then there are those who choose to leave behind some written words for their progeny.

The following stories describe a few of my life's experiences. They were written primarily for "the eight cousins" (our grandchildren) in the hope that someday, they may find within them, one or two useful lessons. I have drawn, perhaps too heavily, on history to avoid the conceit that we are somehow smarter than our ancestors; that we of this generation have somehow been given to see the truth while such insight escaped the notice of our forebears.

A word of caution to the reader: this is a collection of memories. I have attempted to maintain accuracy in the retelling of these stories. But every sentence has not been "fact checked" or researched. Some people have argued that writing about the past, drawing on one's fallible memory, can reshuffle events and paint a somewhat different picture of what happened. Maybe that's why we write memoirs. It gives us a second chance to describe what happened to "the real me." I have exercised every precaution available in my cerebral armory to avoid that pitfall.

Each chapter of this book is a short story. Together they track the flight path followed by my life. The phrase "flight path" has multiple meanings. It refers to (a) my escape from Austria in 1938, (b) the changes, during my lifetime, in direction and velocity taken by four powerful global forces described herein (population, science and technology, political structures, and economic systems), and (c) the pleasure and freedom of flying my own aircraft.

Part One briefly describes my early life and migration to the United States. Part Two focuses on my military service and my career in the U.S. Foreign Service working on economic aid -- primarily in Iran, Turkey, and India-- plus a few of the thirty-seven short-term consultancies on international economic development performed following my retirement from USAID.

Part Three describes my effort to apply the principles of economic aid to a project I undertook privately in the poorer sections of Appalachia. It was a second career for me as I took on the role of an entrepreneur in the U.S. private sector. It offers a few insights concerning the likely future of small-scale enterprise and the government's role with respect to regulation of the economy.

Part Four offers some thoughts that may have relevance to vexing issues in international economic development, politics, and trade. It summarizes some of the key lessons I learned and observations I made with respect to the business of foreign economic assistance, and provides a summary of my conclusions drawn from this body of work. At the end, I offer a few predictions concerning the direction to which present trends are pointing.

ACKNOWLEDGMENTS

It is a pleasure for me to acknowledge the contributions of many to this book. The editorial staff and volunteer readers of ADST, most notably Margery Boichel Thompson and Batul K. Sadliwala, were of great assistance in bringing this book to an acceptable standard for others to examine. Prior to that, for three long years, as the structure of these stories accumulated, first in my brain, then on paper, Ms. S. C. Lynch patiently discussed the thoughts and reflections that have gone into this publication, offered criticism and advice, and encouraged me to continue the process. But, in the final analysis, it was the remarkable people who were my teachers––Oscar Janowsky, Raymond Paige, Lewis Snyder––and those with whom I shared professional labors in the course of my life––Bill White, Emin Boysan, W. Carter Ide, Ray Thurston, Stuart VanDyke, John P. Lewis, John MacDonald, Irving Rosenthal, Hajime Hayashi, Art Wilkin, George Baranik, and Bill Barnhart––that helped me navigate through some difficult passages and caused me to gain many remarkable insights.

Acronyms and Abbreviations

ADST	Association for Diplomatic Studies and Training
AFSA	American Foreign Service Association
AIOC	Anglo-Iranian Oil Company
AID	Agency for International Development
ATA	American Theater Association (India)
BA	Bachelor of Arts degree
CCNY	City College of New York
CIA	United States Central Intelligence Agency
CQ	Charge of Quarters (military term)
CT	Country Team
DEA	Department of Economic Affairs, Government of India
FAO	UN Food and Agriculture Organization
G-77	Group of 77 or non aligned nations
GDP	Gross Domestic Product
IBRD	International Bank for Reconstruction and Development (the World Bank)
ICA	International Cooperation Administration
IMF	International Monetary Fund
IO/STATE	Bureau for International Organizations, Department of State
MA	Master of Arts degree
MATS	Military Air Transport Service
MDG	Millennium Development Goals
MP	Military Police
NCAER	National Council for Applied Economic Research, India

NIEO	New International Economic Order
NYSE	New York Stock Exchange
NYU	New York University
O&M	Organization and Methods Office
ODA	Official Development Assistance
POA	Property Owners Association
PPC/AID	Bureau for Policy and Program Coordination at AID
RCA	Radio Corporation of America
RIF	Reduction in Force
ROTC	Reserve Officer Training Corps, US Army
TA	technical assistance
TMO	Toprak Masuleri Ofici (Turkish grain import and storage agency)
UN	United Nations
UNDP	UN Development Program
UNIDO	UN Industrial Development Organization
USDA	United States Department of Agriculture
WHO	UN World Health Organization

MEMOIRS OF AN AGENT FOR CHANGE IN INTERNATIONAL DEVELOPMENT

My Flight Path into the 21st Century

INTRODUCTION
AND OVERVIEW

*"Life can only be understood backward. But it must be lived
forward."*
--KIERKEGAARD

*EVERY YEAR, IN THE spring, we observe the two-hundred-year-old maple tree
behind our house sprouting its colorful blossoms before the green leaves
make their appearance. All summer, each leaf thrives in its chlorophyll-
tinted anonymous form, surrounded by neighboring leaves, each performing its photosynthetic task of producing oxygen. Throughout the brief
season of its life it basks in the sunshine, plays host to insects and birds,
bends to the winds and storms that fortune and nature inflict on it. But then
comes autumn. The green recedes and each leaf's true, individual colors
break through. Its reds and yellows and browns, which had been there all
along, hidden behind the chlorophyll, become visible, together with the
blemishes derived from its life experience; all is revealed to the naked eye.*

*My life has reached that very point now, no longer any need to hide
behind the chlorophyll. It is a time to reflect on the past, to search for
Kirkegaard's "understandings," before the leaf falls.*

I marvel at my own good fortune when comparing the standard of living
I have enjoyed with that of my ancestors. Lady luck has, on several occasions, granted me wonderful opportunities to improve my well-being. She

has also saved me from what could otherwise have been an early demise. Somehow, fate smiled at me; luck (perhaps along with skill, or perseverance, or who knows what) has brought me safely through life's rough patches.

Here is a photo of my family taken in 1928 in Vienna, Austria, two years before I was born. Of the nine persons shown, only the little boy in the sailor suit, my brother Julius, was still alive as I wrote this.

I was born in July of 1930 and joined this family in Vienna. Now, eighty-four years later, I find myself in Washington, D.C. It has been an interesting journey through time and space. During my lifetime four critical aspects of Western society have undergone unprecedented changes. And there are no realistic possibilities for any significant reversal of these changes that have occurred:

1. On the day the stork brought me into this world, the population of this planet stood at slightly over two billion souls. It had never before been that populous. It would almost quadruple in my lifetime.

2. Rapid scientific and technological discoveries of the Industrial Revolution, said to have begun around the time the cotton gin was invented in 1794, caused this population increase. Clean water, medical treatment for disease, improvements in shelter, and higher food production yields brought about sharply reduced infant mortality, increased human longevity, and created more adequate food supplies. By the time of my birth, despite high worldwide unemployment, many people were able to enjoy new benefits such as x-rays, electric lights, refrigeration, pasteurization, radio and telegraph transmission, airplanes (although the Douglas DC-3 was yet to be built), trains and automobiles, central heating, and indoor plumbing. These new creature comforts contrasted with those that had been available to my forebears in the recent past. The future offered "better living through chemistry."

3. Shortly before my birth, the economies of most of the Western world had fallen into a global depression. Many questioned the reliability and inequality of boom-and-bust capitalism and of the market mechanism. Some saw the Russian Revolution and socialism as the antidote to the abuses of the "robber barons." The magic of mass production, with its economies of scale, and scientific discoveries and innovation were changing the structure of the workplace, as surplus agricultural labor moved to the cities to work in factories. The labor movement was taking hold. Some thought capitalism was crumbling, as Marx had predicted.

4. Twelve years before my birth the political structures of most Western nations changed as well. Systems based on popularly accepted monarchic rule, where occasionally the monarch's absolute authority had been mitigated by restrictions embodied in written or unwritten constitutions, gave way to a radically different system of participatory and representative government, patterned after the systems of France and the United States.

World War I had ended in 1918 and with it the five-hundred-year reign of the Habsburgs, resulting in the dissolution of the Austro-Hungarian Empire. The German Empire had ended as well and Kaiser Wilhelm was gone. The Ottoman Empire, which had ruled the Balkans and the Middle East for five hundred years, had disintegrated. The Russian Revolution (1917) ended the three-hundred-year reign of the Romanovs. For many centuries absolute authority had been vested in the tsar, the kaiser, the king, the sultan, and the shah, and their subjects had generally accepted their authority. Alliances had been formed through the intermarriage of royals. The ruling class had received extensive tutoring in the expectation (or at least the hope) that they would rule wisely. By 1930, it was still unclear how the new democratic structures of government could be made to work in most nations.

Profound changes have taken place in each of these four areas during my lifetime. The enormity of these changes astounds. In the history of this planet no other period of similar length has experienced changes of this magnitude. Technology has achieved advances that were unimaginable in my grandparents' day. We shall return to these four critical aspects of Western societal structure as they evolved during my lifetime and address them again in chapter 12, "Conclusions and Implications for the Future."

During the course of the past eighty-four years, several important course corrections have occurred with respect to my life. At least three derived from unanticipated events that demanded a rethinking, "second thoughts" applied to previously unquestioned assumptions. These incidents, as I relate them, may prove to be useful learning moments for the reader. They certainly were important for me.

A confluence of global events propelled me to attain citizenship in the world's safest, wealthiest nation, one that has offered the greatest opportunities for individual freedom and entrepreneurship. I had the good fortune to engage in two careers: one inside the

U.S. government focusing on international relations, the other as an entrepreneur who built a thousand-acre land development in rural Pennsylvania. These experiences have given me some insight that I would like to share. They may provide some enlightenment about new challenges for our society, some facing us now, and others likely to arise in the future.

Today there are massive clouds on our political horizon. It is as though my life has been timed perfectly to enjoy the benefits of modernization, while succeeding generations will have to face its consequences.

I write this memoir to provide a substitute for the lack of "overlap" in my family. The Talmud tells us that it is the responsibility of each parent to pass on to one's children the clan's (or family's) history and traditions. Before this nuclear age, when families lived closer together, there was more contact between elders and the younger generation. Opportunities to pass on family stories, anecdotes, and ethnic histories abounded. Today, children leave the family home at eighteen, either to go to college or to strike out on their own. The opportunities for overlap have diminished.

I can remember my mother cautioning me that I would some day regret not taking the time to ask about her life and that of my father. Thinking back, I realize that she must have had her own regrets about not making similar inquiries of her parents. That subtlety was lost on me until recently. It is a part of the human condition that we tend to remember the things we do for others and tend to forget the things others do for us. I realize now that I owe these writings to my progeny. Here is my attempt to fulfill that obligation.

PART ONE

THE IMMIGRATION — 1930 TO 1953

1

LIFE'S BEGINNINGS

MY MEMORIES OF EARLY childhood would be a big disappointment to Sigmund Freud. Doubtless, he would regard the dearth of recollections as a sign that, even now, I have not worked out the sources of my dysfunctional behavior. Early childhood for me is a montage of our fourth-floor walk-up apartment in Vienna, Austria, with its gently shaped iron window guards meant to keep me from falling out as I strained to view the taxi rank on the street below, a representation of ultimate luxury we never used. Then there was my brother Julius, my only sibling and nine years my elder, who, according to my mother, could do no wrong––ever, and who practiced the piano in the "entertainment room," where I was not allowed to play. There were his hand-me-down toys that I could never work as well and Dr. Klar, Jul's piano teacher, who tried to give me lessons and promptly gave up. There were also the live-in servant girls who, from time to time, were mysteriously replaced when my brother perhaps showed signs of becoming too interested in them. There are some glimpses of summer vacations spent in the countryside, usually at resorts sponsored by my father's employer, the Phoenix Insurance Company. There are visions of grade school, with but one other Jewish child in my class. (He was my only friend and the limited extent of my social scene). Finally, there was my perpetually ailing father, who died of pancreatic cancer at the age of forty-nine in December 1937.

I have no vivid memory of my father, only that he prayed at home every morning and evening and at the synagogue on the Sabbath. I recall walking with my mother from the apartment to the park. We did not sit on the chairs or benches, as we could not afford the charge to do so. Only occasionally, because of my weariness (or laziness), would we ride the tram to the park, as that fare also was too great an expense.

I believe our family, as was typical of most European families, took primogeniture as the norm. The first-born son was given the best of everything. Jul had enormous musical talent, which had been recognized early. His musical studies and piano playing were always an important part of our family dynamic. And this tendency was intensified by my father's death, which catapulted Jul, at age sixteen, to the position of master of the house.

There was a sense of secrecy that excluded me from matters concerning our family's well-being, probably intended to protect me from the stress of family problems. When my father died, I was sent to a friend's house for several days to spare me the knowledge of what had happened. Jul picked me up days later to take me home via streetcar. I asked him what his black armband represented. He told me it was the latest style. One of my most vivid early memories is the expression on another passenger's face when he said that.

FAMILY HISTORY

Although I did not consider myself to be spiritually linked to the Jewish People, I realize now that my heritage is typical of "The Wandering Jew." I have lived almost my entire life as an American. But had there been no German invasion of Austria in 1938—leading to World War II—I would have lived my life in Vienna. Had there been no World War I in 1914, I would have lived in Czernowitz, a city in the Austro-Hungarian Empire. Had Poland not been partitioned in the 1790s or had there been no Polish revolt against the Russians in 1830, I would have lived my life in Galicia (Poland). My family's roots have been torn up with each new search for refuge.

I have long been fascinated by our family history, particularly the nineteenth-century chapters. Both of my parents, born around 1890, grew up in Bojan (pronounced Boyan), a village near Czernowitz at the eastern reaches of the Austro-Hungarian Empire, and lived there until the outbreak of the First World War. They were in their twenties when they moved to Vienna. What were their lives like in their formative years during that pre-war period, I wonder?

Researching Jewish genealogy in Austria-Hungary before 1786 is almost impossible. It was in that year that it was decreed that all persons in Austria-Hungary must adopt a family name as part of the process of conducting the population census. Before 1786, Jews had no last names. They went by first names only, with their father's name as the second name. There was no "family name." My name would have been Ludwig, son of Jacob (Eliezer ben Jakub). My son's name would have been David, son of Ludwig (Dovid ben Eliezer). The patronym changed with each generation.

Jewish history describes periods of normalcy and good living in various regions that usually ended in violence, such as expulsion (Spain in 1492) or brutal pogroms (Poland, Lithuania, and Russia in the early 1800s). The Jewish community would then uproot itself and settle in another more welcoming region.

After the Spanish expulsion, many Jews migrated to the Dalmatian coastal cities of Italy and to Athens and Constantinople. Most of these cities welcomed them. Some distinguished themselves and became highly successful. Nothing in my family records suggests that my forebears distinguished themselves, either in a profession—such as education—or financially. Somehow, they relocated to the Austro-Hungarian province of Bukowina in the first half of the 19th century, probably from Russia and the Pale of Settlement, to escape persecution.

Edmund de Waal, in his book *The Hare with Amber Eyes*, describes the history of his family, the Ephrussis, who moved to Odessa after Catherine the Great established that city in the early 1800s:

Just as the Rothschilds had sent their sons and daughters out from Frankfurt at the start of the nineteenth century to colonise European capital cities, so the Abraham of my family, Charles Joachim Ephrussi, had masterminded this expansion from Odessa in the 1850s. A true patriarch, he had two sons from his first marriage, Ignace and Leon. And then when he remarried at fifty he had continued producing children: two more sons, Michel and Maurice, and two daughters, Therese and Marie. All of these six children were to be deployed as financiers or married into suitable Jewish dynasties.

Odessa was a city within the Pale of Settlement, the area on the western borders of imperial Russia in which Jews were allowed to live. It was famous for its rabbinical schools and synagogues, rich in literature and music, a magnet for the impoverished Jewish shtetls of Galicia. It was also a city that doubled its population of Jews and Greeks and Russians every decade, a polyglot city full of speculation and traders, the docks full of intrigues and spies, a city on the make. Charles Joachim Ephrussi had transformed a small grain trading business into a huge enterprise by cornering the market in buying wheat. He bought the grain from the middlemen who transported it on carts along the heavily rutted roads from the rich black soil of the Ukrainian wheat fields, the greatest wheat fields in the world, into the port of Odessa. Here the grain was stored in his warehouses before being exported across the Black Sea, up the Danube, across the Mediterranean.

By 1860 the family had become the greatest grain-exporters in the world. In Paris, James de Rothschild was known as the *le roi des juifs*, the king of the Jews. The Ephrussi were *les rois du blé*, the kings of grain. They were Jews with their own coat of arms: an ear of corn and a heraldic boat with three masts and full sails. Their motto, *Quod honestum*, unfurled below the ship: We are above reproach. You can trust us.

I provide this particular description here because it may be that my great-grandfather, Joel Sonnenblum, was party to that grain collection and trading network in the Ukraine at the end of the 1800s until the beginning of World War I.

Beginning in the early 1800s, the Austro-Hungarian Empire offered Jews opportunities to thrive. A visit to the city of Czernowitz (now Chernivtsi) today, even after the Nazi occupation, bears evidence of an enlightened way of life. A large university, built in the 1870s, still operates and the architecture embodies evidence of Jewish influence, with the Star of David incorporated into the design. An international conference on Yiddish as a language was held there in the early 1900s. Before the First World War, Jews exceeded ten percent of the population of the Bukowina province, of which Czernowitz was the center. Although most records and synagogues have been destroyed, much information is still available to demonstrate that Jewish life was safe and prosperous in that region between 1800 and 1914.

The Sonnenblum family (my mother's) lived in Bojan, about six miles from Czernowitz along the Pruth River. How long ago my mother's family had settled there is not clear; but in all likelihood, they had moved from Galicia, with its porous borders in the early 1800s, after the partition of Poland. The Austro-Hungarians were, in the days of Maria Theresa, far more tolerant towards the Jews than were the Russians.

The Sonnenblums had thrived in Bojan and Czernowitz during the 1800s. Great-grandfather Joel seems to have built and operated the town granary in Bojan and was one of the town "elders." He appears in some photographs of the book *Geschichte der Juden in der Bukowina* by Hugo Gold.

My father's family origins tell a very different story. According to our family's oral history, my great-grandfather Eliezer, born in 1825 in a Polish shtetl, was taken in 1833, at the age of eight, by a wagon driver who was passing through the town.

In 1833 there was considerable unrest in the region. Two things happened. The Polish rebellion against Russia, begun in 1830–1831, was brutally beaten back by the Russians in 1833. The other event was a cholera epidemic that was ravaging Eliezer's shtetl. As the story goes, the shtetl's Kabbalist rabbi claimed that God was angry with the shtetl's Jews and had inflicted cholera on them. In order to appease God, several children from the village were to be sent in all directions: to the North, to the South, to the East, and to the West. A more generous interpretation of the story is that the rabbi wanted to save the children, because all the villagers were dying.

Eliezer was one of those children. He was given to a wagon driver who passed through the village and who was willing to care for the child. We know nothing about Eliezer's family, since their name was not provided to the wagon driver whose last name was Rudel. Eliezer, nicknamed Leiser, lived with the wagon driver's family and eventually married one of his daughters (Rebecca Rachel). They remained settled in Bojan. I was named for him.

Jakob Rudel, my father, was born in 1888 of Leah Brender and Isaak Rudel in Bojan. He had a younger brother, Nathan, who studied to be a bookkeeper or accountant. Jakob also went to higher school, perhaps to the university in Czernowitz. He had some legal training before World War I and, as a result, was appointed an officer in the kaiser's army. He would have been twenty-six when the war began.

The Great War, 1914 to 1918, was an enormous negative turning point in the fortunes of my family, as it was with the Ephrussis. Here is another excerpt from de Waal's book, describing the atmosphere at the time the war began:

> On 28th July Austria declares war on Serbia. On 29th July the Emperor declares: "I put my faith in my peoples, who have always gathered round my throne, in unity and loyalty, through every tempest, who have always been ready for the heaviest sacrifices for the honour, the majesty, the power of the Fatherland." On 1st August Germany

declares war on Russia. On the 3rd Germany declares war on France, and then the following day invades neutral Belgium. And the whole pack of cards falls: alliances are invoked and Britain declares war on Germany. On 6th August Austria declares war on Russia….

In Vienna there is fervent support for this war, this cleansing of the country of its apathy and stupor. The British ambassador notes that "the entire people and press clamour impatiently for immediate and condign punishment of the hated Serbian race." Writers join in the excitement. Thomas Mann writes an essay *"Gedanken im Kriege,"* "Thanks Be for War"; the poet Rilke celebrates the resurrection of the Gods of War in his *Fun! Gesange*; Hofmannsthal publishes a patriotic poem in the Neue Freie Presse.

Schnitzler disagrees. He writes simply on 5th August: "World war. World ruin." Karl Kraus wishes the emperor "a good end of the world."'

Vienna was *en jeté*: young men in twos and threes with sprigs of flowers in their hats on their way to enlist; military bands playing in the parks. The Jewish community in Vienna was cheerful. The monthly newsletter of the Austrian-Israelite Union, for July and August, declaimed: "In this hour of danger we consider ourselves to be fully entitled citizens of the state. … We want to thank the Kaiser with the blood of our children and with our possessions for making us free; we want to prove to the state that we are its true citizens, as good as anyone. … After this war, with all its horrors, there cannot be any more anti-Semitic agitation. … We will be able to claim full equality." Germany would free the Jews.

After a terrible four years, here is de Waal's description of how the war ended:

It was a particularly cold winter in Vienna in 1918 and the white porcelain stove in the corner of the salon was the only fire that could be kept going all day and night....

... At the start of the war the house had felt very exposed, a private house surrounded by public spaces. Now, the peace seemed more frightening than the war: it was not clear who was fighting who, and it was not clear whether or not there was going to be a revolution. Demobilised soldiers and prisoners of war returned to Vienna with first-hand accounts of the revolutions in Russia and of the workers' protests in Berlin. There was plenty of "free firing"—random gunfire—at night. The new flag of Austria was red, white and red, and some of the younger and more riotous element found that, with a quick rip and stitch, you could make a good red flag.

From every corner of the old Empire imperial civil servants with no country came to Vienna to find that whole imperial ministries to which they had sent their careful reports had closed....

Vienna, with just under two million inhabitants, had gone from being the capital of an empire of fifty-two million subjects to a tiny country with six million citizens: it simply could not accommodate the cataclysm. Much of the talk was whether Austria was *lebensfahig*, viable, as an independent state. Viability was not just an issue of economics; it was psychological. Austria seemed not to know how to cope with its diminishment. The "Carthaginian Peace"—harsh and punitive—formalised in the Treaty of Saint-Germain-en-Laye of 1919, meant the dismemberment of the Empire. It sanctified the independence of Hungary, Czechoslovakia, Poland and Yugoslavia and the State of Slovenes, Croats and Serbs. Istria went. Trieste went. Several Dalmatian islands were lopped off and Austria-Hungary became Austria, a country 500 miles long. There were punitive reparations.

The war ended on November 11, 1918. The Treaty of Versailles was signed with Germany in June 1919 and the Treaty of Saint-Germain-en-Laye was signed in October 1919 with Austria. It split apart the Austro-Hungarian Empire and designated Rumania as the sovereign for Bukowina. An exodus of Jews followed from Bukowina to Vienna. My father's parents and brother, however, remained in Czernowitz.

The Sonnenblums moved to Vienna some time during the war after their granary in Bojan became "collateral damage." After the war ended, Jakob Rudel followed, in pursuit of Josefine Sonnenblum. The two married in Vienna. It is unlikely that Jakob's parents and brother attended his wedding.

In Vienna, my mother found a job with the Phoenix Insurance Company. After they married, my father also landed a job with the same company. The labor law in Austria required that my mother give up her job, as both members of the family were not allowed to be breadwinners because of the unemployment rate.

Jul was born in 1921 and I in 1930. During the 1920s, the Sonnenblum sisters married men who were either American citizens or desirous of becoming so and moved to the USA. Mom's brother Hermann, the black sheep of the family, left Vienna as well as his wife, for the United States on an alleged business trip and never returned. My parents were content to remain in Vienna during the 1920s and into the 1930s. As their economic status improved, they moved to a more affluent neighborhood, the Seventh District.

In 1924, when Jul was three, my parents, together with Jul, traveled back to Bojan for a visit. That was the last known contact that my father had with his parents and younger brother. When he became ill in 1935, his family did not come to Vienna. When he died, his family did not attend the funeral.

In 1934, my grandmother Feige Sonnenblum died. My grandfather, Yossel (Josef), then decided to emigrate to the United States, where his other two daughters and his son had settled. He tried to persuade my parents to do the same, with some concern that the political situation for Jews was deteriorating in Europe. But my mother had little interest in moving. Finally, in 1935, Grandpa insisted that our entire family apply for immigration visas at the U.S. Consulate. My mother, being an obedient daughter, did so to keep him happy. Unfortunately, Father was not able to pass the medical exam. Once Josef Sonnenblum departed Vienna for the United States, my family promptly put the matter of U.S. immigration out of its collective mind. It was their reluctant accommodation to a parent's wishes that later saved our lives. That was the first of the "second thoughts" that profoundly impacted my life. But more about that later.

The Anschluss

In the school system in Vienna, the grade school teachers remained with the class when students were promoted to the new grade. When I began second grade in September 1937, my first grade teacher moved with our class. His son was also in the class, but he did not include me among his friends. One day in early March 1938, my only Jewish classmate and I were told by our teacher that we could go home because it was a Jewish holiday. That was news to me, but I was delighted to go. My mother was puzzled but, to the best of my recollection, did not get alarmed.

The evening of March 11, 1938, the Austrian chancellor Kurt Schuschnigg went on the radio and acceded to Hitler's demand for *Anschluss* to Germany. The word *Anschluss*, meaning annexation, was the expression Hitler used to justify his conquest of Austria to make it a part of, and subservient to, Germany.

The *Anschluss* occurred on March 12, 1938. It was no longer safe for a Jew to be out on the streets. Our apartment was in the Seventh District, a lower-middle income and not predominantly Jewish section of Vienna; thus nothing untoward happened on our street. However, it was not that way in known Jewish sections. De Waal describes March 12 vividly:

It is as if a switch has been thrown. There are runnels of noise down the street, the Schottengasse echoing with voices. They are shouting, *"Ein Volk, ein Reich, ein Fuhrer"* and *"Heil Hitler, Sieg Heil"* 'And they are screaming *"Juden verrecken"'*––Perish Judah! Death to the Jews!

It is a flood of brown shirts. There are taxi horns blaring and there are men with weapons on the streets, and somehow the police have swastika armbands. There are trucks rushing along the Ring, past the house, past the university towards the Town Hall. And the trucks have swastikas on them, and the trams have swastikas on them, and there are young men and boys hanging off them, shouting and waving....

By 11:15 Nazi flags are hanging from the parapets of government ministries. At half-past midnight President Miklas gives in and approves the cabinet. At 1.08 a.m. a Major Klausner announces from the balcony with deep emotion in this festive hour that Austria is free, that Austria is National Socialist.

There are queues of people on foot or in cars at the Czech frontier. The radio is now playing the *"Badenweiler"* and the *"Hohenfriedberger,"* German military marches. These are interspersed with slogans. The first Jewish shop windows are broken....

All across Vienna doors are broken down, as children hide behind their parents, under beds, in cupboards––anywhere to get away from the noise as fathers and brothers are arrested and beaten up and pulled outside into trucks, as mothers and sisters are abused. And across Vienna people help themselves to what should be theirs, is theirs by right.

Treatment of Jews in Austria got worse and worse over the next few months. *Kristallnacht* burnings of every synagogue in Vienna in November 1938 were the culmination.

The day after the *Anschluss* I went to school. I saw that my teacher wore a swastika button on his lapel and his son, my classmate, a Hitler Youth uniform. We were soon informed that I was no longer allowed to attend my neighborhood school. I was instructed to travel daily to a school across town in the Jewish section of Vienna (Second District). My mother thought it too dangerous for me to do so and made arrangements with a tutor to come daily to our apartment (number 16 Kandlgasse). In June, I went to that special school in the Second District to take an exam, finish my class, and obtain my report card.

My recollections about our escape from Vienna are likely a mix of early memory colored by hearsay from oft-repeated explanations and narrations by my mother and brother, possibly colored by World War II movies and war stories, and, conceivably, by childhood fantasies.

But the basic facts are clear. My father had died of cancer. My mother, a 43-year-old woman, recently widowed, with one dependent son age seventeen and another of almost eight, found herself in an occupied land with something of a handicap: we were Jewish. She had an apartment but was dependent on a widow's pension. Her circle of friends, all Jewish, was small and all equally besieged. She did not trust her neighbors. She had no way to surmise what the future held for her.

Every Jew in Vienna was trying to find a way to leave Austria. The line at the U.S. Embassy was endless with many visa applicants for the limited quotas available. Mother (her nickname was Pepi and I shall call her that from here on) remembered the visa applications we had filed in 1935 at the behest of her father. She now had a "second thought" about that visa application.

Pepi went to the Embassy and was told to stand in the visa line. She explained that she wanted to check on the status of an earlier application. That got her into the visa section right away. She was able to resurrect our old applications. The consul then tentatively slotted us for one visa to be valid in June and two visas for October, contingent on her securing an affidavit from an affluent U.S. citizen to guarantee our financial support in the United States. She was able to get that document from a distant cousin, Pearl Hoffman, who lived in Los Angeles. It was never clear to me why her sisters did not provide that document.

Pepi correctly assessed that Jul, being of draft age, was most at risk, and gave him the June visa. She and I would wait for the October visas. It was mid-to-late March. The challenge was to stay alive and out of trouble until our departure dates. The primary focus was to get Jul out of Europe by June 1.

I don't recall that anything of this was explained to me. Secrecy in my family had always run deep and wide. As I was not attending school, I was confined to the apartment and was told never to open the door to anyone. Occasionally, I would be left at a family friend's apartment while Pepi ran necessary errands.

I have a vivid recollection of one incident. One day the doorbell rang and Pepi did not answer promptly, perhaps hoping to convey the idea we were not at home. I went to the door, looked through the peephole and saw a man dressed in a handsome uniform. I had always been impressed with authority figures and quickly opened the door. At this point Pepi came out and interceded. This man was a member of the German Luftwaffe and his name was Rudel. I have always wondered if this person might have been Hans Ulrich Rudel, the famous German pilot. He explained that he was trying to join the Nazi Party and had been accused of having Jewish blood in his ancestry. He was trying to collect evidence that this was not so and had looked us up in the hope we could help. Pepi did not look Jewish. She was a good actress and put on airs about our family not being connected to his line (certainly true) and therefore assured him we could not help him (also true). Fortunately, he was easily persuaded and left quickly without further investigation with our neighbors, who certainly knew we were Jewish. I then got a very stern "talking to" about opening the door, which I remember to this day.

The Escape

Arrangements were made for Jul to leave Vienna in late May by train through Salzburg to Paris, where he would meet some distant cousins named Patin and then proceed to Le Havre to board the *Queen Mary* on June 1. Pepi then began to make arrangements to pack, store and later ship our belongings to her sister's address in New York City. Obtaining exit visas quickly to travel to Italy was crucial, since it was getting more and more dangerous for a Jew to remain in Vienna. October was a long way off.

Pepi had taken me to the Second District school to take the examination that would show that I had completed my home study for second grade. She turned the apartment over to new occupants, even though they did not pay the *Schlusselgeld* (key money) as was customary. They knew we were Jewish and that we could not complain.

My next vivid memory is the trip by train from Vienna to Italy in mid-June. Pepi packed up what she could and we boarded the train. When the train crossed the border and once the immigration inspector had checked our passport, Pepi thought we had safely made our escape. She then took out her Hebrew prayer book to "give thanks." She noticed one of our compartment mates leave the compartment. Immediately, the immigration inspector returned and asked her if she was Jewish. When she told him we were, he said that Jews were not allowed to enter Italy. Since we had left Austria illegally, being sent back would have been the end of us. We were taken off the train at Udine and put on the next train going back to the border. Fortunately, that train was a local, went only as far as the border, and did not cross over into Austria. We were removed from the train and put under guard with two gendarmes, awaiting the next train that would take us back into Austria.

Knowing what was in store for us, Pepi began to befriend the gendarmes by offering them some of her quality cigarettes. There was a language problem, but she sensed a softening of their stance, as perhaps they did not like the job they had to do. They too, understood what our fate would be, once we returned to Austria.

Pepi then acted faint and asked for water. The guards took us into a washroom and, when we were clearly unobserved, she bribed them (she had some jewelry in her purse) and persuaded them to let us get on a different train that would transit through Italy to France. We assured them that we would not exit the train and would travel directly to France. But we took the train to the next station and changed to another for our original destination, Fiume.

We wanted to get to Fiume (now Rijeka, Croatia) because Pepi had been given the name of a Jewish businessman there. We needed to hide until October, when the U.S. visas would be valid. It was only mid-June.

When we arrived at the station, we placed our luggage into the "left luggage" window and walked to the businessman's work address. I do not remember his name. He asked if we had registered at a hotel, and we told him we had not done so. He said that was fortunate, because if we had, we would have been required to fill out a police record card, which would have been sent to the police the next morning. He then said that the only place we could stay would be at a sanitarium, since their residents were not reported to the police. He made arrangements on the telephone and took us to pick up our luggage and then onward to Abatzija (now Opatija). I think the story we told was that I was recovering from whooping cough and needed rest. We stayed at the sanitarium for six or seven weeks until my mother was able to obtain a Swiss visa.

Our stay at the sanitarium was marked by extreme caution. An eight-year-old does not like to be kept out of sight, and so I doubtless caused my mother some distress, as I constantly wanted to leave our room. The staff was not trusted to know that we were fugitives.

I believe that the help we received from the businessman in Fiume in June 1938 saved our lives. I always wondered about him. In 2009, with my wife, Joan, and our daughter, Ruth Ann, I traveled to Croatia, trying to identify him. We thought the Jewish community in Rijeka might have some record of actions taken by members to help fleeing Jews. We saw, in their synagogue, the names of the 401 members who had been killed during the Holocaust. Perhaps it was one of them. There was probably a Jewish doctor associated with the sanitarium. The businessman might have consulted him about admitting us.

Pepi and I were lucky to have survived. Some will risk their own safety to help others. The Jewish community in Rijeka can take pride in what some of their members did in those times. During our visit, I think we located the sanitarium where we had stayed. The Opatija Hotel has been remodeled, but the old front entrance, which is no longer in use, resembles the place where we lived.

Pepi and I were able to hide there for about six weeks. I remember befriending a boy my age who also spoke German. He was very pleasant, and I spent a lot of time with him, although Pepi was nervous about my being out of the room. One day, he passed on an invitation from his father for us to go for a ride in his family's car. Pepi was apprehensive but I cajoled her into agreeing. As we went through the lobby I pointed out my friend, who was sitting in a big German staff car parked at the entrance. It had a swastika on its door. My mother almost fainted. She stopped and told me to tell them she was sick and could not go. Nor did she allow me to go. I was furious with her but did as she asked.

Pepi came to the conclusion that we could not stay in Italy any longer. She realized that the Italian immigration records of our entry without a record of our exit would, by that time, have put us on the "look-out" list. Where to go? It was late July and our U.S. visas were not valid until October. Switzerland was safest, but the Swiss were granting no visas. She embarked on a plan.

She dressed herself in her most fashionable clothes, put on every bit of jewelry she owned, bought herself a fancy hat, and took the train from Fiume to Naples, the Italian city farthest from the Swiss border having a

Swiss Consulate, assuming it would not be overwhelmed with visa applicants. I do not recall how she arranged to have me cared for during her absence. There she marched into the Consulate, affecting every high-handed air she could muster, and asked to see the consul. The receptionist asked if it was about a visa, and she told her "no."

When the consul admitted her, she explained that her eight-year-old son had just recovered from whooping cough and that her physician advised that he spend ten days in the mountains at an elevation of 1,200 meters. Could the consul kindly advise her on a suitable mountain resort town in Switzerland that met these criteria and had first-class accommodations? The consul pulled out an atlas and searched for a location. Pepi then questioned him about the suitability of the accommodations. The long discussion led to him giving his best advice to this attractive woman, who thanked him profusely and then turned to go.

At the door, she turned to face him and asked innocently, "Do we need a visa?"

"Yes," was the answer.

"Oh," she said. "How does one go about getting a visa?"

"I can give you one," was the reply. And he did.

We left Italy without incident and remained in Zurich until the end of September. Pepi arranged with the U.S. consulate to issue our visas to us in Zurich, and we proceeded to Le Havre, where we boarded the *Isle de France* on October 1.

GROWING UP AS AN "AMERICAN GREENHORN"

After a seven-day voyage, we arrived in New York Harbor at night. I glimpsed the Statue of Liberty and ran to that side of the boat, right into a volleyball net, and got my first black eye. I can remember worrying that the customs inspector would take this as a sign of some contagious illness and that the U.S. Immigration official would not let me debark. Pepi's sister Ethel and her husband, Ludwig Schenker, a successful pharmacist who owned his own pharmacy, met us. We were welcome to stay with them until we could get settled.

Jul had arrived four months earlier and had been living with the Schenkers. He had found work at a local butter-and-egg shop at a salary of $12 per sixty-hour six-day week. Pepi quickly found an apartment nearby on Creston Avenue, bought a couple of beds, and we moved in. She found a job as a seamstress at a women's corset factory. I was registered at Public School 33 on Walton Avenue and became a latchkey immigrant kid.

I spoke no English. Pepi brought me to school and pleaded for them to accept me into the third grade. Mrs. Leibowitz, the third grade teacher, a very gentle soul who spoke passable Yiddish, said she would give me separate help in Yiddish for one month. If, at the end of that month, I could understand her instructions in English, I could stay in her class. If not, I would be put back to second grade. That was a wonderful incentive to learn English. After the month was over, she allowed me to stay in her class.

I have often wondered about Pepi's relationship with Jakob's family remaining in Czernowitz. When Pepi, Julius, and I left Vienna for the United States, was there any thought or concern about Jakob's family? Would she have considered taking her two sons back to Bojan at the time of the *Anschluss* as a way to escape from the Nazis? The Sonnenblum family had all gone to America, and she was alone in Vienna. Upon her arrival in the States would she have made efforts to get Jakob's family out of Europe? No one alive knows that now. It would seem that there was little closeness, certainly no family ties, and possibly ill feeling between my mother and Jakob's family.

My latchkey status was unique in that I did not have a latchkey. After school, I hung around on the street near the house with the other kids on the block until someone came home to let me in. As a result, I got schooled on the street as well as in class. The game among these kids was to loiter in the local five-and-dime and shoplift small toys. When these toys showed up at home I was confronted with a stern talking to by Jul and Pepi. I was told to return to the store, admit my crime, and return the toys. That I did this at the age of eight and a half is hard for me to believe even now.

After that, Pepi and Jul decided I needed supervision that they could not provide. Arrangements were made to place me in an orphanage at the Jewish Children's Home in Newark, New Jersey, when I had completed the third grade in June 1939. They described the plan as a "vacation summer camp" that would last only for July and August while Pepi made a trip to California to thank Pearl Hoffman for providing the affidavit for us. Then I would return home. When I told this to the other kids at the orphanage; they just laughed. This is what we were all told when we came. The other kids said I would remain there until I finished high school. I called them liars and said they would see that my Mother would not leave me. This was the norm in my youth. I was not told the straight facts and had to find things out for myself.

And so the summer came and went, then, the autumn and winter, and then spring and another summer. Telephone contact was too costly. Usually, but not always, Jul or Pepi would come to visit on Sundays, buy me a soda and spend a couple of hours with me. But they always made the trip back to New York City without me. And on the Sundays when no one showed up, I spent the day at the window in the front hall of the orphanage, watching for the approach of the buses traveling from the Hudson Tubes Station in downtown Newark up Clinton Avenue to get the first glimpse of the visitor who, all too often, never arrived.

In October 1940, Pepi married a man named Joseph Rappaport, a businessman with a New York garment district shop in which she was employed. I left the orphanage and moved in with Pepi and Jul and Joe, who had rented an apartment in the Bronx on Ryer Avenue.

Joe Rappaport had not been married before. I should have been grateful to him for having accepted responsibility for me. But there never was the slightest emotional tie between us. In all fairness, I must have been a handful for him and Pepi. I was the appendage to the family. Without me, in all likelihood, Pepi would not have married Joe. Her motivation for marriage was to secure a "meal ticket" for me and for her. Jul was now approaching twenty years of age, had a job, had resumed his music studies, was dating Rita Gillis, and was independent. I was the albatross around Pepi's neck.

Pepi continued to work at Joe's company, the Normandie Stitching Company on 8th Avenue at 39th Street, but not full time. I was receiving more supervision after school. Yet I can remember almost nothing about life on Ryer Avenue. I do recall my mother being a superstitious person. For example, when cutting my fingernails, she would insist on cutting every other nail—never two nails on adjacent fingers. She would say that evil would fall on someone whose fingernails are cut next to each other.

I do not feel nostalgic about life at the orphanage and cannot recall any friends I made there. I was enrolled in a Talmud Torah to prepare for my Bar Mitzvah but hated it. In fact, I have some memories of becoming an anti-Semite. I attributed my uprooting and unhappiness to my Jewish birth and blamed Judaism for my misfortunes. I thought it would be wonderful to shed that stigma and become fully accepted in the world around me.

By the summer of 1941, we moved to another apartment in the Bronx, on Walton Avenue across the street from good old P.S. 33 and very near Pepi's sister's family, the Schenkers. I suspect there was a conflict between Joe and Pepi about that move. Joe's family lived in Brooklyn. He had two sisters, Evelyn and Rose. Evelyn was married to Al Wellington, the proprietor of a store on Canal Street. He and Evelyn had a maladjusted only child named Morrie. Rose was a spinster and behaved like an overbearing shrew. Mom did not want to live near Joe's family and apparently convinced him to move to Walton Avenue. I had just turned eleven.

The advantage that apartment held for me was its proximity to P.S. 33, the grade school I first attended on arrival in the United States. It was located near the A&P store where I could freelance as a delivery boy after school, earning tips from customers. That was my first job. It is also my first recollection of the name of a friend, Edward Daum.

That one year at Walton Avenue was marked by Pearl Harbor on December 7, 1941, the onset of war, and Jul's wedding to Rita in June 1942. It seems to have been a happier period for me.

After Jul's wedding, we moved to a smaller apartment in the Crown Heights section of Brooklyn at 1035 Washington Avenue, near Joe's family. It was a nifty building with a doorman and was just across the street from the Brooklyn Botanic Gardens. Though the building was located only one block from Ebbets Field, the home of the Brooklyn Dodgers, its location did not inspire in me any interest in baseball or other sports. I was enrolled in the seventh grade of yet another school, P.S. 241.

LIFE IN BROOKLYN

The apartment was small. It had one bedroom for Pepi and Joe and a living room where I slept. I rolled a cot into the room each night, folded it up the next morning, and put it away in the foyer closet. There was no privacy. I performed this routine daily from the time we moved in, in September 1942, until I left home in 1948 at the age of eighteen. The neighborhood kids played stickball in the street, and I watched them from my window. I did not take to athletics, perhaps because I was so bad at it; every time I threw the ball it went wide of the intended receiver. In Vienna, my parents always referred disparagingly to the *schtrassenbuben*, the kids who hung around the streets and came from low-class homes.

The neighborhood was solidly middle-class Jewish. Some of the kids in our building had family cars, a luxury at that time. I had jobs after school nearly the entire time I lived in Brooklyn. In grammar school I was delivery boy and stock clerk at a nearby hardware store and a tailor/cleaning shop. Once I entered Boys High School and obtained working papers, the jobs were more lucrative. I worked at the Brooklyn Public Library on

Eastern Parkway and then at the Home Insurance Company in downtown Brooklyn as a mail carrier. We set aside the money I earned and at Easter/Passover, used my savings to buy me new clothes.

New York public schools were organized with three classes of children in each grade. The "brighter" students were in class 1. The "average" students were in class 3 and the "slow learners" were in class 4. On arrival in the USA in 1938, I entered the New York City school system in third grade. By the time we moved to Brooklyn, I was in the seventh grade. I had been placed in classes with the slow learners at time of my immigration. Thus, when I entered PS 241 in Brooklyn my class designation was grade 7-4. The system did not provide for upward mobility.

PS 241 was not a pleasant school. The teachers ran it like a prison. We were marched from room to room in silence, in single file along the hallway walls. Talking or horseplay was not tolerated. I recall an incident when I was reprimanded for chatting while marching in the hallway and being told Pepi had to come to school to discuss my behavior. She was not pleased to do this but accompanied me back to school after the lunch break. The teacher confronted us and reported my latest misdeed. Pepi was silent for a while. Then she turned to me and asked me if I had done as the teacher described. I lied with a straight face and said I had not. Then she turned to the teacher and said, "My son does not lie!" and walked out of the room. It was the only time I can recall that she took my side. That is an important memory for me.

In eighth grade, all students were given an IQ test. I took it and thought no more about it. Then I noticed the teachers began to treat me differently. It was as though I had somehow earned their respect. Among the hundred or so students that made up the eighth grade in classes 8-1, 8-3, and 8-4, I had the third highest IQ score. That was an awakening for me. I gained a growing sense of self-confidence that prepared me to take an increased interest in classes upon entering high school.

Jul and Rita would visit once a week for an elaborate dinner made by Pepi. But after dinner, "court" was held. Pepi would report each of my transgressions of the previous week and ask Jul what he thought. Jul and Rita were put in a terrible spot. Sometimes they would take me for boating off City Island or biking in the parks. Often they would invite me to their apartment. These were wonderful moments. They tried to help me navigate my life around Pepi, advising me that it was pointless to argue with her, as she would surely win. She held all the cards.

I think these bits of counsel helped me get through that period. But the unhappy home life impelled me to push myself to finish high school in three years. I took summer classes and some extra courses each semester. Passing the German three-year Regents exam after only one year of classes helped. The principal of Boys High, Alfred A. Tausk (whom we affectionately called "A square") tried to tell me that these were the best years of life. Why was I in such a rush to finish? I could not reveal the real reason for my hurry.

During my teens, and perhaps even earlier, I had become increasingly hostile to my Jewishness. There was considerable anti-Semitism in the United States, even in New York City. But my resistance to a Jewish identity derived more from the war and the Holocaust. My mother, brother and I were "stateless persons." Austria had disappeared from the world map. We did not belong anywhere. If I had not been born a Jew, I would not have been subjected to all of these hardships, including my relocation to the States. I became aware that Jews had lived extraterritorially since biblical days. In the 1200s they settled in Spain and that lasted until Isabella expelled them in 1492. In the 1500s they were invited to live in Lithuania and made a successful presence there until the Polish Partition (1790s), after which they were brutally repressed by the Russians. In the 1800s Jews were allowed to thrive in Austria-Hungary once more, continuing for more than a hundred years until the First World War. Shortly thereafter, terror returned. Every hundred years or so, it seems, there has been a pogrom and a few million Jews are murdered.

I began to reject anything that had to do with my Jewish heritage and sought to assimilate into the American culture. My father had been Orthodox. My mother kept a kosher home. My stepfather embraced his Jewish and Yiddish roots. My grandfather earned his living as a *shames*, an assistant to the Rabbi in an Orthodox synagogue in Brooklyn. Yet, I looked for reasons to reject all of that. I wanted to assimilate. This was largely because I had seen around me in the United States the assimilation of many ethnic minorities. *E pluribus unum*! Had I migrated to another country, say Germany, Austria, France, even Scandinavia, I would not have chosen to assimilate into those cultures and abandon my Jewishness. But in the United States, assimilation was virtually mandated by the Constitution. And, unlike my black school chums, I needed no skin bleach or hair straightener to shed my Jewishness.

Particularly among my stepfather's relatives, I noticed hypocrisy in the way they treated blacks while wanting to be treated properly themselves by the "goyim" I asked myself, "What's so great about being a Jew? Why do I have to endure all of this anti-Semitic hatred?" I wanted desperately to be a non-Jew, an American. Attending high school in the Bedford-Stuyvesant section of Brooklyn, I caught myself looking at blacks in that community and thinking, "There, but for the grace of God go I!" So, when I began college, I joined the Congress of Racial Equality.

A FREE COLLEGE EDUCATION IN THE LAND OF OPPORTUNITY

These immediate postwar years were truly exceptional, although at the time, very few realized just how exceptional they were. Bill Bryson describes them this way: [1]

I can't imagine there has ever been a more gratifying time or place to be alive than America in the 1950s. No country had ever

---

1 Bill Bryson, *The Life and Times of the Thunderbolt Kid* (New York: Broadway Books, 2007), page 5.

known such prosperity. When the war ended, the United States had $26 billion worth of factories that hadn't existed before the war, $140 billion in savings and war bonds just waiting to be spent, no bomb damage, and practically no competition. All that American companies had to do was stop making tanks and battleships and start making Buicks and Frigidaires — and boy, did they.

I received no counseling or choice for college preparation. It was assumed that when I graduated Boys High in June 1947, I would enroll at City College (CCNY)—as Pepi wished—and live at home. But I had other ideas. If I could find a job and attend college at night, I could leave home right away. I found work as a mail clerk at the International Division of the Radio Corporation of America (RCA) at 745 Fifth Avenue in Manhattan. The pay was a princely $30 per five-day workweek. Pepi was suspicious but I told her it was only for the summer and that I would quit to go to college in September. When September came, I refused to quit and, instead, enrolled in the evening session of Brooklyn College. The logistics of travel to Brooklyn College were simpler as long as I lived at home.

My plan to move out after high school was thwarted by arithmetic. Thirty dollars per week was insufficient to keep body and soul together in New York City. I saved and skimped. I recall that Joe Rappaport insisted I contribute to the household but am not sure of that. I found myself sleeping through evening classes but managed to get passing grades for the six courses I completed in the first year. RCA promoted me from the mailroom and I became an order writer for broadcast audio equipment, selling the identical equipment to the Egyptians and to the Jewish Agency for Palestine (soon to become the new government of Israel). My salary went up to $35 per week.

In the summer of 1948, I met a kindly chemistry professor who taught at CCNY. He asked me some pertinent questions about the structure of my life. I was candid with him. He then told me about Army Hall, a City College dormitory where students could room at very low cost. I could move into a six-person room for $90 per semester. That was something I could afford.

I persuaded my mother that I would do better academically if I lived at school. I switched to CCNY and moved out of the apartment and into Army Hall in September. I had several allies in this argument with Pepi. Joe Rappaport, who had seen enough of me, was one. The others were Jul and Rita. Another was the Reserve Officers' Training Corps [ROTC] recruiter at CCNY, who thought I would make a good infantry officer.

I continued to work for RCA for another year. I was allowed to come in late one morning a week so that I could attend ROTC drill at the college. After all, RCA's president was David Sarnoff, referred to throughout the company as "the general" because he had been given that title during World War II for RCA's military work.

I had taken three years to complete high school (1944 to 1947). It took five years, including summer classes, to complete undergraduate college and ROTC training (1947 to 1952). I have never been satisfied that my BA degree was properly earned because I did the minimum to get through and pass. The pressure of time to earn a living, plus a lack of personal discipline, obstructed the fine educational opportunities offered by the taxpayers of New York City.

Three things made it possible for me to successfully complete my studies. The most important, perhaps, was entering into psychoanalysis in 1950. That process allowed me to clear away some rubble that kept me from focusing on my studies. I had, too often, heard my mother lament my actions and ask two rhetorical questions: "What's going to become of you?" and "Why can't you be like your older brother?" I vowed that I would never put those questions to my children.

The second was a lucky break: being hired by the New York Public Library in 1949. I was able to restructure my schedule to work afternoons and evenings (from 12:30 pm until 9 pm) four weekdays plus 9 am to 6 pm Saturday, so that I could attend college courses in the mornings when I had a fresh mind and could focus on what really mattered.

Third was the small amount of money my mother provided me in my last year of college, 1951–1952, about $400. That supplement allowed me to reduce my work time to 25 hours a week, so I could take a full course load and complete my graduation requirements in five years.

Another piece of luck also played a role in my completing college: the ROTC. I enrolled in ROTC because it came with a uniform. The uniform included shoes and a shirt that could be worn with street clothes. I needed every bit of financial help I could get. Then, in the spring of 1950, I was offered an appointment to the senior ROTC. Now that was a real bonanza, because it paid $27 a month in addition to the uniform. I would get college credit for the three hours a week of ROTC classes, and there would be a six-week summer camp between the third and fourth year at which I would receive full military pay. One had to commit to service in the reserve after completing college, but that obligation was not a big deal in peacetime. I signed up.

I think the date of my signup was June 15, 1950. Nine days later, North Korea invaded South Korea, and the war was on. The draft was invoked, and suddenly everyone was applying for the senior ROTC, since that automatically gave one a deferment from the draft. I was already in.

While at CCNY, my expectations from life were modest. I understood what a white-collar job was. Employment at RCA gave me a good idea of the available choices. My political orientation was toward world federalism. I admired Wendell Wilkie and Norman Cousins, author of the essay "Modern War Is Obsolete," and thought of the United Nations as an organization that could lead to the ending of all military conflict. My interests were international relations and trade. My favorite courses were with Professors Oscar Janowsky and Raymond Paige in the History Department. The chain of events leading up to the Russian Revolution of

1917 fascinated me. It did not occur to me that I could ever qualify to work for the federal government, although I might have had a few fantasies of somehow influencing national or international policy. I credit Professor Janowsky for being instrumental in helping me complete undergraduate school successfully.

I majored in international relations, and after graduation in 1952 I was admitted to NYU for graduate study. I thought international trade would be an enjoyable and challenging way to earn a living. Then, the woman whom I had been dating in my last year at CCNY, Sandra Glickman, persuaded me to take a federal government test called the "Junior Management Assistant" exam. This was a three-tier government entry exam, given nationally once each year. If you passed the first part (four hours), you got on one list. And if you took the second part (another 4 hours) and passed that one, you got on a more select list and were then called for an oral exam. If you passed the oral as well, you were on a truly select list. Every government department would then want to hire you. A total of 17,000 applicants took the test, and 3000 passed the first two parts. The final select list of those who passed the oral exam was 250. I took the exam just to please her, absolutely sure I would fail. Miraculously, I was one of the 250. With this new and heretofore unanticipated opportunity appearing seemingly out of nowhere, I could now consider entirely new career choices.

As I approached the magic date for graduation, it seemed time to propose to the woman I had been dating. Sandra was a New Yorker; she was my age, Jewish, and in my graduating class at CCNY. We seemed to have a great deal in common. And she was prepared for our likely separation while I served the required two years in the army, probably in Korea, after graduation. She was also delighted with the prospect of going to Washington, D.C. after my military service. It seemed such a natural fit. Who knew?

Pepi was very pleased with our marriage plans. As one can gather from this narrative, my relationship with her was quite poor. Neither of us truly understood the other. She saw the forthcoming marriage as an important stabilizer for an errant son. In truth, I had never appreciated the sacrifices Pepi had made for me in Europe during our escape, as well as in the States. For example, she divorced Joe Rappaport as soon as I moved away from home. That should have given me a clue that she married him just to give me a home so that I could leave the orphanage. He was a "meal ticket" and she lived with him for almost ten years for my benefit.

Life during the four years at CCNY seemed tediously drawn out, but after graduation things fell into place. I graduated in the summer of 1952, entered New York University Graduate School in September for one semester, reported for duty at Fort Benning, Georgia, in February 1953, got married in March 1953, and sailed for Japan in September 1953. We enjoyed our life there, which was steeped in the Japanese culture. We represented the conquerors during a period when Japan was beginning to return to civilian rule. (See "My Brilliant Military Career" below). I returned to civilian life after completing active duty in February 1955. One year later, I moved to Washington and went to work at the International Cooperation Administration, the predecessor of the U.S. Agency for International Development.

I felt deep gratitude towards Professor Janowsky. He deserved credit for preparing me to take on my career in the Foreign Service. In 1960, before departing for Turkey on assignment to the U.S. economic aid mission, I returned to CCNY to say farewell. He seemed proud of my accomplishments and pleased that his efforts to help me were well spent. He invited me to have lunch with him in the faculty dining room. I had never before had that honor. At lunch, he asked me if I could shed some light on what seemed to him a peculiarity about President Eisenhower's itinerary on his recent trip to South Asia. Eisenhower had spent only one day in Karachi, Pakistan, but then spent four days in New Delhi, India. "Did that signify a departure from the U.S. position of evenhandedness between India and Pakistan?" the professor queried. I still remember my reply. I reminded him of something he stressed in his own class: that historians sometimes search too deeply into the data and ascribe meaning to random events. "Ike decided to spend all that time in India because he wanted to see the Taj Mahal in Agra," was my response. Sadly, I did not keep up with the kind professor after that. Somehow I got busy. I guess it's what we all do.

END OF THE BEGINNING

This chapter was the story of my first twenty-three years of life. The rest of this autobiography will offer a collection of stories, mostly about people who played important roles in my life. I was blessed to have had as friends and/or colleagues, some wonderful and remarkable human beings, and as my second wife, Joan. With friends like Emin Boysan in Turkey, Carter Ide in Washington and India, Bill White in Ebensburg, Pennsylvania, I formed special relationships that inspired me and taught me the most important of life's lessons.

PART TWO

U.S. GOVERNMENT SERVICE 1953 TO 2002

2

MY "BRILLIANT" MILITARY CAREER
1953–1955

My introduction to "the military life" began when I transferred to City College and, at long last, moved out of my mother's house and into Army Hall at CCNY. The dormitory got its name during World War II when the army used it to house military personnel sent to CCNY for special training. After the war, it was converted into a student dorm and the name stuck, though it was no longer connected with the army.

It was the cheapest place for me to stay but, as stated earlier, I needed additional income even there, which is why I joined the ROTC. This also meant that I would become an infantry second lieutenant in the U.S. Army Reserve when I graduated. But I was not too concerned. No way would the army ever again call up reservists! The final, absolutely last war of our civilization had been fought and won.

Since I was earning the magnificent salary of $35 per forty-hour work-week at the RCA's International Division, ROTC emoluments were of considerable value. Moreover, as a teenager during the war, I had dreamed of being in uniform, flying fighter airplanes and killing Germans. The uniform had more than just a financial appeal to me. It was a symbol of authority and added, I surmised, to my sex appeal.

My attitude toward the U.S. military was always ambivalent, fluctuating from giving hawkish support to U.S. international assertiveness to being skeptical and suspicious of the leadership and their competence. But I never slid into the pacifist or isolationist mode. I did not see myself as a natural-born fighter and never thought of "going RA" (joining the regular army) when I was invited to do so. Yet I consistently believed that every citizen was obligated to follow the decisions made by the country's elected leadership, whether one agreed with those decisions or not. This belief got severely tested during the Vietnam era when the Agency for International Development (AID), for which I then worked, began drafting its personnel for reassignment to Saigon. A number of my colleagues declared they would resign if reassigned, but I held that we were not entitled, morally, to do that.

In May 1950, as I was completing my second year at CCNY's ROTC evening session, we were invited to sign up for the senior ROTC. Most of my fellow students became timid around that time because rumors abounded that the army could call us up once we graduated. I wanted the $27 monthly payment and signed up right away. Well … then came June 24 and the North Korean invasion. Those that had signed up received an automatic deferment from the draft until graduation. The others were called up immediately.

I was ordered to report to the Infantry School at Fort Benning, Georgia, affectionately referred to as "Benning School for Boys," in February 1953.

Life in the U.S. South proved of some interest. My orders authorized travel by train from New York to Atlanta with a change there to another train to Columbus, Georgia. When I got on the train in New York, all dressed up in my new uniform with a gold bar on my shoulder, I saw another CCNY ROTC grad board the same train. His name was Bob Freeman and he was black. We decided to travel together.

We had a four-hour layover in Atlanta before catching the train for Columbus and were hungry. No restaurant would serve two second lieutenants of different skin color, even though traveling together. Finally, we went into the black ghetto and ate at a food stand.

At Benning, the army barracks had been integrated, and Freeman and I found ourselves in the same unit. That training unit comprised about two hundred infantry lieutenants, all ROTC grads from around the country. The Fort Benning school slogan was "Follow Me," and its significance was not lost on us. It meant that we lieutenants would be the first to crawl out of the foxholes and lead the charge on the enemy, and it was up to us to inspire the recruits to follow. We needed to pay attention to the lessons, because there was a shooting war in Korea and we were surely destined to be sent there. This was the limerick on everyone's lips:

> Here lie the bones of Lieutenant Jones,
> A graduate of this institution.
> He died last night,
> In his first firefight.
> He followed the school solution.

One Alabama boy named Steele behaved civilly to Freeman and other black unit members; but at the end of the day, there was debate about the army's decision—on Truman's order—for racial integration. Steele was convinced this would undermine our forces' effectiveness and ultimately lead to miscegenation. These discussions, although courteous and civil, did not sit well with Freeman.

One Sunday, I traveled across the Chattahoochee River to Phoenix City, Alabama, and walked into the city park. There in the pond were two swans swimming together; one black, the other white. The next time we had our day-end discussion, I asked Steele why those swans could do something the citizens of Alabama were not allowed to do. Freeman enjoyed the effort but, in the end, no one was persuaded.

During my thirteen-week training stint at Fort Benning, I realized that an infantry second lieutenant was in a vulnerable position in combat and that there was indeed a serious combat situation in Korea. I recalled stories my cousin, Sam Korn, told when he returned from the Pacific Theater in 1945. He had served in the Army Air Corps during World War II as a blister gunner on B-24s. He was lucky to be a blister gunner and survived forty missions; the nose gunners and tail gunners usually lasted no more than five missions.

I thought about what it would be like to lead a platoon of combat infantrymen in Korea. It struck me how dependent I would be on the units on either flank. Returnees I met at Fort Benning would describe the advantage of fighting next to a Turkish unit, because they could be counted on to hold their positions and provide support if there was trouble. I think it was at that point that I began to size up my fellow infantry lieutenants. Would this guy with whom I was enjoying a drink at the Officers Club hold his position when things got bad? The second question was even more demanding; would he come to my assistance if I got into trouble? These were not academic issues. It was spring 1953 and the war was in full swing. Somehow, these two questions have lingered in my mind since then. I often find myself considering whether one of my friends could meet that very high bar; and this has kept me from forming strong ties with all but a handful of people.

After training, in June 1953, I was assigned to Camp Roberts near Paso Robles, California, for three months of troop duty. It was there that my hearing was damaged. I was posted for four days as a safety officer in a training exercise for combat on towns. The army had built a "plank village." Houses were made of plank boards with no sound baffling equipment, and recruits were shown how to fire automatic weapons from upper floors. I did this for six hours a day for four days, and my ears were never the same again.

In September, I was assigned to the Far East. Departing the continental United States by Military Air Transport Service (MATS) for Yokohama, I was expecting to be assigned to Korea but was placed instead at the Sasebo Replacement Depot on Kyushu Island, across the straits from Pusan at the very closest point to the Korean Peninsula. A ceasefire had been declared two months earlier. Troops in Korea were being rotated and fresh troops sent in. The replacement depot handled that pipeline, and I was a company officer there. No one knew how long the ceasefire would hold. It was dull work, but the town of Sasebo and the exposure to Japanese culture were refreshing. Moreover, if we could find and secure living quarters off base, our families could join us––at government expense! I took advantage of this, rented a Japanese-style house (glass and paper sliding doors, tatami mats on the floor, and a coal-fired hot bath), and sent for Sandra and our car.

Sandra and the car arrived in January 1954. For a few months, the routine was boring but pleasant. Sasebo is located about sixty miles from Nagasaki, where a Madam Butterfly House had been built in a park. Puccini had never traveled to the Orient, yet the Japanese had built this tribute to his opera after the atomic bomb had leveled the city. A decent road existed between Sasebo and Nagasaki, with many ceramics factories along the road. Apparently there had been a large migration from Korea about a hundred years earlier, and the people settled in that area brought their ceramic skills with them. There was a U.S. naval base in Sasebo, with a naval air/sea rescue unit. I took some helicopter flights as they practiced "auto-rotating." That should have scared me out of my wits. Instead, I found myself enjoying the thrill.

The duties were certainly not taxing for a junior officer at a transit point for replacement troops going to Korea. Men would come in by train from Yokohama and be quartered there for about three days while drawing combat uniforms. After getting their medical shots up to date, they boarded the Pusan ferry that shuttled back and forth between Sasebo and

Pusan. Disciplinary problems that arose had to be settled before the recruit was sent on.

The army had built a large, well-equipped and well-staffed hospital in Sasebo during the early years of the conflict to treat U.S. military evacuees from Korea. It was still standing at the ready in case shooting resumed, but business had come to a standstill because there were no evacuees. The medical staff were bored and in search of things to do. If any transient soldier needed medical aid, the hospital staff would vie for the chance to practice their skills. These were the folks I tended to hang out with, more than the Replacement Depot staff.

The army required all troops to receive a one-hour class on current events having to do with the conflict each week. This was the Troop Information and Education (TI&E) class, delivered like a homily according to the guidance prepared by the Pentagon. It fell to me to deliver this weekly lecture in the post's large auditorium. I had always been a collector of off-color jokes and decided to deliver a "joke of the week" for each class. I must say, in all modesty, that show became a big drawing card for my lectures. Even the post commander would come from time to time.

One day, the lesson to be given was the reasonableness of the U.S. official position that Taiwan was the legitimate government of China while "Communist Mainland China" was not and that the Chinese troops who counterattacked when our forces got close to the Yalu River did not reflect the true wishes of the Chinese people. I had real problems with that. I thought we should have recognized the Communist Chinese government before they entered the Korean War. Technically my presentation followed the script, but I got hold of a big map of the region, pointed to the vast areas of China controlled by the Communists and, perhaps tongue in cheek, said everyone in the audience was to ignore that territory and focus instead on this little island called Taiwan, which was sure to recapture all of that other territory pretty quickly. A number of fellow officers, those who had fought the Chinese in Korea and then rotated back to Japan, really took umbrage.

That was a lesson for me. It's difficult, perhaps impossible, to embrace someone who has shot at you.

I also learned a little about the Uniform Code of Military Justice. The company commander handled Summary Court. General Court required a lawyer from the Judge Advocate General's Corps (JAG) to defend and a JAG lawyer to prosecute. But Special Court Martials required only two officers with some familiarity with the Uniform Code of Military Justice to argue the case before the court, one each for prosecution and defense. I was made a "special defense counsel," was handed "the book," the Uniform Code of Military Justice, and told to "study it before next Friday," when I was to handle my first defense case.

It took a while to figure out how the system worked and several soldiers that I defended were easily convicted (as they should have been). But then I tired of losing. I was next assigned the case of four soldiers caught sneaking off post with army blankets, on the way to the nearby brothels, intending to do some trading. The men had been caught by Japanese guards employed by the post Military Police.

It was the practice for the accused to sit to the right of the courtroom at a desk with his attorney. The first two questions to any witness called to testify were (1) state your name, rank, and serial number or identify yourself; and (2) do you know or recognize the accused? If so point him out. The witness would simply point to the table on the right side to answer the second question. I became aware of my own difficulty in distinguishing one Japanese from another and was sure the Japanese guards had the same trouble with Caucasians. I recruited three soldiers that looked similar to the defendants and designated them as assistant defense counsels to sit with me and the four accused. Well, after getting the defendants off, I was quickly reassigned to take the other side as a prosecutor.

I view my army assignments over the entire first year of my tour as fortuitous, considering the other possibilities available. It is said, correctly that "timing is everything." I was lucky never to have served in combat. The ceasefire could have happened later or might not have held. I might have been sent directly to Korea to a front line unit. So many fatal or near-fatal things could have happened to me but did not. While posted at Sasebo, lady luck really smiled on me.

In 1952, MacArthur had signed the peace treaty with Japan that ended martial law. Previously, each military commander had full authority over all matters in his territory. After that, the Japanese were allowed to reestablish their provincial government departments and take jurisdiction for their own affairs. As might be expected, military commanders got themselves into trouble by trying to impose their will on local affairs, as they had been doing for the previous seven years following Japan's surrender. To solve this problem, the wise men of Camp Zama, the Tokyo headquarters of Far East Command (FECOM) decreed that a civil affairs officer should be assigned to each military post commander to help him stay out of trouble. How to find enough civil affairs officers to do this? Search the database of officers in Japan to see who had graduated from college. The IBM cards were sorted, my name popped up, and I got a new assignment. Two weeks' training in Tokyo, and Sandra and I moved to Camp Gifu on Honshu Island, about 50 miles north of Kyoto, Japan's cultural capital.

Camp Gifu had an airstrip that had been used to train kamikaze pilots (how does one train a kamikaze pilot?) and was now the headquarters of the Third Marine Division. For some reason, the army was placed in charge of housekeeping for the Marines, and Colonel Phipps was in charge of the army contingent. The base employed 2000 Japanese to operate the infrastructure (fire fighting, road repair, utilities, and perimeter security) and do all the needful for the Marines. It was here that I was told to help the good colonel keep the peace between America and Japan.

Sandra and I and our two dogs were given housing on the base. I was placed in charge of the newly created Civil Affairs office and reported to a really decent guy, Major Wilson, the base comptroller. I was also responsible for the Labor Office and worked with the Fiscal Office, headed by a

Lieutenant Hall. He turned out to be the oldest son of the Hall family, the creators of Hallmark greeting cards.

Gifu was famous for cormorant fishing. Each evening, boats with metal baskets of burning charcoal on a pole attached to the bow, surrounded by cormorants with metal rings around their necks tethered to the boat, would drift downstream with the current. The birds would fish but could not swallow the fish because of the iron ring around their necks. These fish, with cormorant beak marks, would be highly prized in the market. It was quite a spectacle to watch in the evenings.

It was a most enjoyable time for me. I remember many stories about those days. Some are silly, like the special assignment I did for the post's executive officer to investigate the loss or waste of several thousand dollars' worth of food. The exec charged the commissary officer with this loss, because a freezer broke down. It turned out the commissary officer, upon learning of the defrosted food, shifted the menu to serve the defrosted food several days earlier than scheduled. He then reprogrammed the originally scheduled rations to a future date. There was no loss. I could not get the exec to understand this until I wrote it up in a fancy report that he was required to forward up the chain to the next higher command. He then gave the commissary officer a commendation.

Another time, when I was CQ (charge of quarters), I hosed down a Marine barracks. Every so often the Marines would pull the barracks fire alarm as they arose in the morning for reveille. A full alert on the base resulted, and the fire truck would come screaming out of the firehouse to respond to what always turned out to be a false alarm. The CQ (there is always an officer on duty at the base 24/7) would also have to go to this show. At five a.m. the humor of all of this was somehow lost on me. After the third time it happened on my watch, I told the fire crew to hose down the barracks. I told their first sergeant I smelled smoke. Colonel Phipps got a call from the two-star commander of the division complaining about this, and I was called on the carpet. But there was never another false alarm on my watch.

However, the most important lesson for me was learning the dynamics of providing technical assistance in a different cultural setting. That lesson was to serve me well in my later economic development work.

During the seven-year period of martial law in Japan, particularly after the outbreak of the Korean War, our bases in Japan employed more and more Japanese workers to replace military staff performing routine duties. These employees received health benefits. Each army post contracted locally with Japanese health clinics to provide annual screening, particularly for tuberculosis, which was still rampant in Japan. I recall that the army was paying $6 per employee per month for provision of these health benefits. With the signing of the peace treaty, the responsibility for managing the health contract was now that of the prefectural government, headed by a Japanese civil employee named Unosan. After I took over the Labor office, I decided to inspect this clinic. I asked the base medical officer, Captain Segal, to accompany me, even though his responsibilities were limited to the health of military personnel and not the 2000 Japanese employees. What we found was appalling.

The place was filthy, not just unsanitary. The sewer drains had been stopped up for weeks. The supplies of medicines were somehow "not there." But worst of all, the annual chest x-ray was done with something that produced a 35-millimeter slide, and there was no equipment to read the slide at full size. They viewed the slide with an eyepiece. And on that view, it was determined whether or not the employee had contagious TB.

I decided to raise hell with the prefectural chief. My Japanese staff cautioned me about this and warned that there could be a serious romp if I did not handle the "face" issue properly. They suggested, and I agreed, that the information should be leaked out to the Japanese employees so they could see our action as being in their interest.

When the scheduled meeting was held, six people from the Japanese prefectural staff showed up. We did the "tea thing" and then the senior Japanese official made a profuse apology, said the Japanese government wanted to learn from us, and asked us to provide detailed recommendations for actions to be taken. There were two note takers on his staff and they hung on every word. We offered to send our fire engine (the one that hosed the Marine barracks) to blow out the sewer drains, and Captain Segal offered to help locate an x-ray machine that would do the job. All employees were later reexamined and a large number were found to have contagious TB. The medical supplies were rebuilt after the Japanese officials ended their sale on the open market.

No one on our side was confused as to how the Japanese felt about us. We were an enemy that had defeated them. But they saw in our presence a way they could improve themselves. The lesson was clear. If a society wants to change, it will take advantage of external resources. If not persuaded that change is in its interest, the society will continue to follow its old patterns, and no amount of aid can make a difference.

Not every encounter went as successfully as that one. On another occasion, a delegation of employees asked to meet with us. Their complaint was that we had hired non-Japanese to work on the post and that was not acceptable so long as there were unemployed Japanese citizens. I said that we were doing no such thing and asked for the names of non-Japanese that were hired. A list of thirty or so names was presented. These turned out to be residents of Japan whose families had moved to Japan from Korea a century earlier. Although born in Japan, they were not accepted as Japanese, nor identified in official records as such.

Here is a story on a more positive note. Sandra and I hired an artist to build and paint a *biobu*, a wedding screen to hang on our wall. It was about 6 feet wide by 3 feet high, consisted of four panels with a black lacquer frame, a three-inch gold brocade border, and a scene painted in the center. It took some time to persuade the artist that our taste did not run to cherry blossoms. We desired a scene from Japanese traditional history. The artist produced a scene with a lake, an island, a Shogun's palace with different levels that allowed figures to be seated around the Shogun according to rank, a bridge painted in vermillion, and some trees, both on the island and on the other side of the bridge.

We liked it very much and placed it on our wall. Every Japanese who saw the picture, irrespective of their economic or social status, from Unosan to my staff to the garbage collector, was able to interpret the scene exactly the same way. It takes place in the eighth century because vermillion (the bridge) is Chinese red, and the Chinese were dominant in Japan in the eighth century. Everyone spoke about the boat with the ladies on the lake while there was no boat visible in the painting. Apparently it was the usual way the Shogun and his nobles spent an afternoon. The point is, the history and culture of the Japanese is known not just to the upper class but is inculcated by family, clergy, and educational institutions at all strata of society.

A final lesson learned was how complex life can be for Japanese who are exposed to and involved in disciplines that have global interaction. One of the Japanese professionals on my staff in Gifu, a man named Hayashi, was an exceptionally gifted man who came to the United States in 1956 to attend university. He had no money but was determined to obtain an education in the States. He enrolled at Michigan State, was awarded scholarships, and completed his BA, MA, and his PhD in biochemistry in seven years. In 1962, he returned to Japan and married his betrothed (she had waited for him for seven years), brought her to the States, worked at Henry Ford Hospital all his life, and became an authority on organ transplant rejection remedies. He raised two children, both girls, in the States. Each daughter went back to Japan but could not reconcile herself to the form of life there and did not find a mate. Both returned and married here.

At the end of my two-year tour of active military duty, Sandra and I boarded a troop ship in Yokohama, sailed for twelve days to San Francisco, and returned to New York City. I was separated and returned to civilian life on February 1, 1955, having suffered nothing more than a slight loss of hearing. I remained in the active reserve, was promoted to captain, and then ended my military involvement in 1960 by transferring to the inactive reserve. I am proud to have served in the U.S. military.

3

THE U.S. FOREIGN SERVICE – MY INTERNSHIP – IRAN 1956–1960

SANDRA'S FAMILY HAD FOR many years been living in a fine apartment in Parkchester, a well- maintained cluster of high-rise apartment buildings in the Bronx, owned and managed by the Metropolitan Life Insurance Company. Housing in the New York City area was scarce, but Met Life provided priority to children of current residents. Sandra's family submitted an application on our behalf, and we were granted an apartment. That was a huge break because these apartments were rent-controlled. I found a job in the Wall Street area with an import-export firm, registered at New York University to complete my MA program, and waited for "the call."

That call was to be from a federal government agency in Washington, D.C., to schedule an interview in September 1955 for an entry-level trainee position. In fact, several calls came from different agencies because the Civil Service exam I had passed before entering active military duty (the Junior Management Assistant exam) put me on a select list for entry-level federal professional positions. But I had some clearly defined goals. I had no interest in working for domestic agencies but did not want to go into the traditional Foreign Service either. Rather, I was interested in Truman's

Point Four Program, giving aid to newly independent countries, the former colonies of the European imperial powers.

When the United Nations was first formed in 1945, there were fifty-one members. Today it has 193, a large number of them former colonies. During my college days, I took a course at CCNY in Imperialism and World Politics with my inspiring professor Oscar Janowsky, and developed a passion for righting the wrongs of European imperialism. I wanted to help these former colonies establish their own identities and economic viability as independent nations.

The Marshall Plan had been operating for nearly seven years and showed signs of being a huge success. Programs for Greece and Turkey had begun in 1946 with a political agenda, namely to head off the Soviet-supported local Communist parties. The Point Four Program started rolling in 1950. By 1955, the Greece-Turkey program had achieved some success and was folded into the International Cooperation Agency (ICA). That was the agency I chose. After a trip to Washington in September for an interview, I began work in February 1956. I completed my coursework at NYU and Sandra and I gave up that great Parkchester apartment and moved to Silver Spring, Maryland. This change of employment involved a significant cut in pay. I started working at ICA as an "Intern."

THE APPRENTICESHIP

Eleven years had passed since the end of World War II, about the same length of time between my birth date and the end of World War I. And what a huge difference there was in the approach of the victors to the vanquished. Thanks to the dominance of the United States, there were no demands for reparations to be paid by Germany and Italy. Instead, the Allies, mostly the States, provided funding to rebuild the economies of the Axis powers. Maybe the human species does learn from its mistakes after all.

The political and economic climate following World War II was remarkable. The dollar was almighty, and the United States and its citizenry were looked upon by the entire world as beneficent, benevolent, and generous people. The Lend-Lease accounts were wiped clean. The United States began making its payments under the Marshall Plan for reconstruction of Europe's war-torn economies in 1947. By 1955, the United States was giving aid to virtually every country that thought itself entitled to its own color on the global map.

More important, it seemed to me that these flows of aid were, at that time, not taken for granted by most recipients and were rarely, if ever, demanded for. Many senior aid representatives were recruited from the upper reaches of the academic community and transferred laterally from other U.S. government departments. They were often highly accredited and respected. As a result, they had significant influence with the aid recipients. The Eisenhower administration encountered little public resistance in the United States to large appropriations for these programs in the 1950s. I had landed a job in a growth industry.

Even with general public support for economic aid to these former colonies (or as they were often described, victims of "imperialism"), the program had some detractors. One of my earliest memories during the six-month orientation and training process was a visit to the Capitol galleries to listen to the House debate on the ICA appropriations bill. A congressman from New Jersey was delivering an oration reflecting his concern that we were providing aid to India while their representative at the UN General Assembly, V. K. Krishna Menon, was criticizing just about everything the United States was doing, particularly our resistance to communist China's admission to the UN. I remember him saying, "In my district, when we buy a vote, it stays bought!" He simply could not understand how India could get away with biting the hand that fed it. The Appropriations Bill passed easily.

The ICA was the U.S. government agency responsible for all U.S. economic assistance. It was a consolidation of earlier federal government agencies, such as the Foreign Operations Administration, the Marshall Plan, and the Inter-American aid agency that had been established long before to help Latin American countries. President Eisenhower had appointed Harold Stassen to pull these disparate organizations together. Congress had given him special authority to waive the laborious and time-consuming Civil Service employment process for terminating Civil Service employees, and he set about firing some of the best, albeit Democratic, appointees. The mood in ICA was dark when I was recruited, even though John Hollister had by then replaced Stassen as head of ICA.

ICA was a "temporary" agency. It was understood that this meant we were to work ourselves out of a job, no small feat for any bureaucracy. The Marshall Plan had been successful and was to be concluded. The work with the former colonies was to be short term. Everyone thought our work could be completed within ten years. In fact, I can remember one of the conclusions of a 1957 evaluation team that examined our economic aid program to Pakistan. U.S. aid levels would increase, reaching about $100 million by 1960. The aid level then would decline over the next five years until it ended. At that time, no one really gave much consideration to the idea of providing continuing annual resource transfers to these developing nations for poverty alleviation.

The "congressional presentations," the administration's annual requests for continued funding of ICA, used that same approach, arguing that ICA was trying to work itself out of its job, to justify the new funding requests. More or less, the more liberal members of Congress were usually sympathetic to continued aid funding proposals based on economic development rationales while more conservative representatives seemed more responsive to strategic arguments. ICA presented arguments for both sides of the isle, often drawing on the perceived threat of Soviet expansion. Many of the country-specific aid requests would begin their narratives with some variation of the statement, "Country X is strategically located between country Y and country Z."

What surprised me most in the first months of training was how technologically behind the curve Washington was. In my work before joining the government, I learned that brokerage houses on Wall Street calculated every client's margin account value at the end of each business day. The next morning, there would be a statement of the surplus or deficit in that account resulting from the daily change in the stock or commodity prices, plus the changes resulting from the trading done by the client. At ICA, program expenditure data was not available until six weeks after the actual expenditure took place. We are talking here about the Treasury Department's actual disbursements.

IRAN DESK

After eight months of training in the Office of Organization and Methods (O&M), I was assigned to the Iran Desk as assistant desk officer. The desk officer was W. Carter Ide, and this was another lucky turn for me. He was my first "government boss" and a wonderful one. He became my mentor for the four years I remained on his staff, and well beyond throughout my career. We became good friends for the rest of his life. Carter had worked in Europe on the Marshall Plan, was as sophisticated about this new business of foreign aid as anyone could be at that early stage, and seemed to enjoy my naïveté. He had been one of the old-line employees that were "Stassenated,"(his employment summarily terminated by Harold Stassen), but then rehired after John Hollister took over the agency. To round out my education, our secretary, Agnes Daugherty, a redheaded Irish woman of some seniority who understood well how the agency operated and was perfectly suited to keep a junior officer in line, also guided me.

Our aid program to Iran in 1956—when I first appeared on the scene—had many political and military overtones. It had started in 1949 as a modest technical assistance effort. The shah of Iran, a young Swiss-educated lad, was known to be a weak-willed, vacillating ruler compared with his father, the all-macho, powerful, and ruthless Reza Shah, who had ruled with British guidance before World War II and died during the war. The royal family, notably the shah's sister, and the political elite had become highly corrupt; popular support for the regime was beginning to erode.

Some Iranian History

Iran, the former Persia, has an interesting history. During the 1800s, Britain had treated the country as a buffer between the Indian subcontinent and Russia. It had worked out an understanding with the tsar that Britain would confine its operations to the southern portion of Iran, near the Persian Gulf and along the border with India, while Russia would operate only in Iran's north, along Russia's own southern border, in Azerbaijan, and along the Caspian Sea to the Afghan border. The two imperial powers cut the same deal on Afghanistan, giving that country a buffer status as well. The center of the country was left to the Iranians to rule without outside interference. In this way, the two world powers hoped to avoid any skirmishes between their respective business traders and troops.

In 1906, Iran's shah, Muzzaffar-al-Din Shah Qajar issued a proclamation establishing the Majlis, Iran's parliament. A constitution was adopted to allow for popular elections, restricting the vote to the elite and educated over the age of twenty-five. The Majlis was given some powers, but ultimate authority rested with the shah.

At the end of the Second World War, the Iranians successfully negotiated a deal with the Soviets to have them vacate the northern regions of Iran. The British had discovered oil in the south in 1906 and were not about to give that up. The Anglo-Iranian Oil Company (AIOC), ostensibly in partnership with the Iranian government but actually run by the British, maintained control in the south. That company had been operating in Iran since its first successful oil well, the Masjid Suleyman well, began producing oil in 1906. Since its first day of production, that single well had produced 17,000 barrels of oil per day, every day of the year. No pumping was required; the underground pressure was sufficient to power the off-take. Several hundred wells were put in place, and oil gushed from them. The

AIOC had full control of Iran's oil production and marketing. A royalty to the government of Iran was paid for each barrel of oil extracted, but this royalty payment was a mere token of the market value of the oil, priced in 1956 at the wellhead at $2.04 per barrel.

The Cold War competition between the Soviet Union and the "free world" intensified during 1947 through 1950 with the Berlin Blockade, the attack on South Korea by North Korea, and the fall of Czechoslovakia, Poland, and Hungary to Soviet client-state status. The Soviets were supporting the communist parties in Greece and Turkey, hoping that these countries would also become part of the Soviet bloc. They provided financial support to Iran's communist party as well (the Tudeh Party), in the hope that Iran would gain full independence from the British and also join the Soviet orbit.

Iranians observed that as former colonies gained independence throughout the world, many of them were taking on the form of democracy; individual freedom and universal suffrage for the citizenry was growing. Pressure on the Iranian government mounted as anti-establishment representatives were voted into the Majlis. The young shah gradually relinquished more of the monarchy's controls to the Majlis. Mohammad Mosaddegh became prime minister on April 28, 1951, largely with the support of the Tudeh Party.

On May 1, 1951, Mosaddegh seized and nationalized the AIOC. Once the oilfields had been nationalized, the British managed to get all other participants in the international oil business to boycott the Iranians and, for two years (during the Korean War), this issue was a flashpoint on the global agenda.

History books like to use the following language, or something similar, to characterize what happened to resolve this dispute: "Mosaddegh was removed from power in a coup on 19 August 1953, organized and carried out by the CIA at the request of the British MI6, which chose Iranian General Fazlollah Zahedi to succeed Mosaddegh."

That statement is taken from Wikipedia and seems to have become the conventional wisdom in the public mind as well as in Western academia. The entire blame for the ouster of Mosaddegh is laid on an action of the U.S. CIA and the British MI6. The recent Hollywood film *ARGO* used that same scenario as a part of its introduction. Even the comedian, Jon Stewart has taken this on and has included an apology to the Iranians for U.S. actions in one of his monologues.

I was not on the scene until October 1956 but had occasion to discuss these events with those who were there, indeed, with some of the principal actors, such as the CIA chief of station in Tehran. I had been assigned to serve on a senior evaluation team in early 1957, and spent four months examining the U.S. military and economic assistance program for Iran. My take on the events surrounding Mosaddegh's fall from power is quite different.

The U.S. government cleared my MA thesis, "U.S. Economic Assistance to Iran ––1951 to 1959," for submission to New York University on July 24, 1959. It deals with the events leading up to the fall of Mosaddegh on August 19, 1953. My thesis did not mention any CIA involvement, or it would not have been cleared for release. Still, the events described in the thesis can assist in surmising what role the CIA could have played.

The conventional wisdom, suggesting that the CIA organized and executed the coup without support or direction from the Iranian authorities, implies that somehow hundreds of U.S. military personnel were injected into the streets of Teheran and went around killing Mosaddegh's followers. That is utter nonsense.

The CIA station chief had a close personal relationship with the shah for many years. They played bridge every Friday night. The US government's main concern was that the Tudeh (Communist) party would seize power and that Iran, with its oil reserves, would become a Soviet client state. The United States and Britain saw the shah as the only legitimate domestic political force that could challenge Mosaddegh and the Tudeh party.

The shah took the decision to dismiss Mosaddegh as prime minister and sent him a *firman,* or royal decree, delivered by Colonel Nassiri, commander of the Imperial Guard. When Nassiri arrived, Mosaddegh had his guards arrest him. At that point, the shah asked the United States and Britain to help him. The CIA was then authorized to rally those Iranian troops and civilians loyal to the shah, bribing them where necessary, so as to restore the shah's authority over the prime minister.

There is a clear record that the United States and Britain encouraged the shah to dismiss Mosaddegh and assured him of support if he did so. But does that rise to the definition of a coup? The shah had absolute control and power in Iran. He appointed Mosaddegh to the position of prime minister in 1951. He then dismissed him in 1953 and remained in power. How can that be described as a coup?

CIA documents leaked to the *New York Times* in 2000, particularly the "history" written by Donald Wilber, paint a picture of agents manipulating the entire scene. But these descriptions need to be evaluated with the understanding that the writers had something of a cowboy mentality and visualized themselves and events in an unrealistic light. Regrettably the *New York Times* reporters did not do this. The dominant ingredients that sustained the shah's power and position in 1953 were the same ingredients that sustained the imperialist powers in Iran for the previous century: money and bribery. The United States provided those ingredients in support of the shah and the British.

Some historians have concluded their analysis along the same lines. In 2004, Mark Gasiorowski, a political scientist at Tulane University, and Malcolm Byrne coedited *Mohammad Mosaddeq and the 1953 Coup in Iran* arguing that "the climate of intense cold war rivalry between the superpowers, together with Iran's strategic vital location between the Soviet Union and the Persian Gulf oilfields, led U.S. officials to believe that they had to take whatever steps were necessary to prevent Iran from falling into Soviet hands." While "these concerns seem vastly overblown today," the pattern of contemporary concerns—"the 1945-46 Azerbaijan crisis, the consolidation of Soviet control in Eastern Europe, the communist triumph in China, and the Korean War, and with the Red Scare at its height in the United States"—would not allow U.S. officials to risk the Tudeh Party gaining power in Iran. Furthermore, "U.S. officials believed that resolving the oil dispute was essential for restoring stability in Iran, and after March 1953 it appeared that the dispute could be resolved only at the expense either of Britain or of Mosaddegh." Gasiorowski and Byrne conclude, "It was geostrategic considerations, rather than a desire to destroy Mosaddegh's movement, to establish a dictatorship in Iran or to gain control over Iran's oil, that persuaded U.S. officials to undertake the coup."[2]

Faced with choosing between British interests and Iran, the United States chose Britain, Gasiorowski said. "Britain was the closest ally of the United States, and the two countries were working as partners on a wide range of vitally important matters throughout the world at this time. Preserving this close relationship was more important to U.S. officials than saving Mosaddegh's tottering regime." A year earlier, British Prime Minister Winston Churchill used Britain's support for the United States in the Cold War to insist the United States not undermine his campaign to isolate Mosaddegh. "Britain was supporting the Americans in Korea, he reminded Truman, and had a right to expect 'Anglo-American unity' on Iran....The two main winners of World War II, who had been Allies during the war, became superpowers and competitors as soon as the war ended, each with their own spheres of influence and client states. After the 1953 coup, Iran became one of the client states of the United States."

In June 2009, President Barack Obama in a speech in Cairo, Egypt, talked about the U.S.-Iran relationship and mentioned the role of the United States in the 1953 coup saying:

---

2 https://en.wikipedia.org/wiki/Iran–United_States_relations - as of May 2, 2014

This issue has been a source of tension between the United States and the Islamic Republic of Iran. For many years, Iran has defined itself in part by its opposition to my country, and there is indeed a tumultuous history between us. In the middle of the Cold War, the United States played a role in the overthrow of a democratically elected Iranian government. Since the Islamic Revolution, Iran has played a role in acts of hostage taking and violence against U.S. troops and civilians. This history is well known. Rather than remain trapped in the past, I have made it clear to Iran's leaders and people that my country is prepared to move forward.

Nevertheless, this carefully crafted language implies that, in 1953, there was such a thing as a "democratically elected Iranian government." Is that really what Iran had there?

MY WORK ON THE IRAN DESK

After the fall of Mosaddegh, the shah agreed to a settlement with the British oil company whereby the profits of future oil production and sale would be split on a 50/50 basis. The oil fields began cranking up operations in 1954. The United States then increased the economic aid program to about $50 million a year.

Simultaneously, we initiated a military construction program to build fortifications in the Elburz Mountains with the far-fetched rationale that, if the Russians attacked by a land route across Iran for the purpose of seizing the Suez Canal, the Iranians would stop them as they climbed through the Elburz Mountains. It was far-fetched because both the Russians and we knew that the way to attack a target so that the attacker had control of the skies over the target was to establish an "air head" and fly the troops into the assault area. I had learned that at Fort Benning in 1953 during my military training. The 82nd Airborne Division was set up for exactly that purpose. The 1948 Soviet blockade of Berlin, during which we airlifted supplies— including coal— for months to that city, proved this tactical concept.

There was no question in anyone's mind that the Russians could maintain control of the air space around the Suez Canal, if they chose to do so. But the main consideration for the program was that we were supporting the shah's hold on power, and that the aid program was an important tool to help do that. Given the uncertain allegiance of Iran's military leadership to the shah during the Mosaddegh period, getting the Iranian military out of Teheran and into the mountains was seen as a viable way to support the shah. Giving the generals some new military toys to play with was a cheap way to do this.

Each annual cycle for the congressional appropriation request would yield the same conversation between the Defense Department desk officer for Iran and me. "How much do you need in local currency (which was generated by our economic aid program) to complement your military construction for this year?" I would ask. "How much have you got?" would be his reply. It finally hit me. The military never acknowledge they have set up all the defenses they need. Preparing for an attack is a never-ending job. The military are indoctrinated to stop preparing defense positions only once the first wave of the enemy begins attacking. What's the point of asking them how much is needed when they operate under this mind-set?

By the end of 1956, oil production had resumed and reached the 1950 quantitative production levels. As a result of the new 50/50 split, Iran's share of the revenues increased by a factor of eight from its pre-nationalization level. Nevertheless, U.S. aid continued at the new higher level set in 1954.

The program had another problem. The head of our aid mission in Teheran, from 1953 to 1955, was William Warne, a former assistant secretary of agriculture who had once had a run-in with a congressman named Porter Hardy. Hardy was now chairman of a congressional sub-committee that had oversight of ICA appropriations, and he decided to launch a congressional investigation into the Iran aid program (some say, to get at

Warne). The Iran desk at ICA was required to research and respond to all the inquiries that Hardy's committee directed at ICA.

Under Carter's guidance, I was not only doing the leg work to fend off these attacks on the program, but was also helping him handle day-to-day operational tasks (i.e., approval of projects and funding) associated with running a program with about 200 technicians and their families living in Teheran and ten provincial sub-offices.

The country desk officer is at the center of action. He is, at once, the mission director's spokesperson in Washington, and the key staff person for that country on the staff of the regional assistant administrator of the agency. Nothing happens with that country's program that does not require his input. The mission director expects him to lobby for the actions of the mission that need Washington's approval. The regional assistant administrator asks the desk officer to provide independent advice on these same issues. The allegiance of the desk officer is therefore divided.

There are many personnel tasks associated with 200 Americans stationed at the aid mission. But there is a personnel office to handle that. The different technical projects are each backstopped by the respective technical offices. But the most powerful weapon in the desk officer's arsenal is the annual budgeting process. He is responsible for vetting the mission's budget and advising the Washington bureaucracy on the content of the congressional presentation justifying the next year's funding requests. This was an area in which I excelled. I could find soft spots in the proposed budgets from a mile away.

There was also a country desk officer at the State Department. State wanted desperately to influence— actually, to control— ICA's funding and programming decisions. In those early days following the Marshall Plan's success, ICA was able to keep control of its programs. Later, in the 1970s, the center of power and decision making shifted to the political side.

I loved the work and was glad to put in ten to twelve hour workdays assisting Carter. A year later, Carter was promoted to chief of the Greece,

Turkey and Iran Division and I became the "acting" Iran desk officer, even though my rank (GS-9) was way below the rating for the job (GS-14). That was all right with me, since it meant I could get promotions as soon as I met the time-in-grade eligibility requirements.

Carter's circle of friends was from the Marshall Plan. Many had served in Europe following World War II and now held senior policy-level positions in Washington. Carter could pick up the phone and "check things out" to get some inside news before information became generally available. He was also a "hand wringer." When analyzing the facts to draw a conclusion, he would examine every aspect from every angle before announcing how he stood on an issue. I would want to get on with it, but he would be very careful in his deliberations. And then, when he would let me know his reasoning and give me my marching orders, often, a couple of hours later, he would come to me with yet another previously overlooked argument that could tilt the conclusion the other way. This process could go back and forth several times; and often, my mind felt like a Ping-Pong ball.

Here we were, in a world where every day the population was growing and the poverty levels are deepening as the gains from investment were eaten up. The U.S.S.R. was daily growing in power and becoming a bigger threat. Technology's relentless march was concentrating greater and greater destructive power into smaller and smaller containers ... and our responses to these challenges were so slow. I tended to rush to judgment; Carter was more deliberative and perhaps that made us a good partnership. I was a brash young upstart who regarded the passage of time as the enemy of development.

Carter was also a much more forgiving person, more accepting of the limitations of others than I. I remember having a row with a woman who worked in another office because she had not done what she had promised. Carter was very cross at me and I was just as furious. I finally said, "She is just a mental cripple!" He softly replied that we were all mental cripples, of one sort or another.

MY FIRST PROGRAM EVALUATION

Within three months of my assignment to the Iran Desk in late 1956, our program was selected for an in-depth evaluation. Two senior officers, Ray Thurston, former deputy chief of mission of our embassy in Greece and Hugh Farley, former director of ICA's mission in Lebanon, plus a staff assistant— me— would spend four months, including a two month trip to Iran, to provide a definitive examination and assessment to the State Department senior staff and other key administration personnel of our assistance efforts in Iran. Somewhere in the vast storehouse of government documents is a file of "memoranda of conversations" that covers what every person with whom we conversed during the four-month evaluation mission said to the team. I know that for sure because I wrote every blessed one. What an eye-opening experience it was for me. Before we left, we talked not only with every person of substance dealing with Iran in ICA and the State Department, but all the other actors who had something going in Iran including CIA, Departments of Defense, Commerce, Agriculture, and the White House.

This evaluation, besides equipping me to do my job as Iran Desk Officer for the next three years, also provided me with a wonderful education about political-economic program evaluation techniques. This was to serve me well later in other assignments. Throughout my career in the U.S. Foreign Service, and then during the subsequent twenty-two years during which I performed more than three-dozen consultations for international organizations, my work often involved special evaluations of economic aid programs (See chapter 10, below).

The evaluation team took a full four weeks to get briefed in Washington. This was followed by an eight-week tour throughout Iran, visiting nearly every one of the ten ICA provincial offices, and then another four weeks in Washington to write our report. Four such teams would be doing this in four different aid recipient countries. When we returned, there was a serious peer review process of each team's findings, overseen by C. Tyler

Wood, one of the most experienced ICA officers. He had been the head of the U.S. aid mission in Seoul following the Korean War and was a close confidant of General Maxwell Taylor (who had replaced MacArthur). The word "superficial" was used often during those peer review sessions to characterize a team's unsubstantiated allegations. These reviews were an effort to sharpen the teams' conclusions. These reports were highly classified and, unlike other evaluations I was to perform in my later years, were read widely by senior administration officials.

The substance of our aid, leaving aside the military construction program, was well conceived. Technical assistance was concentrated in the field of public administration. Young bureaucrats were trained in western techniques to manage the responsibilities of government, including the financial system and oil revenues. There were also projects to support Iran's own efforts— funded with oil revenues— in agriculture, health, rural water supply and electrification. On the shadier side, there was some advisory and equipment support for the civilian police. There was some suspicion that a part of this support was actually reaching the SAVAK, Iran's secret police in the Interior Ministry.

LAND REFORM IN IRAN

The big problem, from a long-term perspective, was the need for land reform. Iran still had a feudal system. The land owning gentry had legal title to massive numbers of villages and to all their cultivable lands. Many useful services were provided to the tenant farmers such as the extension of credit for seed and fertilizer. Often, the landowners marketed the crop after harvest. The landlord controlled irrigation flow in that he maintained the qanāt tunnels. And for these services plus the ownership of the land itself, the landlord retained most of the proceeds from the crop sale.

Briefly, the old feudal system called for crop proceeds to be divided five ways; one fifth each for land ownership, provision of seed/fertilizer, water rights, animal-drawing power, and labor. If the tenant farmer owned the animal used for cultivation, he would get 40 percent of the sales proceeds. The landlord would usually provide the fertilizer and seed, and maintained the qanāts, which provided the underground water. Of course he owned the land. That entitled him to 60 percent of the proceeds from sale. Though clearly exploitative, this system was not as bad as some other ancient Western feudal systems.

The social structure of this system was equally exploitive. The landlord was the judge and jury for any disputes on his land and villages. Often he would exercise his prerogative, when a village girl got married, to deflower her before the wedding. If Iran were to become a modern nation, this system would have to change.

It has often been said, "Fools rush in where angels fear to tread." Into this quagmire, the naïve Americans came running. The evaluation team strongly recommended that we press the shah to undertake land reform. I have come to believe this U.S. assisted land reform effort was directly responsible for antagonizing Iran's religious establishment and gave rise to Khomeini and the mullahs. The *Khalq*, the Iranian religious establishment, owned or controlled a substantial number of the forty-five thousand villages in Iran. The land reform effort took away their traditional revenues, which had been used to fund the same things every religious order funds: their mosques for prayer, their madrassas for religious education and charitable work.

The following paragraphs have been extracted from Wikipedia. While there is no guarantee that every detail is accurate, the general tenor of the description seems valid:

> In 1957 martial law was ended after 16 years and Iran became closer to the West, joining the Baghdad Pact and receiving military and economic aid from the US. In 1961, Iran initiated a series of economic, social, agrarian and administrative reforms to modernize the country that became known as the Shah's White Revolution.

The core of this program was land reform. Modernization and economic growth proceeded at an unprecedented rate, fueled by Iran's vast petroleum reserves, the third largest in the world. However the reforms, including the White Revolution, did not greatly improve economic conditions and the liberal pro-Western policies alienated certain Islamic religious and political groups. …. In the 1970s leftist guerilla groups such as Mujaheddin-e-Khalq (MEK), emerged and attacked regime and foreign targets.

—∞∞∞—

Here is another description of the effect of the land reform program contained in Wikipedia:

The White Revolution received most of its criticism from two main groups: the clergy, and the landlords. The landlords were angry about the land reforms because their land was bought by the government and then sold in smaller plots to the citizenry at a lower price. They also did not appreciate the government undercutting their authority when it came to dealing with peasants or land laborers.

The powerful Shi'ah clergy were also angered at the reforms that removed much of their traditional powers in the realms of education and family law, as well as lessening their previously strong influence in the rural areas. A "large percentage of the upper echelon of the clergy came from landowning families" deeply affected by the reform and much absentee rent income went directly to the clergy and their institutions. The rents from an estimated 10,000 villages whose rents helped finance the clerical establishment were eligible for redistribution.

The most important and relevant consequence of the White Revolution and the reforms it brought was the rising popularity of

Ruhollah Khomeini. Khomeini started out as a member of the clergy who followed the practice of "quietism", not getting involved with the government or political affairs. With the growing corruption of the Shah and the implementation of reforms through the White Revolution, Khomeini grew to be an outspoken political enemy of the Shah. The White Revolution was the catalyst for Khomeini's change in thought. Once Khomeini, as a respected member of the clergy, started to openly oppose the Shah and call for his overthrow, people of all different professions and economic status began to see him as a figure to rally behind.

Though the White Revolution contributed towards the economic and technological advancement of Iran, the failures of some of the land reform programs and the partial lack of democratic reforms, as well as severe antagonism towards the White Revolution from the clergy and landed elites, would ultimately contribute to the Shah's downfall and the Iranian Revolution in 1979.[3]

<hr />

In evaluating Iran's land reform efforts, one should consider the difficulties encountered in Europe in the 1800s, particularly in Russia, when similar reforms were implemented to free the serfs. Then, imagine how difficult it would be to implement such reforms in Iran, one of the world's most corrupt societies.

The former landlord was given twenty-five year government bonds in payment for his land. Then, other mechanisms had to be established to provide those services to the tenant farmer that had been previously provided by the landlord. Credit for purchase of seed and fertilizer was needed. An agricultural bank was established with branches throughout Iran. If the branch manager demanded a payoff to make the loan, as would often be the case, the often illiterate borrower might think he did not have

---

3 https://en.wikipedia.org/wiki/White_Revolution as of May 2, 2014.

to repay the loan because he had bribed the manager before the loan was made. Additionally, the farmer would then have to purchase the seed from a supplier and obtain timely delivery. Subsequently, the tenant farmer would have to combine his crop with others in order to market it. A cooperative might have to be established. Every step of the way was fraught with corruption.

Ray Thurston, the senior evaluation team member and I got along exceedingly well. Our friendship continued long after the evaluation ended. After completing this evaluation he spent four years in Paris as political counselor to General Lauris Norstad, the commander of NATO. Then he went on to become ambassador to Poland and then Haiti.

Ray had a number of important contacts in Iran from his earlier Foreign Service assignments. Hassan Ali Mansur, later the prime minister (who would be assassinated in 1965), was one of the young Iranians our evaluation team met, dined and drank with during our two-month stay in Iran. He was not in government then, was highly critical of the shah, particularly his immediate family, including the shah's sister who seemed to be involved in every corrupt transaction of significant magnitude.

The evaluation caused some minor readjustments to the aid program. Its biggest benefit was that it educated me in the details and rationale of our efforts and I could use that background in my daily work with Carter.

From 1957 to 1958, I earned rapid promotions. Carter continued to serve as chief of the Greece-Turkey-Iran Division (GS-15). Even though I was promoted regularly, I was still too junior for the Iran Desk position (GS-14). In 1959, a more senior officer was placed into the desk officer job and I had to step back to act as his assistant. That was gut-wrenching for me.

Also, around that time, my marriage with Sandra was coming apart and I was getting counseling. Being required to serve a guy who knew less than I about the job squashed my ego. In one session with my therapist, I related a dream in which a small plane piloted by my new boss was flying low, in trouble and crashed into the window of our apartment. Somehow, it teetered there and my boss was unable to get out. I reached over to help him but the plane then tilted and lost its perch on the window and fell to earth with my boss still in it. The therapist said I pushed my boss over the edge. I denied it, pointing out that I tried to save him. He smiled and asked me, "So... who wrote that script?"

Sandra had found work in Washington as a stockbroker. There is no point in belaboring the problems of our marriage here. There are always at least two sides to this kind of issue. We had a wonderful time in Japan during my military assignment. But once we settled in Washington, things got unstuck. There were no children to complicate things. In mid-1959, we separated and divorced in 1960. My determination to end the marriage convinced my mother that she had been right all along in thinking her "number two son" was unstable.

One of my friends in the army reserve unit to which I was then assigned, a lawyer named Marv Perlis, helped me secure an "Alabama" divorce. In those days, many states made it difficult to obtain a "no fault" divorce, except in Alabama. Since it was unseemly for a gentleman or a lady to appear in court, the attorneys conducted it all. Neither party had to make a physical appearance. Being in the state for twenty-four hours satisfied residency requirements. I flew down to Birmingham, took a taxi to the attorney's office, signed some papers and handed the attorney our signed agreement. That was it. He did the rest.

There were some amusing scenes around the period of the divorce. Sandra tried to project a public image that "Lu had lost his senses" and was acting irrationally in wanting a divorce. "Wasn't he undergoing therapy to deal with his craziness?" She would continue to be the rational one and get on with her life, as though Lu had just gone on a "long trip."

Shortly after the divorce, Jul was scheduled to perform a new opera, *Bomarzo* written by the contemporary Argentine composer, Ginastera, at the Lisner Auditorium in Washington DC. Jul asked me if

I was coming to the performance and I respectfully declined because I knew this was an atonal, disharmonic piece. I was not interested in listening to an entire evening of twentieth century contemporary music. We arranged to have lunch together on the day of the opening, just the two of us.

We met at a restaurant and I could see that Jul was troubled by something. After talking about the divorce, which had become final about a month earlier, he confessed that he and Rita were to attend a pre-performance dinner at Sandra's apartment and that she had made a theater party out of the event by buying tickets and inviting all of our mutual friends, both to the dinner and then to the performance.

WOW! So then, I changed my mind about going to the performance. Jul got me two tickets and I invited the attractive woman I was then dating to accompany me. Jul, to his credit, decided to skip Sandra's dinner that evening. But I went to the show, and had a ball during each intermission, meandering the isles and the lobby as my friends darted away from me. I, of course, would give chase and, when my charmer and I caught up with them, would go into my spiel that I did not realize they liked this very modern music. "Had I known," I would say, "I would have gotten you complementary tickets to the show." I relished the experience!

Carter was absolutely wonderful to me, knowing I was going through a rough patch both at home and also with my new boss. He covered for me and treated me very gently.

In early 1960, State, Defense and ICA undertook another set of Country Program Evaluations. I applied for reassignment to that new program so as to get out of the other difficult relationship in my life. My experience with the Iran evaluation qualified me to be detailed to State for six months to do two evaluations (U.S. military assistance to Belgium and to the Netherlands). I had a truly enjoyable experience with that. I describe the details of these evaluations in chapter 10, which deals with the broad and important subject of evaluations.

I had also been slated to take an overseas assignment. Once my divorce was final, I requested one with the ICA mission in Turkey. In late summer 1960, I transferred to the Foreign Service Reserve and was posted to Turkey. A new chapter in my life began.

IRAN EPILOGUE

Recently, diplomatic relations between Iran and the West, particularly the United States, have been in the news. The economic sanctions imposed by the UN, the European Union and the United States have brought the Iranian government to the negotiating table with respect to their nuclear weapons development program. The September 2013 issue of *Foreign Affairs* contained an essay analyzing the philosophy and outlook of Iran's supreme leader, Ali Khamenei. That essay moved me to offer some thoughts for the public dialogue based on my earlier experiences. The letter sent to *Foreign Affairs* in September 2013 may be found as Annex 1. I also took issue with Stephen Kinzer's book, *The Brothers: John Foster Dulles, Allen Dulles, and Their Secret World War,* as well as the New York Times book review by Adam LeBor in terms of the treatment of the so-called Iran Coup (See Annex 2).

The search for truth is fraught with obstacles. Historical records should always be treated with suspicion since it is the victors who inevitably write them. Iran's recent history seems to have been rewritten to describe the fall of Mosaddegh as an American coup targeted at destroying a fledgling Iranian democratic government. That rewriting of history is a fiction, which should not be allowed to stand.

In the foregoing pages I have attempted to put the actions of the U.S. government in Iran in proper context, as I witnessed it. The latest sport among some academics, as they survey events through their rearview mirror, is to attack decisions taken by our government during a completely different context of time. I often want to tell them that some of the very decisions they are now attacking have kept them safe. Several have taken the CIA documents leaked to the *New York Times* in April 2000 and have woven a story that vilifies the U.S. action to support the shah in 1953.[4] Shah Pahlavi was indeed as much an autocrat in that period as his father had been before the war and, for that matter, as is Iran's current "Supreme Ruler"— Khamenei. The shah's dismissal of his own prime minister, however, does not rise to the definition of a coup.

Ryan Crocker, a former United States ambassador to Afghanistan and Iraq, has been quoted as follows:

> (T)he United States must make clear that we do not seek to overthrow the Iranian regime. Iranian paranoia on this issue is virtually limitless and understandably so. In 1953, the American and British intelligence services ousted a democratically elected Iranian prime minister, an episode that very few Americans remember and no Iranian will ever forget. [5]

I'm sure the last phrase of this statement is true. As for the rest of the quote, we have the Steven Kinzers of the world, as well as certain New York Times reporters, to thank for the popular acceptance of that oversimplistic interpretation of history. As this book is about to go to press (July 2014) another article in the July/August issue of *Foreign Affairs* attempts to dispel the popular myth about the "CIA coup in Iran." That article, written by Ray Takeyh, comes to a similar conclusion to the one I have offered above. After documenting the events and the exaggerated role ascribed to the CIA, he writes this final paragraph:

> Whatever the reason for the persistence of the mythology about 1953, it is long past time for the Americans and the Iranians to move

---

4 See Web site on Iran – Overthrow of Mosaddegh http://www2.gwu.edu/~nsarchiv/NSAEBB/NSAEBB435

5 *New York Times*, November 4, 2013

beyond it. As Washington and Tehran struggle to end their protracted enmity, it would help greatly if the United States no longer felt the need to keep implicitly apologizing for its role in Mosaddeq's ouster. As for the Islamic Republic, at a moment when it is dealing with internal divisions and uncertainties about its future, it would likewise help for it to abandon its outdated notions of victimhood and domination by foreigners and acknowledge that it was Iranians themselves who were the principal protagonists in one of the most important turning points in their country's history.[6]

Yet, one wonders why many scholars give a free pass to the actions of the Moscow-financed Comintern during the six or so years following the end of the Second World War in countries like Greece, Turkey, Iran, Czechoslovakia, Poland, the Baltic states, Bulgaria and Yugoslavia. If American foreign policy can be called "interventionist" what should one call Soviet policy in those days?

---

6 *Foreign Affairs*, July/August 2014

4

TURKEY: 1960 – 1962

A WATERSHED IN MY life was my assignment for a two-year tour of service at the USAID mission in Ankara, Turkey. I had learned the foreign aid business over the last five years and understood how Washington worked. I had developed a favorable reputation within the agency and launched on an exciting career path. My marriage to Sandra had been ended and I was a "free" man; I had completed all work for my MA in International Policies at NYU, including the thesis requirement. I had sufficient income to have some degree of financial independence for the first time in my life. The assignment as assistant program officer at USAID Ankara put me to work under some very experienced, smart and capable people. It promised to be challenging and interesting in a country that was very important to the United States. And it was not too far from Europe, convenient for travel purposes. It was, in every sense, a fresh start to my adult life.

In September 1960, I purchased a Peugeot 403 for delivery in Paris and set out on a drive through Europe, Yugoslavia and Bulgaria into Turkey. The USAID mission got me a classy, two-bedroom, furnished apartment within walking distance from my office. First order of business was a visit to the military Post Exchange (PX) located in the center of Ankara to buy new supplies and adult toys (i.e. a neat hi-fi system) to complement the furnishings. Next was the recruitment of Gulsun, an elderly, slightly crippled (she had a pronounced limp) but sweet, devoted woman as my full-time housekeeper. Boy-oh-boy … at the tender age of thirty, I had arrived!

Turkey was, at that time, a major recipient of U.S. military assistance. It sits on the border with Russia (indeed, Mount Ararat is right there). The U.S. military plus our National Security Agency (NSA)—sometimes referred to as "the world's eavesdropper" —had set up electronic listening posts in the Turkish city of Trabzon to tap into Soviet military and intelligence communications. The U.S. Air Force had air bases in Turkey; the Navy had a large presence in the port city of Izmir. A U.S. Air Force hospital was located right in the middle of Ankara. We were a close ally of Turkey and were very well connected to their military establishment.

In May 1960, three months before I arrived, the Turkish military staged a coup and overthrew the civilian government. This was an internal matter for the Turks and the United States was not consulted. The head of the junta, General Cemal Gürsel, had thrown the entire civilian cabinet into jail on an island in the Sea of Marmara called Yassiada and was putting each minister on trial for corruption and misappropriation of public funds. Former Prime Minister Menderes, Finance Minister Polatkin and Foreign Minister Zorlu would eventually be executed in September 1961 by hanging. One month later, in October 1961, the military returned power to a civilian government after adopting a new constitution. At the time of my arrival, it was not clear how many of the cabinet would be punished. On the domestic political front, things were tense.

Our economic aid to Turkey had three components. The first was a technical assistance program in the areas of agriculture, education, public administration, and health. The second was a "PL480" food import program, which shipped surplus U.S. agricultural products, like wheat, to Turkey. Payment to the United States was allowed in local currency (liras) that was then spent, for the most part, on economic development projects in the country itself. The third component was a capital assistance program to finance commercial imports needed by Turkish industry and for which Turkey did not have sufficient foreign exchange. My assignment in the USAID mission's program office put me at the center of these activities.

And what an illustrious group of colleagues I worked with. Stuart Van Dyke was the mission director; Wade Lathram, his deputy, also served as economic counselor at our embassy. Roger Nelson was my direct boss and Ernie Stern was the mission economist. Ernie would later become executive vice president at the World Bank. Each one of these persons had long pedigrees and had distinguished themselves in executing important professional assignments for the U.S. government. None were defensive and were always open to new ideas to improve our operations. I felt truly fortunate to be given the opportunity to work with this group.

THE REMARKABLE EMIN BOYSAN

One of my early assignments had to do with the capital assistance program. This assignment led me to meet Emin Boysan, one of the most remarkable persons I have ever met in my long life and professional career.

The program was quite simple and straightforward. The aid mission economists would sit with their counterparts in the Turkish government to analyze Turkey's import needs for the next half year, calculate the likely foreign exchange earnings and then commit U.S. aid to cover the shortfall. The mission would then issue "U.S. Letters of Commitment" that could be used by the Turkish government to fund specific categories of imports. The problem was the time lag between the two governments reaching an agreement and the actual import of the product.

Let's say the relevant period of import shortfall we were trying to cover was July 1961 to December 1961. The analyses might be done in April - May 1961, based on data from 1960. The letters of commitment would be issued in late June. Then the Turkish Ministry of Finance in Ankara would take its time to authorize the Central Bank headquarters in Istanbul to begin issuing its own letters of credit to the importers. Only then would the Central Bank headquarters begin allocating smaller amounts to their branches in distant cities, always holding back an amount in case it was needed elsewhere. Once these allocations were made, each branch would issue letters of credit to its customers. Information from the branches concerning the rate at which they issued letters of credit would take weeks to get back to Central Bank headquarters in Istanbul. Inevitably, each party in the allocation chain would have held back a small amount in case it was needed to cover a shortfall elsewhere.

In the meantime, staff at the aid mission would be trying to calculate how much aid would be needed for the following six months. There was little knowledge of how much was still unutilized from previous letters of commitment. Invariably, due to the conservatism of central bankers, a significant portion of these funds was never used. The result was a pipeline of U.S. aid that had built up. These funds accomplished absolutely nothing for Turkey.

My task was to find a way to speed up the fund allocation process and to generate timelier reporting on the utilization of these U.S. letters of commitment. Changing the system would require an agreement among several Turkish ministries and agencies.

The Finance Ministry called a meeting and I accompanied my boss, Roger Nelson. That was where I first met Emin Boysan. He stood at 6 feet 5 inches and weighed perhaps 250 lbs. He was in the prime of life, full of energy, the picture of the Anatolian warrior: a big round head, eyes that took in everything and a smile that lit up the room. He had recently returned to the Commerce Ministry after a four-year assignment as commercial counselor at the Turkish embassy in Tokyo. His English was impeccable.

After some discussion, the meeting agreed that the problem lay with the Central Bank. That conclusion was facilitated by the fact that the Central Bank had no representative at the meeting. The minister of finance phoned the governor of the Central Bank to tell him that he was sending Emin, and Naci Tibbet from his own staff and me to Istanbul to try to solve the problem and "requested" him to extend all courtesies and cooperation to us. The three of us arranged to meet in Istanbul.

Suddenly, I found myself on my first mission. Roger offered to let one of his locally hired staff, a very capable fellow named Bahadir Colgar, accompany me. The exercise lasted two weeks. The Central Bank governor, Fikri Diker, did give us full cooperation. He assigned a senior officer, Bekir Sami, to pave the way as we dealt with the bank's senior staff. We brought in the local IBM representative to help us design a reporting system using IBM punch cards and got the Central Bank to adopt a more efficient and rapid allocation system to move funding authority to its branches. A "state of the art" computer reporting system was instituted within the Central Bank to generate weekly reports on letters of credit issued against the U.S. commitment letters. We returned to Ankara to be greeted with much hoopla and fanfare. The mission was considered to have been a great success.

Those two weeks in Istanbul allowed me to get to know Emin.

The first thing I realized was that everyone had some family link in Istanbul except I. Each member of our group boarded at some private residence. Even Bahadir stayed with relatives. Emin, however, took keen interest in my personal needs to make sure I had companionship and did not feel abandoned. He hovered over me to make sure I did not get into any trouble. I do not remember eating one meal alone. We worked long hours. In the evenings, he joined me for dinner, walks around the city, visits to coffee houses, the underground bazaar and the like.

On the job, when we encountered resistance to some request for information or to run a test or to gain access to some bureaucrat who was not particularly seized with the importance of our efforts, Emin became "the enforcer." He certainly knew how to be persuasive and was able to use his knowledge of the system to get things done. He seemed to have convinced himself that I was capable of solving the problem for the benefit of his country and dedicated himself to make sure I succeeded.

Then came the weekend. Our work was still not complete, but I had scheduled a date with a lovely lady in Ankara on Saturday. At our regular Friday morning meeting, I announced that we would take a break and resume work Monday at noon. Everyone was agreeable except Emin. "But our work is not finished," he said. "Well," I said, "it will have to wait." I had other priorities to attend to. I asked Bahadir to buy me a ticket for a flight back to Ankara but Emin, instructed him not to do so. We went back and forth on this, each of us getting more adamant, with several interjections in Turkish among the team members, until finally, Emin said to me, "If you purchase a ticket, I will have to telephone your ambassador to inform him that you are not being cooperative with this mission." Later, Bahadir would report to me that, in some of the intervening dialogue in Turkish between Emin and Naci, Emin referred to me as "this infidel" and made clear to the others that I was not about to be allowed out of his control.

So I picked up the phone, called Ankara, and cancelled my date. We worked through most of the weekend. I was not a happy camper. But, during any leisure time, particularly that Sunday when the bank was closed, Emin took me on outings in a car he had secured from the Central Bank. We drove along the Bosporus to excellent seafood restaurants that he knew. He did all he could to make sure I got over my snit.

The closer we got to successful completion of our work, the more excited he became. I had conceptualized the kinds of reforms that were needed. The IBM representative figured out the technical aspects of the system that needed to be adopted. But it was Emin who understood all that was happening, figured out where the institutional resistances lay and how to overcome them. I knew I had gained his respect. Soon I began to appreciate his capabilities as well. Over that two-week period, we had many chances to talk about things other than our work: our private lives, our world outlook, our likes and dislikes. By the time we headed back to Ankara, we understood and respected each other. I cannot say we liked each other. Not just yet.

—◦◦◦—

The cancellation of my date in Ankara was a bit of a blow for me. In the few months since my arrival, I had developed a complicated social life. Having recently been divorced after a seven-year-long failed marriage, I thought it was a good time to sow some wild oats. Ankara was a good place to do this.

Two weeks after arrival, on a visit to the U.S. Embassy, I found myself walking up the steps behind a very shapely woman, also recently arrived and working in the Economic Section. From my vantage point, I noted she had great legs. Her name was Joan Fogltanz. I say, "was" because eventually it would change to "Rudel."

The social circuit for those of us holding diplomatic passports in Ankara was wide ranging in that many of the embassy and USAID secretarial staff dated Turkish men and women. In Joan's case, she had met a handsome fellow named Erdoğan Ulus; he had a terrific job as General Gürsel's press secretary. There were lots of social gatherings at which we singles would dance, and eat and drink and generally have a good time. We frequented several upscale restaurants with music and dancing, such as Sureya's and Karpich, where Westerners would gravitate to on weekend nights.

I had met a Fulbright fellow named Malcolm Rivkin who was doing research in Ankara. He was heavy into learning the Turkish language and had engaged a private local tutor named Asuman Kilich. In addition to being a gifted artist, she was bilingual. It was also clear that she was a very charming and attractive lady. I met her at Mal's home and soon made it a point to date her. That was when I learned she was separated from her husband, a prominent journalist, who had been in the Menderes cabinet as the minister of information and broadcasting. He was currently detained in that jail on Yassiada Island with the rest of the overthrown cabinet. She had a six-year old daughter and needed the work to care for herself and her child. She had many friends in high places, including senior personnel at our embassy, and often attended parties given by the diplomatic set. Soon, our dating became a topic in the Ankara gossip mill.

I provide this background because it all has something to do with that fateful date I cancelled due to Emin's insistence I stay the weekend in Istanbul.

The closeness of the U.S. military with the Turkish military allowed for some amusing interchanges, especially among the "Intelligence" community. My dating the wife of a former cabinet minister seemed to touch a nerve among some of my "betters" at the embassy. It was not "consorting with the enemy," still the current government saw those who held office in the former civilian government, and their close family and associates, as "out of favor." Questionably, here was a young American officer spending time with one of them.

But then, a couple of weeks before going on the assignment to Istanbul, I asked Joan to go out with me and we went to Sureya's to have dinner and to dance. She had been seen at Sureya's numerous times in Erdoğan's company. We sensed some flash bulbs going off while we were dancing and, the next morning, on Erdoğan's desk, there was a photo of Joan and me.

Now this was really interesting stuff for the intelligence set. One can imagine that people whose job it is to keep track of unusual linkages and odd behavior among the diplomatic set might be curious about this channel from Altimur Kilich's wife, Asuman, to Lu to Joan to Erdoğan to General Gürsel.

My date was to have been with Joan on that fateful Saturday because I had begun to think about her a lot. I was still playing the field, but Asuman and Joan were becoming my dates of choice. I was reluctant to break the date with Joan, because this would give Erdoğan a free opportunity. What games we play when we are young!

⸺⸙⸺

Emin's family was truly exceptional. Ilhan, his wife, was a gracious and handsome woman, a youthful "grand dame." It was obvious both came from good Turkish Anatolian stock. She had immersed herself in Japanese art during their four-year tour in Tokyo and was teaching a group about flower arrangement and bonsai growing. They were a very popular couple among the Western diplomatic circuit.

After our Istanbul project, Emin and I would see each other more frequently, sometimes on business, but more and more on social occasions. He and Ilhan would join me and a young woman for an evening of dinner and music. On the first such outing, everything seemed friendly and we enjoyed the evening. Then we scheduled another evening and I showed up with a different young lady. That evening also was pleasantly spent. But then, Emin pulled me aside and told me only when I settled down and selected ONE woman to date, he and Ilhan would again join me for evenings out. Until I did this, he was not going to expose his wife to my behavior. He was jovial and his tone was friendly, but one could not help but sense a cold Anatolian wind emanating from his broad, warm Western smile.

Each week, after we had returned from Istanbul, we would await the new Central Bank report on utilization of our aid. Naci Tibbet was the conduit for the reports, and they were delivered by messenger from his office directly to mine. After a couple of fitful starts, the reports began to become more understandable and reliable. Once the routine was established, I bowed out of the circuit and the reports went to the economists who needed that information. New tasks were given to me and my business contacts with Emin diminished.

One day, Emin asked me to lunch to discuss a sensitive problem. Would I be willing to make a copy of the weekly report from the Central Bank for him? He would send a messenger for it. If I could give it to him in a sealed envelope, that would solve the problem. I was aghast. Why did he not get a copy from Naci Bey? It seemed the minister of finance had classified the report secret, and it could not be released to any other Turkish ministry outside the Finance Ministry.

So, I went to see Naci. After the usual two cups of tea, I asked why Emin was not given a copy of the report when it was being released to me. "Oh, you are an American," he answered. "You can have anything you want. If it were not for the Americans, the Russians would have taken the Bosporus and the Dardanelles. Your bases are protecting us. You can have anything." That was the mood of our relationship with Turkey in 1961. I played the game and accommodated Emin's request, no questions asked.

I wanted to understand the Turkish national character. Turkish value systems gave high marks to the qualities of bravery, loyalty, honoring one's word and less to intelligence and business acumen. The only time Emin ever had harsh words for me, once I had gained his trust, was in 1974 when the United States did not come to the support of Turkey during the Cyprus Crisis. The United States tried to mediate the dispute between the Greeks and the Turks. It was inconceivable to Emin that we would not fully support Turkey in light of our close relationship and mutual trust. With the Turks, you are either with them or you are considered the enemy. We were seen to have broken our "trust" with them.

Atatürk had taken control of Turkey in 1923, after the demise of the Ottoman Empire. The sultan was deposed, the Caliphate was abolished and Atatürk led a successful defense against Greece's attacks on Anatolia. Although virtually a dictator, he used his power in a manner that won general admiration and was able to transform Turkey into a strong, modern, nation-state. He visualized the future of Turkey to be linked to Europe, considered Turkey's religious establishment a threat to the adoption of Western values and decreed that there be a separation between the government and the Mosque. All persons were to be equal before the law irrespective of their ethnicity. Atatürk used the army to safeguard Turkey against both foreign enemies and those he considered domestic enemies.

Emin was devoted to these ideals. He had faithfully served as a civil servant under the administration of Prime Minister Menderes but understood that the army needed to clean up the corruption that had flourished under the civilian government. Now he was doing everything in his power to support the new military government.

National character, or the underlying value systems which can often explain behavioral differences among peoples, has fascinated me since taking classes at CCNY in the 1950s with Professor Louis Snyder. It runs the risk of tending to stereotype national groups but still, in my opinion, is a useful tool to help understand group reaction in different societies to similar events. Here is what I wrote about the Turks in 1964 in a paper for a class during my graduate studies at University of Michigan:

National Character

It might be well to recognize certain general national character-istics which, in the opinion of the writer, go a long way to explain some of the peculiarities of the GOT's (Government of Turkey) offi-cial policies concerning economic development.

(1) The Turkish military have traditionally been the elite of the society. Throughout Turkish history it is notable that any great ben-efits derived by Turkey have been through military successes.

We do not see Turkey as a leader in the field of culture or ideol-ogy. We see no great principles, ethics or intellectual achievements coming from this group; nor has Turkey attained glory from its politi-cal systems. Rather, the success enjoyed by the society has invariably been derived from its military achievements. It was once said in jest that Turkey's most fruitful investment during the last 15 years has been the Brigade it sent to Korea to fight under the United Nations command. The prestige won for Turkey by that single enterprise has served it well in attaining global popular support, thereby assuring substantial economic assistance.

Thus, the qualities on which military successes thrive, i.e., cour-age, honor, loyalty and inflexibility to external pressure are to be found throughout the society.

(2) The desire to Westernize is all pervading. Thrace, that small piece of land on the European side of the Bosporus, provides the rationale for the Turk to consider himself European rather than Middle Eastern. Irrespective of his short-run economic interest, he wants more than ever to join the European Economic Community

(EEC). When Besim Ustunel, one of Turkey's leading economists, prepared a study in 1961 which suggested that Turkey's economic interests would not be served by membership in the EEC, the report was greeted with public outcries and severe criticism.

It is paradoxical then that the Turks should also be suspicious of, and hostile to the foreigner. This hostility doubtlessly dates back to the exploitation by the Europeans during the latter part of the 19th and early 20th centuries at the time of the capitulations. Foreign investment is suspiciously looked upon as exploitive. It is believed that the foreign investor must be deriving a greater return from his investment in Turkey than he could derive in his own country and consequently is "exploiting" the Turks.

(3) Hostility towards foreign investment also finds its roots in the Turk's concept of social justice. He instinctively rebels against inequities in the distribution of wealth and resents those who seek what he considers to be "excessive" profits. This attitude may stem from those profits reaped by the Concessions during the period of the capitulations. It may also be due to the known malpractices of the private entrepreneur (tax evasion, poor working conditions, low pay for workers, profiteering during times of shortages). It may reflect a bit of chauvinism since most entrepreneurs in Turkey are members of minority groups (Greeks, Jews and Armenians).

Somehow one suspects that the attitude toward social justice may transcend all of these rationalizations. For example, pervading the government's mining policies there are clear indications of bias against permitting a private individual to dig into Turkish soil, glean the valuable material contained therein and sell it (even worse, export it) for a personal profit. There is the belief that these valuable deposits belong to all of Turkey and should therefore be used for the benefit of the entire nation. The explanation that the nation receives its share in the form of taxes does not seem to satisfy them.

Interwoven in this concept of social justice is a paternalism that calls upon the government to protect the illiterate workers and peasants from the exploitation inherent in industrialization and to tolerate inefficiency and low productivity.

These general observations undoubtedly oversimplify and exaggerate these qualities. Nevertheless, I believe some strains of these characteristics will be found to run through modern Turkish history and may be helpful in gaining understanding of the impediments to their development.[7]

———

And so it was, in that culture and environment that I worked as a change agent for the U.S. economic aid program. Over the next two years, I would grow to love and respect the Turks.

I often wondered about the basis for the history of conflict and hatred that prevails between the Turks and the Greeks. After all, they are neighbors and will continue to live in proximity of each other. What can explain this deep and long-running feud? Perhaps it can best be explained by the difference in their respective national characters. The Greeks are a "cerebral" people. They have a long history of intellectual accomplishment. Their architecture, literature, theater, philosophy, mathematics and scientific achievements, all speak to enduring intellectual prowess. There have been a few wars in which they have excelled but their strategy can include strategic withdrawal, in essence, retreat from an overwhelming enemy to "live and fight another day." They embrace Greek Orthodoxy.

The Turks, on the other hand, list their accomplishments almost exclusively through the martial arts. Turkish literature and poetry are comparatively less rich. But they ruled the Middle East for five hundred years. And they have done so very well. Their value system extols bravery, honor

---

7   Ludwig Rudel, "Development Planning in Turkey," May 1964, unpublished paper for Prof. A. Basch, Economics Department, University of Michigan.

and loyalty—all battlefield virtues. They consider retreating in the face of enemy fire to be a heinous vice. A majority of Turks are followers of Mohammed. These two wonderful societies, with these differences in outlook and approach, have found their interaction fraught with hundreds of years of conflict. How sad.

Emin and I hit it off better and better. His service in Tokyo during the 1950s, as a member of Turkey's diplomatic corps, had given him lots of exposure to American and Western behavior. I had been invited to try out for a part in a play to be performed by a local amateur theater group in Ankara. It was a mixed group of Turkish and American actors that was scheduled to perform "Once More, With Feeling" by Harry Kurnitz and I was cast as Maxwell Archer, the comic role created by Walter Mathau. Emin and Ilhan were into theater and so we had another common interest. Also, I had become more focused on Joan and we were seeing each other regularly. That meant that Emin was willing to double date with us.

The theater piece got good reviews. Joan and I gradually became "an item." We took weekend trips together across the mountains north of Ankara, past Mount Uludağ to the Black Sea and its black sand beaches (Akcakoca), camping in ancient bat-filled caves along the Mediterranean's coastal cliffs (Antalya), Bursa and its warm baths, Lake Abant in the mountains (with the Boysans) and Konya to see the whirling dervishes. Other wonderful trips were to Istanbul – the Golden Horn, Topkapi Palace Museum and Saint Sophia mosque, the Bosporus and its great seafood restaurants and, finally in September 1961, to London where I bought a new Jaguar, and drove it back to Turkey via an extended tour of Europe. That trip with Joan scandalized the entire embassy staff.

I continued to do my duties as assistant aid program officer, evaluating projects and extending funding to successful projects. My success in solving the capital imports funding pipeline build-up had established my reputation as a "hands-on" implementation facilitator, both at the Ministry of Finance and at the embassy and aid mission. Soon, every time some project got stuck, I was called in as the troubleshooter.

The U.S. General Accounting Office (now called the U.S. Government Accountability Office) had selected the Turkey aid program for an in-depth evaluation. This is a large and powerful watchdog organization working directly for the Congress to evaluate how effectively its funding appropriations were being spent. A team of six auditors was hard at work trying to find fault with what the executive branch was doing. I was asked to be the coordinator for this review. It was tedious work to search the files for documents and information about funding decisions made and the results yielded by these projects. Still, the task gave me some useful insights into the techniques (and pitfalls) of evaluation and this was to serve me well later in my career.

It took the audit team two months to do their research and another six months to write their report. By the time their draft report was finally submitted to our mission for review and comment, I had already completed my tour and been reassigned to Washington. But the AID mission director called me back to Ankara to draft a response to the report. That was really fun because I was able to provide responses that put their major conclusions into question and eventually succeeded in scuttling the report. One score for our side!

One day, Emin announced that he was being reassigned from the Commerce Ministry to become director of an independent government agency called Toprak Mahsulleri Ofisi (TMO). This agency had charge of all government grain buffer stocks. It bought from the farmers or imported wheat, and then sold it on the open market in the cities to the bakers. This was a very important and politically sensitive job and involved a balancing act between the farmers/producers in the countryside and the bakers/consumers in the cities. The agency was under pressure to pay the farmers a sufficiently high price to keep them happy, and then, to sell the wheat in the cities at low prices to keep consumers from rioting. It was responsible for the import of all food grains, primarily from the United States under the surplus agricultural commodity sales program, to maintain a buffer stock to keep prices stable. This was a big promotion for Emin. He was assigned his own car and driver and was invited to all the big diplomatic and government social functions. He also had to travel a lot. Still, we managed to spend time together and spoke freely about politics and development in Turkey.

Joan and I were getting a bit of "heat" from some members of the embassy for our so-called "disgraceful behavior." I sought Emin's counsel as to how to handle that. Aside from the "scandal," it did not help that Joan was a practicing Catholic and I was a divorced Jew. Emin seemed torn, just like the monarch in *The King and I*, caught between rapidly changing Western mores and Turkish formality. But he showed himself to be a friend, giving helpful advice even though such advice ran counter to the rules of his own upbringing.

Joan and I had slowly come to the realization that our love was too powerful to cast aside when our tours ended. We each finally understood and agreed that we must marry. What at first seemed an impossibility gradually became an improbability, then a possibility, a likelihood and finally, an inevitability.

There was the tortuous process of informing my family about Joan and about our plans. All of this had to be done by what is now referred to as "snail mail," each letter taking about a week to get to its addressee. I had to explain myself to Pepi and to Jul and Rita. My mother was quite upset that I would be marrying someone who was not Jewish. It was not an easy sell. But the great distance between our families and us was our friend. There was nothing that they could do to stop us.

In May 1962, Joan and I took the "Orient Express" from Istanbul to Zurich and got married at the City Hall. The room we rented was very modest indeed. Joan still remembers the plaid linoleum on the floor. But we were in love and did not care. Arranging to meet all of Switzerland's marriage rules and requirements was quite an ordeal but we had lots of friendly support from the U.S. consulate. I even managed to get the authorities in Vienna to promptly send a copy of my birth certificate to Zurich after we discovered it was needed. Finally, after three days of back and forth between the consulate and the Marriage Bureau, the "bonds" were posted at City Hall for all to see, and the appointment with the marriage officiator was set for the following Monday. We headed to a tavern, ordered fondue and several bottles of the local wine, got plastered and waited for Monday, when I would make an "honest woman" of Joan.

The Rosenthals, friends who were also posted at the aid mission in Ankara, had purchased a car for delivery in Dusseldorf. They coordinated their trip with ours and met us in Zurich, serving as witnesses at our wedding. They then accompanied us on our honeymoon as we drove back to Ankara together.

Our arrival in Ankara as "husband and wife" was a great relief to the more conservative (and senior) members of the embassy and aid staff. They threw a big wedding celebration for us and the gossip mill began looking elsewhere for its feeding needs.

Two important events occurred shortly after we returned from Zurich. One was a letter I received from Rita that informed me that an exploratory operation on my mother had disclosed that she had cancer of the stomach. There was no hope of stemming the growth and her life expectancy was to be less than two months.

The second event was a series of screaming cables from the U.S. Department of Agriculture (USDA) that informed the embassy that the government of Turkey had fallen in arrears on payments for recent shipments of surplus U.S. grain. USDA was threatening to stop deliveries. The embassy was instructed to make a demarche to protest this default. The person who was smack in the middle of this problem was, of course, Emin Boysan. Now it was his turn to seek my help.

How did this happen? It seems that it all derived from the good news that Turkey was enjoying a bumper harvest of domestic food grain. In previous years, there had been a deficit between the annual crop yields and the demand for grains that was balanced by imports of U.S. surplus grain. TMO would bring in the grain, store it in its silos for a short time but the demand was always such that it turned around and sold the grain, thereby generating the cash needed to pay into the USDA accounts. With this year's (1962) high crop yield, the USDA imported grain was building up in TMO storage facilities and no cash was being generated. Emin had no cash to pay for the imports. Yet, TMO needed to build up the buffer stocks for the winter.

The good old American way would have been for the Finance Ministry to lend TMO some working capital. The ministry could borrow from the Central Bank or just print money. But that would have run counter to an agreement Turkey had made with the IMF to avoid monetary expansion as part of a stabilization program. Turkey was stuck between a rock and a hard place. Emin would have to go to Washington to work out an agreement.

Without a word to me, Emin went to the U.S. ambassador and asked for my services to accompany him to Washington, D.C. as an advisor to help him in these negotiations. I learned this from Wade Lathram, the deputy aid mission director, who also doubled as embassy economic counselor. This was a highly unusual, indeed, unorthodox request. How could an American officer, working at the aid mission, be seconded to the Turkish government to sit on that side of the table in these negotiations? But ambassadors do not like to say "no." And so, in mid-October, Emin, Hayrettin Osansoy and Naci Tibbet of the Ministry of Finance, plus a couple of lower-level aides and I flew to Washington.

Before leaving I spoke with my bosses—Mission Director Stuart Van Dyke and his deputy, Wade Lathram—about the role I would play in my advisory capacity. They found the whole situation amusing for several reasons. The State Department Turkey desk officer who would chair the negotiation was George Churchill. His last assignment had been in Ankara as economic officer at the embassy and he had been Joan's boss. He was also a good friend of mine. He would be sitting across the table from me, flanked by many persons from USDA who were taking this "default" a lot more seriously than anybody at State or USAID. I asked Van Dyke what difference it made to any of us whether the Turkish lira funds were deposited or not, since we were going to use them to pay for new economic development projects for Turkey. He smiled and pointed out that a legalism was the problem. The law requires that these deposits be made. "Besides," he said, "if you are going to put a clause in the agreement that they are going to deposit 'pizazas,' at least we should insist that the pizazas actually be deposited. The Turks should be able to work it out."

We took a suite of four rooms plus a sitting room that contained a television set, for our entire delegation at a second-class hotel in Northwest Washington within walking distance of the State Department. Emin and Hayrettin immediately visited their embassy to brief their ambassador. They were assigned a couple of his staff to join the meetings scheduled for the next morning at the State Department. I was not invited to join Emin at the meeting with his ambassador. When they returned, we unpacked and had a light supper before retiring. I woke up early the next morning, walked out to the suite's sitting room to see Hayrettin, in his pajamas, sitting in front of the television set, staring at the color pattern. It was 5:45 a.m. and the station was to go on air at 6 a.m. Television was an exciting new item for the Turkish delegation.

After watching the news, we went to our first meeting. In those days, there were no security scanners at the entrance to the State Department. We walked into the building and I led the group, which now included a couple of Turkish embassy people as well, directly up to the assigned conference room. There sat my buddy, George. As predicted, he was flanked by several USDA accounting types plus a lawyer from the general counsel's office.

Everybody had his turn setting forth their respective positions. I just smiled and waited to be asked a question. But nobody asked anything of me. After everyone had his turn, Emin explained the bind the Turks were in. The USDA expressed sympathy but explained their dilemma. The meeting then adjourned. Everyone agreed to consult with their superiors (in

Emin's case it meant cables to Ankara) and scheduled another meeting at the same place, for the morning of October 22.

I decided to use the intervening weekend to go to New York City to see my mother. I knew it would be my last visit. She was in the hospital. My brother was very kind and attentive. We discussed my marriage to Joan and Pepi's condition. No one had told her she was dying or that she had cancer. I went along with the story that the doctor who had done the exploratory had left a lot of scar tissue and that was the source of her pain. After I returned to Ankara, I learned that, shortly after my departure, Jul checked her out of the hospital. She was moved back to her residence hotel where she was receiving full-time assistance. She died peacefully several weeks later. I felt no loss, no sadness or remorse then. I had never appreciated what she endured for the sake of my welfare, remembering only her disappointment and displeasure with my actions and behavior.

Monday morning October 22, we again headed to the State Department and resumed discussions. Emin had been able to somehow work a deal with the Ministry of Finance to come up with some funds. The proposal was to stretch out the payments so that the arrears would be deposited over an extended period of time. Within a year, it was proposed that the shortfall would be made up. That seemed to be acceptable to our USDA accountants. It was similar to a deal that might be struck today with a sub-prime mortgagee.

Emin, Hayrettin and I returned to the hotel suite very much pleased with ourselves. We broke out some alcohol and sat down to watch the evening news. It was announced that President Kennedy was scheduled to give an address at 7 p.m. And so, we watched as the president announced the quarantine of Cuba. It was the beginning of the Cuban missile crisis. Emin was standing directly next to my chair. When Kennedy threw down the gauntlet to Khrushchev, Emin's eyes glistened; he showed a broad smile as he hit me on the shoulder and shouted, "Well, it's about time you Americans stood up to them. Now we will see how they will run!" Here was the fierce Anatolian warrior, ready to fight the good fight.

After Kennedy's speech, we talked into the night. All that uncertainty! None of us were aware that Turkey would be very much involved in these negotiations between the United States and the Soviet Union during the critical next few days. We all knew that the NSA was operating an electronic listening post in Trabzon, a remote city along the Black Sea near the Soviet border. But it appeared that we had missile launchers there as well. Part of the deal to get Khrushchev to back out of Cuba was for us to remove those missile launchers in Turkey.

We also talked about our respective ages. Emin said he did not know exactly how old he was. It seems he was born around 1912. In those days, it was the practice in the Ottoman Empire for parents not to register their sons with the authorities for several years after birth. The Ottomans would draft the boys into the army at age 16; so by holding off the birth registration, the boys had a chance to grow up at least to age 18 before being drafted. Because of this practice, Emin thought he might be around 50 years old. I was just 32 and so there was definitely a seniority issue between us.

We were scheduled to fly back to Ankara the next day. In the morning, as we were each packing our things, Emin came to me with a handsome new garment he had bought for his wife. Quietly, so none of the others could hear, he asked me if I would be willing to pack the garment in my suitcase. "If I have it in my suitcase, the customs inspector in Ankara will open my case, see it is a newly purchased garment, close the case and smile or wink at me. That will mean he has done me a favor and he will then later come to me for a favor in return. You are traveling with a diplomatic passport. They will not open your suitcase."

I took the garment from Emin and assured him I would take care of it. That became our ultimate bonding. Loyalty and trust had been established. From that moment on, Emin would refer to me by the Turkish word for "younger brother," and I always thereafter called him "ahbe," meaning older brother.

We returned to Turkey with another success story. But I found Joan in the U.S. military hospital. She had suffered a miscarriage during my absence, as had Sue Rosenthal. When I had departed for the United States, I had no idea either woman was pregnant. Joan's miscarriage had an emotional impact on me. It also taught me something about the chemical changes in a woman's body during pregnancy and their effect on her emotional well-being in the event of loss of the fetus.

The Rosenthals will continue to cross paths with Joan and me, almost as though it were written in the stars, for the rest of our lives. We were scheduled to depart Turkey in early December, and so the farewell parties began. Joan and I were happy to move on.

The farewells with Emin were more emotional. He and I somehow knew that our friendship would not end, as most "foreign service friendships" do, when people rotate away from a posting. In fact, four years later in 1966, Emin was assigned as commercial counselor in New York City and would stay there for five years. His daughter, Neely, would marry a German and move to Dusseldorf. His son, Arif, would marry an American and move to Stamford, Connecticut.

After Thanksgiving, we packed our things, got into our Jaguar and drove to Izmir. We watched the car get loaded onto a ship and then boarded the ship to sail for Venice, then drove to Le Havre, checked into a first-class stateroom on the SS America and sailed for New York City.

It had been a wonderful two-year assignment with many opportunities to understand Turkey's amazingly complex culture. The work experience helped prepare me for positions of greater responsibility and enhanced my reputation within USAID. By the end of my tour, I had also improved my financial position.

Most significant was my second try at matrimony. The satisfactions derived from my new marriage with Joan were to be greater than I had any right to expect. I had found my soul mate.

Emin and I remained in contact. My final visit with Emin was in Stamford in 2004 when he and Ilhan came to the wedding of Arif's son. He was still the "proud Turk warrior" although his health was failing him. He refused to accept any support from his children, even though inflation in Turkey had eaten away at his savings. He told me that he had had many opportunities to get rich while he managed TMO because Turkish ship-owners offered bribes to obtain contracts to carry imported grain to Turkey. The prime minister once personally requested that Emin award a contract to one of his friends. Emin refused and threatened to resign if he were compelled to make that award. He had preserved his honor, but had to live his retirement on very modest means. He died shortly after that meeting.

Although we hailed from very different cultures, in some sense Emin was my colleague, my teacher, my mentor, my companion and, to be truthful, my brother as well as my father figure. He loved his country and his family, in that order. He will remain in my memory so long as I live.

TURKEY TODAY

I have often thought about Turkey's June 1960 military coup, just three months before my arrival there. Did this action set back the maturation of Turkish democracy and economic growth? I do not think so. There is sufficient evidence that the Menderes government, although democratically elected, was heading in the wrong direction. Certainly my Turkish colleagues were not disturbed by the military's intervention. Within two years, civilian government was restored and the military quickly exited the political scene.

Observing the current political state of play in Turkey as I write this, in the midst of the turmoil in Egypt and other nearby nations as the "Arab Spring" evolves, I am impressed with the resilience of the reform measures instituted by Atatürk about ninety years ago. Some have expressed concern over the government's seeming regression with respect to fundamental Islamism, evidenced by the behavior of Prime Minister Erdoğan and the recent break in relations with Israel. The Turkish military, which overthrew the civilian government again in 1971 and also in 1980, has lost its influence as a "defender of the Atatürk Revolution," probably because it focused too much on enhancing its perks and privileges instead of remaining aloof of politics and adhering to Atatürk's mandate. But three generations of Turks have now matured and been educated since the Caliphate was abolished. I am hopeful Turkey's internal political dynamics will bring about a rebalancing of the linkage between the State and the religious establishment to resume its earlier direction towards a secular, modern, democratic society. Europe's resistance to allow Turkey membership in the European Union even though it is a member of NATO has exacerbated Turkey's sense of isolation and pushed it to seek alliances with its Arab neighbors. It is clearly in Europe's self-interest to embrace Turkey as a full member of the European Union.

There are signs that Egypt may be following Atatürk's model to bring about modernization of its society. The election following Mubarak's overthrow was premature and allowed the Muslim Brotherhood, the only organized political force, to win while its various opposition groups were too fractured to compete. The military have ousted Morsi, the winner of that election, and have called for the drafting of a new constitution and new elections. Those "procedural purists" who are uncomfortable with this action as a violation of democratic procedure have ignored the actions of the Morsi regime to impose the power of the State to enforce their religious beliefs.

My own view of the actions of the Morsi government is that it followed the typical pattern of African democracy – one person, one vote, one time! It would be well to remember that Hitler was fairly elected by popular vote to the German Chancellorship in 1933, just 15 years after the Treaty of Versailles removed the kaiser. If the German army had interceded to contain the Nazi Party after that election, as the Egyptian army has with respect to the Muslim Brotherhood, the history of Europe might have played out very differently in the twentieth century.

5

INDIA –HIGHLIGHT OF MY CAREER 1965 TO 1970

It is not good for the Christian soul
To hustle the Aryan brown,
For the Christian riles and the heathen smiles
And it weareth the Christian down.
And the end of the fight is a tombstone white
With the name of the dear deceased.
And the epitaph drear: "A fool lies here
Who tried to hustle the East."

RUDYARD KIPLING

RETURN TO WASHINGTON

During my tour in Turkey, John F. Kennedy was elected president. He brought into his administration "the best and the brightest." That phrase has now evolved into a damnation of the folks who pulled us into the Vietnam War. Still, Kennedy understood the importance of bringing along to Washington a group of hand-picked, like-minded, talented administrators to implement his vision of what the world should look like five to ten years hence. He drew heavily on the universities, the business community, even the judiciary, to breathe fresh competence and ideas into the federal bureaucracy he inherited from Eisenhower.

He drew up new legislation for the U.S. economic assistance programs and established the Agency for International Development (AID) to manage these programs. That legislation, passed in 1961, still provides the operating mandate for U.S. economic aid today. And he brought Fowler Hamilton, Bill Gaud (who gave up his judgeship to follow Kennedy), Alex Vagliano and Rod Wagner (out of JP Morgan Bank) and others of that caliber to take on senior positions in the new aid agency. Kennedy's enthusiasm was contagious. The best talent in the country was ready to uproot at his call and go to Washington to work for him. John Kenneth Galbraith left Harvard University to take the ambassadorship to India. John P. Lewis left Indiana University to serve on Kennedy's Council of Economic Advisers (and was later appointed director of our AID mission to India). Dean Rusk became secretary of state and Chester Bowles became the deputy secretary. Each of these luminaries recruited others to join them.

When I returned to Washington in 1963, I found vibrancy and a sense of purpose in AID that was inspiring. I was assigned to the Near East and South Asia Bureau's Capital Loan Division headed by Alex Vagliano. It was easy to put in ten hour days as well as weekends to be a part of this enterprise. After some time, I was given a training opportunity to study for one year at the University of Michigan to earn an MA in Economics. In the spring of 1965, I was assigned as chief of the program division at our mission in New Delhi.

INDIA

The five years in India were wonderfully rewarding, both professionally and personally to me and to my family. Superb opportunities were granted to me to contribute substantively to India's economic development. Sadly, I am disappointed at how few of the concrete accomplishments derived from these efforts have withstood the test of time. I was sent to be a "change agent" to one of the world's most populous societies, with a highly sophisticated three-thousand-year long history of its own. I was a thirty-five year old mid-professional serving in the foreign service of one of the world's two superpowers. There was not one ounce of humility in me as I approached this daunting task.

This was no ordinary time. Here is the scene I found as I approached this assignment in early 1965, following my year of advanced study in economics at the University of Michigan.

This was India twenty years after the end of World War II, eighteen years after achieving independence from Great Britain, boasting a population of 550 million. It had just lost its long serving prime minister, Jawaharlal Nehru and, amazingly, had peacefully passed power to Lal Bahadur Shastri, a man recognized to be a temporary selection, a caretaker, as the Congress Party sorted things out among its leadership. After two hundred years of colonial subjugation, India was trying to make democratic political rule work. The country is a large land mass, comprised then of seventeen states speaking about thirteen discreet languages with a population suffering, then, from a high level of poverty and illiteracy. Giving support to this fledgling effort at democratic rule was a key element of our policy toward India.

Its Hindu and Muslim populations were deeply affected by religious and ethnic tensions. Within the dominant Hindu population there was strong adherence to its ancient caste system. Historically, the caste system defined communities into thousands of endogamous hereditary groups called *jātis*. The *jātis* were grouped by the Brahminical texts into four caste categories, the *varnas* viz. *Brahmins, Kshatriyas, Vaishyas,* and *Shudras.* Certain people were excluded altogether, ostracized by all other castes and treated as untouchables. Many Hindus looked upon India's Muslim population, who had opted not to join Pakistan, with suspicion and hostility.

India had taken on a position of leadership in the "Third World," the Group of Seventy-seven that was attempting to play an intermediary role between the world's two superpowers, the United States and the Soviet Union. India's economic policies were driven by a socialist-leaning central planning approach, with the central government attempting to own or control key industrial sectors. The United States had been shipping large-scale surplus agricultural commodities under its PL 480 program and India had willingly become dependent on these virtually costless imports, focusing its own resources instead on investment in industry, predominantly in the public sector.

It did not help our political relationship with India that its ambassador to the United Nations, V. K. Krishna Menon, had been regularly castigating the United States from the UN General Assembly's podium about perceived U.S. political and economic misdeeds, particularly non-recognition of the Communist government of China.

The political climate in India was relatively stable, with the Congress Party in control. But there was a strong left-leaning wing inside that party, as well as a Communist Party that controlled Kerala and West Bengal. Many in India, particularly those in the upper classes that had attended the London School of Economics during its heyday as the bastion of Fabian socialist thinking, believed, or at least suspected that Marx was right; capitalism was crumbling and socialist economic structure would be the world's future. The Soviet Union was seen as the forerunner of this inevitability. After all, what was wrong with the concept, "From each according to his ability; to each according to his need"? These views were not unlike those that had been held by people like Arthur Koestler in the States during the 1930s. Koestler and his colleagues had had an awakening in the 1940s, had seen the flaws in the Soviet system and became virulent anti-communists. It probably takes longer for disillusionment to take hold in a relatively rigid society.

India had been receiving economic aid from the United States since 1950. Begun modestly as a set of technical assistance projects under Truman's Point Four Program, it had grown manifold over the succeeding fifteen years. A large USAID mission occupied Faridkot House, a former palace in New Delhi of the maharajah of Faridkot. Many American experts were posted at numerous agricultural colleges and technical institutes throughout the country. The magnitude of U.S. economic aid to India in 1965 totaled about $400 million and about two hundred American technical experts were posted there. Aid had significantly increased in 1962 after China and India went to war over a boundary line dispute in the Himalayas.

Chester Bowles was serving as our ambassador and John P. Lewis was AID director. Both had been appointed within the last twelve months. Their appointments had an important underlying basis: a willingness by the president to consider a major new effort in support of India's economic growth. This idea was called "The Big Push."

In 1960, John Lewis, then a professor of economics at University of Indiana, had traveled to India to perform a study for the Brookings Foundation on India's economic development efforts. By the time the study was published in 1962 (with the title "Quiet Crisis in India"), Lewis was serving in the White House on J.F. Kennedy's Council of Economic Advisors. India's leadership had an "etatist" bias towards government ownership and operation of the means of production, to control the commanding heights of their economy, and was moving that society toward the Soviet economic orbit. Lewis' study concluded that scarcity of foreign exchange was forcing India to ration its resources and thus adopt socialist policies rather than rely on open markets to allocate its scarce foreign exchange. If enough resources could be made available to flush through the system, India could liberalize its foreign exchange allocations for imports through the private markets. The entire direction and thrust of its development approach could change. This "Big Push" could move it away from the current socialist approach to economic development. Lewis was offering a way out. The findings of Lewis' study stimulated a major review of our aid policies toward India.

Eventually, the president told Lewis to go to India and see what he could do to make it happen. Bowles was given his assignment for several other reasons, but was sympathetic to the Lewis approach and understood Lewis' access to the White House. Bowles realized a closer aid relationship would help stabilize our political relationship as well, given India's open and not-so-open conflicts with its neighbors, Pakistan and China.

THE TECHNICAL ASSISTANCE EVALUATION TEAM: 1965

On arriving in Washington from Ann Arbor with my family, a newly minted MA in Economics in my pocket, I was assigned to be the chief of AID's Program Office in India. Before moving the family to India, I was asked to serve on a five-person evaluation team to review the mission's technical assistance programs. It was a wonderful opportunity to learn about the programs for whose financial management I would be responsible, and to be allowed to devote the time and thought needed to understand its relevance and effectiveness, and to influence its future shape, priorities and direction. In light of the high-level interest in the India program and the possibility of a shift in our overall approach, the team was comprised of representatives from the White House, the Bureau of the Budget (today it is called the Office of Management and Budget) and the chief of AID Washington's Technical Assistance Bureau. The evaluation team would be briefed in Washington, then spend one month in New Delhi and complete its report before returning to Washington.

The general scope and focus of our technical assistance program was seen to be sound. There was no surprise about that. The problems found by the U.S. staff that arrived in India in 1950 to begin the program had not disappeared. Some adjustments, based on our experience over the preceding fifteen years, needed to be made.

Our agricultural assistance needed to be shifted to deal with agricultural policy formulation at the ministry-level, rather than focusing on continuing institution building for agricultural research and extension.

There was a need for education reform so that India's school system would lead those who completed universal compulsory primary schooling to find advanced educational and vocational training opportunities that would produce the skilled manpower India would require in the near future. The improvement of teacher in-service science training was recommended.

The team endorsed public administration assistance to the India Planning Ministry.

Two more recommendations were made. Projects in the health sector were endorsed with the recommendation that family planning be added to the program with priority gradually shifting to the new activities. It was recommended that our assistance to the India Malaria Eradication program (which relied heavily on the use of DDT) be phased out and that India take on the responsibility to complete the work. It was envisioned in the 1960s that the world would rid itself of malaria in a short time. As we all know, that did not work. Today, the Gates Foundation has again taken on this ambitious effort.

As an example of just how complex the process of development can be, consider the story of our efforts to transfer to India the U.S. concept of agricultural extension service and its links to Land Grant Colleges. The United States had become a dominant agricultural producer to a large extent because of the system of Land Grant Agricultural Colleges and their role both in research and in supporting the agricultural extension systems, giving hands-on assistance to farmers. These extension services managed by State and Federal governments showed local farmers how to increase yields by using new practices developed at the colleges. This system was to be transplanted to India.

One of the first projects started under our early aid program to India was the establishment of seven agriculture colleges, (one in each of seven major agricultural states) each supported by a U.S. agriculture university. The first phase was the bricks and mortar; building the physical facilities. Phase two was training faculty at the U.S. sister universities and the development of curricula modeled after the U.S. curricula but focused on Indian conditions. Phase three set up the selection process for student admission to these colleges. Each class was selected giving preference to the most competent students from each region who had completed middle school. When teaching began at each institution, faculty from the U.S. universities would supervise the class performance of the teachers to upgrade their performance. We were building brand new institutions, a process that can take decades.

Our evaluation of the project concluded that the system for selection of students had a major design flaw, in that those students who attended and completed middle school, and were thus selected to go to the agricultural college, were from upper caste families. The poor farming families could not spare their children to be educated, let alone complete middle school. The students from upper caste families had their mind set on being employed in a government office, sitting comfortably behind a desk after college graduation. They were not thinking about working in the fields with the farmers.

These institutions had been in operation for the better part of a decade and were doing useful research, yet their students and graduates were having little impact on the farmer and his practices. How to get the graduates to roll up their sleeves, put on farm clothes and get into the field? That problem was eventually solved in a very unexpected way. I will describe it later in this chapter when discussing the PL 480 program and the "short tether policy" imposed at the start of the September 1965 India-Pakistan war.

Later on in my tour as chief of the Program Office, I had occasion to visit one of the colleges (Kharagpur) to deliver a talk and to get an update of progress since the evaluation. A luncheon was scheduled and I was asked to sit at the table of the students from one of the dormitories. I was told that each dormitory had a plot of land on which the students grew vegetables as a part of the hands-on learning process. The school held an annual contest to see which dormitory had the best crop output. The students who were sitting at my table proudly told me that they had won the contest three years in a row. I asked to what they attributed their outstanding results. They told me that they have employed the best *mali* working at the college. A *mali* is a paid gardener-laborer. That was their idea of hands-on agricultural work.

The evaluation team had concluded that U.S. assistance to this project should be terminated since it had run for fifteen years. It was thought that the Indian government and the institutions should be able to stand alone without further help. I am not particularly proud of that conclusion. I believe it takes a long time to build successful institutions.

One of the key recommendations of the team was to concentrate the program, as much as possible, in a few priority areas so as to avoid scattering our efforts too widely. AID had developed some overzealous practices that arose from its well-intentioned efforts. As the global development experience grew, the Washington aid bureaucracy tried to replicate successful projects implemented in one recipient country by advocating the same kind of projects in other aid recipient countries. These "special pleaders," as they became known, would advocate for their pet projects to be included in every mission program, resulting in the dilution of the mission's resources, and therefore its effectiveness.

The evaluation team presented its findings and recommendations to the AID mission and returned to Washington or, as some wag put it, "rode off into the sunset" like the ending of a typical Western. I joined my family—Joan had been struggling to attend to our two infants, aged sixteen and six months, in temporary furnished quarters—and prepared to fly back to New Delhi to take on my new job in the Mission Program Office.

PROGRAM OFFICE CHIEF: 1965 TO 1967

After a stop in New York to say farewell to Jul and Rita, as well as to show off our two beautiful children, we boarded a Boeing 707 Pan American number 2, which took us through Frankfurt, Beirut, and Tehran, finally arriving in New Delhi at 4 a.m. No matter which airline or flight one selected, it seemed one arrived in New Delhi in the middle of the night, as though the runways had been rolled up in daytime to protect them from the mid-day heat.

We had an advantage over others who also arrived in New Delhi for a first-time posting. I had already selected a house to live in and had hired staff during my short-term assignment with the evaluation team. The house was furnished, and a full-time staff of three—a bearer, a sweeper and an ayah—plus a part-time *mali* and a part-time *dhobi* (laundryman), were already on the job as we debarked from the airplane. My hiring skills were soon shown to be lacking. During our first dinner party, the bearer dropped a piece of chicken cacciatore down the back and into the dress of the guest of honor. Joan soon made the necessary personnel changes and we lived in comfort for the next five years.

It was June 1965. The U.S. economic aid program to India had three major components; (1) technical assistance, (2) capital assistance, and (3) PL 480 grain imports. As a result of the work of the evaluation team there was general agreement within the mission and also with AID Washington concerning the funding level and substantive modifications of the Technical Assistance (TA) Program. The mission was in intense discussion internally and with the Indian government regarding the capital assistance program with respect to funding the "Big Push". Everyone knew John Lewis had a direct line into the White House and would be in a good position to sell the president on whatever conclusions these negotiations would yield. Finally, with respect to the PL 480 program, Washington had authorized our embassy to negotiate a multi-year grain shipment program at levels somewhat higher than previous years. We had bought into the Indian Planning Ministry's idea of assuring adequate food supplies through the PL 480 program so the Indians could devote their resources to capital investment in industry. There were also early signs that India's 1965 crop was beginning to suffer from drought conditions.

During the summer, skirmishes took place along India's border with Pakistan. These incidents escalated to an all-out war in September with each side losing almost four thousand of its troops. Suddenly, all bets with respect to U.S. aid were off. LBJ was never an enthusiastic friend of India's, in part because of his annoyance with Krishna Menon harping criticism of the States at the UN. He argued that if these poor countries could afford to engage in a war, our economic aid was not needed. All assistance was suspended, including grain shipments under the PL 480 program.

Suspending aid is similar to changing the course of a large ocean liner. It happens very slowly. There are goods in transit; there are signed contracts for goods and services that are firm commitments, there are personnel already hired; there are Indian trainees in the United States in the middle of training programs. But once the White House gave the instruction, no new commitments could be made. With the weather turning ever worse for India's grain crop, the most critical action had to do with PL 480 grain shipments coming from the States.

The proposed multi-year PL 480 agreement that had been under negotiation was dead in the water. There was a "grain pipeline," a set of ships, trucks, rail cars and barges that moved grain from USDA storage silos to the ports of Bombay, Calcutta and Madras. At any one of these ports, ships could be seen lined up and waiting for berths to offload cargo. There was slack in this pipeline but if loading in the States was interrupted, soon that gap would occur on the Indian side. With Indian crops suffering a drought, a massive famine was in store. By way of reference, it is estimated that the 1943 famine in India resulted in three million deaths.

The Indians were furious at this. Bowles and Lewis lobbied the White House to relent, once a ceasefire was achieved. Eventually, LBJ agreed to allow new shipments on a month-to-month basis, so long as the shooting did not resume. This was called the "short tether policy." In fact, the grain pipeline was never interrupted, in large part due to the persistent efforts of Bowles and Lewis to press the White House for a resumption of grain shipments as it became increasingly clear that a severe drought was likely. The Indians, however, had learned a lesson. They decreed that they would never again become dependent on a foreign power for their food supply.

This anger had some serendipitous effect on our TA program. Agriculture Minister Chidambaram Subramaniam shook the lethargy out of the government agencies and galvanized every resource to increase India's agricultural production. Fertilizer and new high yielding varieties of seed (recently developed at international research institutes) were acquired and delivered to farmers in time for planting. The graduate agricultural extension workers were pushed out of their government offices into the field. The agricultural universities were utilized for their intended purposes. In short, the agencies did all the things our technical people had been advocating before the crisis developed, albeit out of anger over our cavalier policies. The Green Revolution had begun.

Slowly, as tensions between Pakistan and India eased, conditions returned to normal. But the damage to "the Big Push" had been done. We were getting more involved in Vietnam after the Gulf of Tonkin incident. The mood about international economic aid in Congress had turned sour. The bilateral approach was being replaced by a more multilateral one, with the World Bank taking on a larger role in organizing aid donors. Most importantly, there was a drought and consequent crop failure in India. A major growth push cannot occur in the midst of famine. John Lewis' goal of achieving a breakthrough in India's economic development was frustrated yet again. During the next two years our mission's approach adjusted to these changing conditions.

My job in the Program Office was to manage the finances and contribute to the effectiveness of the TA program. Since all federal agencies operate on annual appropriations, each mission had to submit, on an annual basis, funding requirements for the next year in order to be incorporated into AID's funding request to Congress. The Program Office drove that exercise. Actually, since there was a competent, well-trained Indian support staff doing the needed routine work, I could devote my time to the substance of the program, implementing what our evaluation report had concluded and recommended.

Occasionally, my job would provide an opportunity for personal amusement. One day, while walking along a street in "Old Delhi," I ran into a Hindu mystic, covered in ashes and offering his services as an astrologist and predictor of the future. As I passed him, he grabbed my hand, looked at my palm, and exclaimed, "Sahib, you are going to get an important telegram about money!" I smiled and replied, "But, my friend, I get a half dozen telegrams about money every day!"

Here are a couple of stories about my work and our life in New Delhi during those first two years.

TECHNICAL ASSISTANCE AND CAPITAL ASSISTANCE

One of the quantitative, macroeconomic methods used at that time to determine the likely impact of a particular annual aid level was to calculate the economy's "capital/output ratio." One analyzed the economy's past performance in terms of the output resulting from a given amount of investment. All other things remaining equal, the economy was therefore expected to yield a certain increase in GDP for a given level of capital investment. This would provide confidence in the calculation of the impact of a given injection of aid.

The TA program was intended to change that ratio by improving the economy's productivity so as to yield a greater amount of output per amount of investment. It was a long-term effort to yield gains somewhere down the road. There is a lot of drudgery associated with changing behavior. It is less glamorous than calculating an aid recipient's capital assistance requirements. The senior staff was much more interested in analyzing the "big numbers." I was more intrigued with TA implementation and what was required to change outdated and inefficient practices.

Perhaps a concrete example might clarify how capital assistance and TA are two prongs of the same fork to achieve economic development, are complementary to each other and, at the same time, tend to be substitutive. During the torrid summer heat of 1966, I had placed my wife and three children at Kasauli, a hill station in Himachal Pradesh, just north of Chandigarh, about a three-hour drive from Delhi. I would drive there on Friday evening and return to Delhi Monday morning. I drove that round trip on four consecutive weekends.

The Indian highway department was improving four points along the hundred-mile stretch of road to Chandigarh. There were a total of fourteen earth-moving machines (dozers, graders, rollers, back-hoes, etc.) operating at those four locations. These were expensive, imported machines, a very large layout of foreign exchange capital. I would count the number of machines that were actually operating at each construction site every time I passed by. The maximum number of machines actually moving, on any one of those eight trips, was four. On one of those trips there were no machines moving at all, even though there was labor sitting around waiting for something to happen.

This story reflects the built-in inefficiencies in the road construction system. If TA could improve operations and management of road repair work so as to double the usage of the equipment, the amount of capital needed to achieve the same output would be cut by half. Well, perhaps not that much because the equipment would wear out faster. But surely there would be some capital savings. Investment in TA to increase productivity is a wonderful way to reduce capital requirements for an economy that is severely short of foreign exchange.

MY COUNTERPART

My first problem was finding someone in the Ministry of Finance's Department of Economic Affairs (DEA) who was mentally engaged with this process to work with. I found myself dealing with a senior official who had previously served with the rank of ambassador in the Indian Diplomatic Service. He saw his current position as a demotion and had no interest beyond requiring us to adhere rigidly to procedural practices, none of which seemed destined to yield any developmental changes on the Indian side. After making several attempts to engage him, I raised the issue with the mission's front office. My boss, Ernie Stern, was the mission deputy director. He joined me at one meeting with my counterpart, saw the problem, and raised the issue with the secretary of DEA who quickly assigned a much more dynamic and forward thinking officer, G.V. Ramakrishna. (He later became governor of the Reserve Bank of India). I developed a good professional relationship with him that helped significantly.

The summer science institutes program was one of the most successful TA projects in the education sector. Our techies in the Education Division figured out that there were many science teachers in the States who were available during the summer and would love a trip to India. Lots of local currency was available from the PL 480 grain sales that could be used for airplane tickets and hotel bills in India. The Indian science teachers could benefit from a four to five week refresher course, if it could be organized.

Seventy such classes were given each summer at Indian teaching facilities, many in the Himalayas where the weather was decent and the scenery spectacular. Teaching aids developed by U.S. teachers were distributed to the Indian participants and could be taken back to their schools after course completion. The results were outstanding. The project had a huge multiplier effect and helped improve the quality of Indian science teaching. It was such a simple idea, yet so effective with minimal cost to the U.S. taxpayer other than the stipends given to the U.S. science teachers.

Another excellent project was the support given to the Indian Education Commission by top flight American educators to analyze and design India's school system. A key political commitment of the Indian government was providing every child with a six-year primary education. But what was to be the next step for these children? How many places could

India afford to offer its vast population in grades seven to twelve? What of the economy's manpower needs over the next twenty plus years? What kind of vocational and professional training facilities should be established to provide for these needs? This activity played to the orientation of India's "national planners" who were attempting to husband the nation's available resources and meet the skilled labor needs of its rapidly expanding work force.

During this period, the TA program was expanded to include a major activity in nutrition planning, an ambitious effort to help the Indian government ease or eradicate malnutrition in the population, focusing on children under the age of five. In the States, there is an entire industry devoted to reducing levels of saturated fat and other unhealthy ingredients in the food we eat in order to combat obesity. In India, given the prevailing poverty, food needed to be nutritionally fortified or at least directed to the most vulnerable groups. However, a magic ingredient to increase nutritional value of food does not exist.

I had originally opposed this newly proposed effort because of the evaluation team's concerns that the TA program would become too fragmented. The team recommended that resources be concentrated in just a few sectors to husband the mission's management capabilities. Fortunately, I was overruled and Alan Berg came out to India to design a superb program that was absorbed by the Indian government and continues to operate today. Many in India are alive today because of this TA program.

THE USAID PROGRAM TO INDIA IN 1966

In the course of my travels across India to examine the various components of our program, the mission and embassy often asked me to explain the program to its beneficiaries. Annex 3 reproduces a speech I gave at the Indian Institute of Technology in Kanpur in 1966 that provides a comprehensive description of this huge and costly program. It describes its composition and magnitude as well as its history since the

aid program began in 1951. It provides a candid account of its achievements and limitations but also discusses the so-called "strings on aid"
that have been alleged to be included in our program. One aspect of that
presentation deals with the cessation of US aid in 1965 when the war
with Pakistan began.

THE RUSSIANS

One person, who seemed to seek me out among the "artsy folks" with
whom we mingled, was a young Russian named Ilyintsev. He claimed
to work in the Cultural Affairs Section of the Soviet embassy. He would
attend all the plays the American Theater Association would stage but also
appeared at other functions, (i.e.; music, dance and theater). He always
made a point to strike up a conversation whenever we met and it seemed
we were bumping into each other ever more frequently. As a member of
the USAID senior staff, I was expected to be watchful for such efforts to
make contact. The rules were very clear. I must inform our intelligence
folks about every event in writing.

I stopped by to ask our spooks what they knew about Ilyintsev. I
learned he was with the GRU, the Soviet military intelligence. Why was he
working me? Who can tell? So I invited him to have dinner at our home. It
turned out to be a fun event for me.

He arrived precisely on time, brought Joan a small gift and immediately reacted to Joan's speech pattern. He explained that he had been one
of the first exchange students to study for one year at Yale University several years earlier and had found he had a knack for identifying American
regional accents. He could tell right away that she grew up in New York
City. We said that was not so. He looked startled and then said, "Oh, but
then you went to college in New York." Again Joan said no. He was really
perplexed. He kept up his questions along the same line. Eventually his
problem became clear to me. He was describing Sandra, my first wife. He
had done for me what I had done for him. He had consulted my dossier

in his intelligence section. Unfortunately for him, the dossier was years out of date.

I then thought it might be useful to ask him if he could get me information about Soviet aid to India. After all, he and I were both in India to help with its development efforts. I would gladly give him all of my data to describe our aid programs (all of our aid information was unclassified). Would he be willing to share his information about Soviet aid? He promised to do so.

The next time we met he could only offer me a couple of pamphlets printed in Moscow about Soviet aid in general. Soviet aid to India was almost entirely military assistance and was therefore highly classified. There was no way he could share that with me. From that point on, whenever we met at some function, we would smile at each other and the conversation was always the same lie: "We must get together really soon," one of us would say to the other. "Yes," would be the reply, "very soon."

THE ZABLOCKI VISIT

In early 1966, we received an official visit from Congressman Clement Zablocki, of the House Foreign Affairs Committee. He was very important to us because his committee had oversight of our aid program. A briefing was scheduled for a Saturday morning in the ambassador's conference room, located behind the "bronze eagle" hanging on the front of the Embassy building. From the large windows of the conference room, one looked out through the eagle and at the front steps and lawn of the Embassy.

Ambassador Bowles was out of station, and so we lesser lights had to do our best. As we droned on about India and our aid relationship, it was clear Zablocki was hardly listening. He was distracted by what he saw through the window, in front of the embassy. There were several young Americans marching in a picket line with signs protesting our involvement in the Vietnam War. When our briefing mercifully ran to an end, we asked him whether he had any questions. He immediately pointed to the picket line and demanded, "Who are those kids out there?" We allowed how they were probably Fulbright students here on a study grant. He wanted their names-- particularly if they came from Wisconsin, Zablocki's home state. He kept calling them "those Madison radicals." It was the beginning of our tribulations with South Asia and the "Domino Theory."

Shastri's Succession

The ambassador's conference room was one of my favorite places. I have fond memories about it because I admired the way Chester Bowles fostered cohesion among the various components of his Country Team (CT). He had a superb ability to get the best out of his staff, and I enjoyed a few good laughs in that room.

In early January 1966, Prime Minister Shastri made a trip to Moscow; the Soviets were acting as intermediaries to settle the conflict with Pakistan. On his returning flight to Delhi, he suffered a heart attack. The aircraft was diverted to Tashkent, where he died. His flight returned with the body and India went into a short period of mourning But the question of succession was on everyone's mind.

The CT's senior staff would meet regularly each week in the conference room. Often, at the ambassador's request, a senior officer would prepare a presentation about a subject of common interest. It was a technique Bowles used to build cohesion among his team. It was common for the presenter, when using audio-visual charts for these presentations, to have them made up by an AID audio-visual technician named Frank Wilder, whose primary job was helping train staff at the Ministry of Information and Broadcasting. Frank was a very decent person and would also help at the presentation. As a result, he became something of a fixture at these weekly meetings.

At the weekly meeting following Shastri's death, the subject of his succession was the hot topic. Each of the embassy's senior staff had a different theory, based on rumors circulating among their respective contacts. The defense attaché thought it would be Chavan, the minister of defense. There was also the minister of labor, a leader of the untouchables who had a very powerful following. Each senior officer speculated about his or her favorite candidate. Suddenly, Frank Wilder popped up and said, "Mr. Ambassador, I was working at the Ministry of Information and Broadcasting yesterday. They say Indira Gandhi will become the next Prime Minister." There was an outbreak of laughter from all the "experts" around the table. "A woman prime minister in this country?? Ha, ha. Sit down Frank and stop being ridiculous." He was right, of course. Indira Gandhi was designated prime minister the next day.

U.S. AID TO INDIA IN EARLY 1967

Here is how things were playing out at the AID mission in early 1967. The "short tether policy" with respect to PL 480 food grain shipments was over. India's grain harvest was exceptionally low due to the drought and we were shipping 8 million tons to fill the gap.

The "Big Push" was, at a minimum, placed on hold but there was a general sense that the mood in Washington had changed, and there was little likelihood that large-scale capital assistance to India could ever be revived. Bowles and Lewis had assembled an outstanding team to work with the Indian government in wrestling with development aid needs, but the Indians were preoccupied with the possibility of mass starvation if the crop failure exceeded India's ability to get food through its ports.

It was getting close to the end of my two-year tour of duty. We had arrived in May of 1965. I was scheduled to depart for home leave in May of 1967. For various reasons, I did not want to return to Delhi to continue as chief of the Program Office for another two years. At one of Lewis' seminars, there was discussion about assisting India to increase its exports, thereby earning the additional foreign exchange the "Big Push" would have delivered, had things not gone awry. I found that discussion exhilarating and allowed that I would like to participate in such an effort. I had a bit of experience in the import-export-shipping business after leaving the army in 1955, working in New York for an import-export house. I was asked to design a TA project that AID could implement.

THE BIHAR FAMINE OF 1966–1967

At the AID mission and the embassy, there was a great deal of nervousness about a possible famine. If a major famine occurred with large-scale loss of life even while we were supplying India with huge quantities of PL 480 grain, AID would surely be severely criticized in Congress and the press over our handling of the aid. The famine of 1943 saw three million starvation deaths. We needed to monitor the food situation and the Indian government's efforts, particularly in the Ganges Plains (Uttar Pradesh and Bihar) where the crop failure was severe. The senior staff designated Alan Berg to take overall responsibility for this. Another officer, Robert Satin, was asked to spend time in Lucknow and I was designated to do the same in Putna. Beginning early March 1966, each Monday, Bob and I would get on the puddle jumper flight from Delhi to Calcutta. He would get off at Lucknow. I would go on to Putna. Each Friday afternoon we would return to Delhi to report to Alan and then the CT. The Program Office staff did all the necessary work to keep everything functioning in my absence.

We helped the Indian authorities set up operations centers in Lucknow and Putna, the capital cities of Uttar Pradesh and Bihar respectively, to collect and monitor the reports coming from their district collectors. We also helped them analyze the time series data for food supplies, crop yields and water table changes. If a community ran low on food, the villagers would wait for the next shipment. But if a community's water table dropped below the well levels, the villagers would move. Trying to find them so as to provide them with food and water then became a big problem.

The chief minister of Bihar had an aircraft and pilot at his disposal. There was a legitimate need for that since the Ganges cuts Bihar in two and there are few bridges across it. I made use of the aircraft and pilot to visit district collectors and orient them to send accurate reports of local conditions. I made sure the operations center's staff analyzed the reports and fed the results to those who were responsible for distributing the food shipments.

Even though some Indian press reports alluded to famine deaths, it has been well documented that our food aid averted what could have been a major humanitarian disaster.

During this time, I prepared a TA project proposal for a new project to stimulate India's exports. Lewis took it to Bhoothalingam, the secretary at DEA and also to K.B. Lal, the secretary of the Ministry of Trade, for their review. After getting clearance from the mission, but not the Indian government, it was sent to Washington for review and approval.

After eight weeks of flying into and out of Putna, Rod Heller, the mission's legal advisor, took over for me. My family and I left India to begin our home leave. Joan, our three children under the age of four, plus Joan's sister, Marlene, and I traveled to Thailand, Japan and Hawaii and then back to the States.

EXPORT INDUSTRIES EXPANSION

Virtually all of the Indian professional, educated people with whom we worked—our counterparts in the government, those in the artistic community, the businessmen and those in the media—were clearly of the upper castes, many of them Brahmin. We Americans were always treated with respect and courtesy, as one might treat a rich uncle. But there was an underlying attitude, bordering on condescension, towards those who had not been bestowed the benefits of a sophisticated and mature culture or civilization. The Brahminical culture seemed to carry with it an aura of self-content and certainty such as one might reasonably expect from membership in a long-established society with deep roots. When temporarily forced to deal with someone from a more "primitive" culture, they simply knew better.

Brahmins did not perceive themselves, as we did, to be burdened with historical baggage. Rather they viewed themselves as having been given by their gods to understand more about life than we did. I later encountered similar attitudes in China. "What do you know about Tibet? We ruled Tibet six hundred years ago, before Columbus sailed the ocean blue!"

It was in this cultural context that the design of an export industries expansion project had to navigate. India's leaders displayed four hostile attitudes during the 1960s. These were:

1. "We know fully well what is holding back our export earnings. It is the import restrictions and barriers to trade imposed by the developed nations to protect their own markets. If you want to help us earn more foreign exchange, do something about those restraints to trade in your own country." Not only in India but also in many other developing nations there was a tendency to externalize their problems.

2. "You send all these technical experts to 'help us.' But we have plenty of our own technical experts here. We do not need foreign technical experts. If you really want to help us then use your aid to finance the import of new high tech machinery and equipment to produce for the domestic and, if necessary, for export markets." A typical response based on a false sense of self pride. Later, in the 1980s, I heard the same words in Egypt. Mubarak had been asked to use World Bank loan funds to pay for technical experts. He refused, unless the financing was shifted to a grant basis. "These experts come to Egypt only to look at the pyramids," he is quoted to have said.

3. "We believe our future lies in a policy of 'import substitution' rather than export promotion. We want to produce products domestically to replace the things we are importing." This was a mantra of the Nehru/Mahalanobis school of central planning.

4. "The future lies in a 'New International Economic Order' with greater equality among nations. The world is moving away from free market

capitalism, with all of its built-in inequalities, toward a more equitable socialist system where governments, elected by the people will control the economic high ground and prohibit profiteering." This argument did not lose force in India until 1991, after the Berlin wall came down and the Soviet Union was seen to have become a failed socialist experiment.

I rejected the underlying assumptions behind each one of these views. Nevertheless, given their prevalence, it was clear that any assistance we provide to the export sector would have to depart from the usual TA format, whereby the government would formally request assistance. The Indian government refused to sign a project agreement requesting assistance. This was an American initiative. The structure of the project had to be modified by limiting the amount of technical expert input and overseas training. In effect, I was to be the expatriate technical expert. The government chose to tolerate our efforts, realizing that there would be untoward consequences for U.S. aid to India if they raised objections.

Having sat in the Program Office for the previous two years, I knew which resources were available to me and which were not. Dollars were in short supply; Indian rupees were available in plenty. If hiring foreign technical experts to give advice about trade matters to the government was a non-starter, could we get Indian experts up to speed to do that?

THE COMMODITY SURVEYS

Here is the strategy we followed. If the government would not listen to American policy advice, we would find a way to use Indian qualified experts to collect hard information about international markets and producers in competing supplier nations, and inject this into India's public discussion on trade. We would facilitate the public discourse between Indian exporters and policy makers.

First, we selected the major traditional export products of India's export basket—jute, tea, cashews, shellac, leather, and textiles. Then we added some new products that seemed to have found their way into India's export statistics (seafood, machine tools, fruits and vegetables). Could we organize a study group, for each of these commodities, to travel, first, to the markets to learn how India's products are positioned there compared with similar products of India's major competitors? Then, we could send this group of Indian researchers to the competing supplier countries to see what they could learn about the competitor's production process. Out of this research, the study group would be expected to make recommendations about how India's exporters could improve their competitive position in the market place.

Each commodity study group would be a team of Indian researchers from an Indian consulting firm. The Indian consulting industry was in its infancy. Large industrial groups, generally family owned (Tata, Birla, Sarabhai, Mafatlal), were in the process of establishing consulting companies, primarily intended to serve their own company needs but also willing to do outside work. Independent consulting firms were establishing themselves to serve industry (Dastur, Laroya/LC Jain, Gallup). There were also a number of well-run research institutes serving particular sectors (Central Leather Research Institute, Indian Institute for Foreign Trade) and there were several top-rate management institutes (Indian Institute of Management, Calcutta, National Council for Applied Economic Research-NCAER). These research groups would be hired, each to perform one study, and be provided with one U.S. expert in that particular commodity to help them gain access to information sources in the markets and in the competing supplier countries. We provided them with a detailed outline of the areas to be researched and the findings expected from their work (see annex 4). We never argued about cost, making clear to each group that we were willing to pay for quality work but that we would hold them to deliver the quality of work that could reasonably be expected of them. We gave them plenty of time to perform. And we assured them that their work would be handsomely bound and widely distributed. Ample press coverage and an opportunity to present findings to senior government policy makers and the industry for which the report was targeted would be provided. All raw data and analytical back up work would also be published. If others wanted to review the data and draw different conclusions, access to the team's raw data would be readily available.

Virtually all the costs could be met with rupees. The U.S. expert's stipend would be in dollars as would be the per diem of the team while traveling abroad. But the fee to the Indian research team, the airline tickets, and the report preparation costs were rupee expenses and we had lots of those.

I was to quality control the operation. We selected the research teams with great care and funded them liberally. They did not need to cut corners to complete their work. We then secured an expert in the trade of that particular commodity to work with the team. He was their encyclopedia about the product being researched. He had no vote with respect to the team's findings, but he would be required to write a one-page critique of the team's work and that critique would be published as an introduction to their report. That provided another quality check built into the system. We were rarely disappointed with the performance of the teams. One of the positive effects of this project was the enhancement of the capabilities of India's consulting industry.

Support from AID Washington for securing the U.S. experts was excellent. For example, for the study of spices we found someone who worked for McCormick Pepper; for shellac, we secured the services of someone who actually traded in shellac. These specialists knew the markets, the competing suppliers, and could guide our Indian research team to meet the right people. The only expert we were not able to supply was for the textile study. The fee to pay for a textile expert was considered too sensitive for inclusion in our dollar expenditures for fear it would upset U.S. textile producers. So I went to Geneva and got UNCTAD/GATT International Trade Center to finance a British expert. This worked out successfully.

AID's contracting philosophy deserves some mention here. There is an old joke about two astronauts about to go for a flight to the moon, one asking the other if he realized that their space ship had been built by a set of contractors, each of whom offered the lowest bid. When selecting Indian consulting firms to perform the commodity surveys, their first proposal would invariably be under-budgeted, woefully inadequate to produce the quality of work we needed. I had to persuade them to budget sufficiently to fully perform their required tasks. The AID contracting officer would press me to go for competitive bids but I refused. Fortunately, the funding was almost exclusively in Indian rupees and so the normal U.S. government contracting rules could be relaxed. Had there been no rupee availability, I would not have been able to achieve the quality of work that came from these firms because I would have been required to use competitive bidding procedures.

Every one of these surveys was presented to government policy makers in a large meeting chaired by Secretary of Foreign Trade K.B. Lal. The research team was given an hour to present its findings followed by questions and discussion. An open meeting was held, usually two weeks later, for the relevant members of the export community. The press was always present at those later meetings. Several hundred copies of the report were printed, including the raw data and analysis compiled to support its findings. The reports were bound handsomely (usually four volumes) and distributed free of charge to almost anyone who asked for them. The underlying assumption was that this entire exercise would add to the public discourse on India's export problems with the hope that something would come out of it. I cannot say with conviction that anything really did.

At some point during the five-year life of the project, I was asked why I chose to research these particular commodities. I answered that I did that for the same reason Willie Sutton said he robbed banks: "That's where the money is!" Interestingly, one of the major conclusions of these studies was that the most likely opportunities for export growth lay in the non-traditional offshoots of the country's traditional export lines.

SUSPECTED OF BEING A SPY

As if the conditions of service for this project were not difficult enough, what with the Indian policy makers' attitudes and their unwillingness to sign a project agreement, I did the very worst thing possible to create yet more hardship for myself. I hosted a party.

Diplomatic life in Delhi was full of parties because maintaining one's contacts was part of the job. These cocktail parties were so prolific that it was not uncommon to attend several in one evening. It would be difficult to have a serious conversation with someone because the other person's eye would rove over your shoulder to see who else of importance had entered the room and to decide when it was time to take up with another who carried more "gravitas" or could give information that could be reported back to one's superiors. My preference, when possible, was to host small dinner parties to avoid that part of the drill.

We had recently returned from home leave and had a few social obligations to fulfill. One was the top Indian government official with whom I worked in Putna on the famine watch before departing for home leave. He had recently been assigned to the position of joint secretary in the Interior Ministry. I also owed a dinner to Angus Thurmer. Angus was the deputy head of station for the CIA. He was a very personable guy, played polo at the exclusive Delhi Polo Club, and had been "declared" to the Indian government by our embassy— meaning the Indians knew him as an administrator in the intelligence world. Unfortunately, my colleague from Putna, newly assigned to the Interior Ministry, knew this and immediately concluded that I too must be working with the CIA. It seems that word was then sent to K.B. Lal, who informed the staff that I might be a spy. Whenever I went to the office of my counterpart in the Ministry of Trade, a very nice guy named Banerjee, he would always find a reason to leave.

I resorted to conducting my business outside of the ministry, working with the private sector. After we had some success with the presentation of the commodity studies to the public, the press, and also to the ministry,

Lal told Lewis that I had been suspected of being a CIA plant but that they finally concluded the CIA could not possibly be that interested in India's export problems. From that point on, I was able to deal with the ministry officials once again. Eventually, they went so far as to sign the project agreement request. That action gave me confidence that my work was being recognized as making some small contribution to the Indian development scene.

THE EXPORT PROMOTION COUNCILS

At the research groups, I worked with some very talented people such as Nayudama of the Central Leather Research Institute in Madras. He later died as a passenger on the Air India flight from Canada that was blown up during the Sikh rebellion that followed the attack on their temple in Amritsar. It was the loss of one of India's finest minds. I also worked with Bhoothalingam, who retired as secretary of DEA and became head of NCAER; Eric DaCosta, head of Gallup Organization; Sreedhar, of Dastur Co. (he later took an assignment with the World Bank, a most coveted job for any person from a developing nation); and Sharma of Sarabhai's Operations Research Group.

The project was very popular among the leaders of Indian private sector industry. Our help in making a case for private sector expansion before government policy makers was appreciated. As the press picked up on our activities, I found my fame spreading and enjoyed the access proffered to me. Godrej would often come to Delhi from his base in Bombay, and would drop in for lunch.

But powerful as these industrial leaders were, they were concerned that their actions might offend the all-powerful government policy makers. This caused them to limit their efforts, to make a weak case for the actions they knew were necessary to achieve a break-through in export growth. An example was the commodity study on marine products.

The Ministry of Trade had set up about twenty-five export councils. These bodies were similar to what we in the United States know to be private business associations. The councils' purpose was to provide feedback to the ministry and to act on behalf of the entire community of producers of a particular export commodity. The government provided some annual funding to each council to meet a portion of their administrative expenses. The councils were often used by the government to channel information to and from the exporters on actions needed to support the industry, such as requesting a special allocation of foreign exchange that might be needed to import some vital raw material or machinery. One of these was the Marine Products Export Promotion Council.

We had done a commodity survey on marine products and it turned out to be a horror story. The producers were unable to increase exports for a whole panoply of reasons. The twenty-fathom offshore belt had limited shrimp beds and the government shipyards were producing small trawlers that could not operate in deeper water. Thus, as boats were added to the fleet, the catch per boat went down while the total catch of the fleet remained the same. The Indian government had discovered shrimp beds in the 40 to 60 fathom belt in international waters (these depths required trawlers of better than 110 feet length) but would not allow leasing of foreign trawlers with foreign crews for fear the location of these beds would be revealed to non-Indian fishing fleets. There were no trained Indian crews to run such large vessels. The Indian government's state owned shipyards at Bombay, Mazagon docks, had the capability to produce only one kind of trawler of the required size. But it had been designed by a Norwegian expert and was intended for North Atlantic service with all the ice breaking and power loading that such work entails, while the Indian waters needed light weight, efficient "tin cans" to do the job. Meanwhile, these beautiful, succulent, high value shrimp were dying of old age in their shrimp beds.

Our report had not yet been presented to the Ministry of Trade but our research crew had discussed its findings with the council.

I visited the council in Cochin and attended a meeting at which a list of things to request of the Ministry for the following year was being prepared. Instead of addressing the real issues plaguing them, their request was limited to a few modest proposals for training abroad and foreign exchange allocations to buy imported nets for the existing fleet. I was aghast and asked why they do not "speak the truth to power" by requesting the kind of help that would really make a difference in production and exports. They replied that, if they did that, those who evaluated their request would throw out their entire request and the small amount of support that was intended for them would be given to some other council. Only after we presented the study team's conclusions to the ministry would the council support those findings.

The Indian staff of my little operation was outstanding, even in comparison with the excellent local staff of the Program Office because I took a couple of the most talented and ambitious people with me. The head was a young fellow named Jerath. After the project ended he shifted to the Canadian high commission and again distinguished himself working on processing and vetting Indian applicants who applied to migrate to Canada.

And then, there is the story of P.N. Arya. Arya worked in the Program Office while I was chief. He often got into difficulty with others on the staff and was about to be discharged when I set up the Export Industries Division. He asked me if I would hire him. I had mixed feelings. On the one hand, he was clearly very competent. On the other, he was highly abrasive and did not do well following orders when he did not agree with them. His difficulties lay with his relationship with our senior Indian staff. I decided to take him on after he assured me he would follow my instructions fully and faithfully.

One subject that intrigued me, ever since my run-in with Ilyintsev, was India's economic relationship with the Soviet Union, particularly its bilateral trade and aid, including military aid. I asked Arya if he would study that question, taking advantage of all public information sources plus any he could access within the government through his own personal contacts. He took to that assignment like a duck to water.

With virtually no supervision, other than to answer his questions when he came to a roadblock, he put together a very thorough report. It used some highly sophisticated analysis of the India–Soviet bilateral trade regime, what was basically a barter system. He also uncovered a pattern by the Soviets that delayed the arrival of India's karakul shipments to Europe sent through the Soviet Union's rail system. It seems these shipments, which competed with Soviet sales in the same market, repeatedly got delayed in transit and arrived too late to be included in the auctions. The study also showed an annual trade gap between imports and exports with a value of 50 million dollars in favor of the Soviet Union. That would account for India's military purchases, always hidden from view. There was no grant aid that we could find. When Arya's work was complete, I took it to our spooks to check the data against theirs. They confirmed that his material was consistent with theirs.

What to do with this document? How to use it? Would its distribution result in more attacks in the left wing press against the imperialist Americans? I took a copy over to P.C. Alexander, the joint secretary in the Ministry of Trade with responsibility for trade with the Eastern bloc countries. Had he any interest in this document? One of my local staff had just done some research for me to satisfy my curiosity. Alexander was about to leave for Moscow to partake in the annual trade negotiations. He was busy but said he would look at it if he had time. The next day, we received a call from his office for fifteen additional copies. With that many copies floating around, I was sure it would get to the press. To keep faith with my colleague Ramakrishna, I had to transmit a copy to DEA. A few days later, Alexander's assistant called for another ten copies. I waited for the next shoe to drop from the Indian left wing press.

It never did. There was no press report about this document. Ever. It did not exist. The absence of any stories about it in the news media made it clear to me that the left-wing press attacked our programs only when it was convenient for the Indian government.

Life in India for the Rudel Family

All work and no play make Lu a dull boy. I threw myself into my work. And life was good. We lived in a small air-conditioned house in a new, upscale community called Haus Khas, not far from the Qutub Minar. Each morning, a car and driver would pick me up, pick up other mission personnel on route and deliver us to the office. Each evening, it would return me to my home whenever I chose to finish work. We had a big black Ford station wagon, which Joan used to transport herself and the family around Delhi. It was the vehicle of choice among the mothers because it could haul a dozen small kids in the back. Those were the days before car seats and safety belts. Now I shudder at that image of Joan dropping the tail-gate to disgorge all those little tykes at Playhouse Nursery School.

Joan was pregnant again. Our third child would be born in India on Valentine's Day 1966. David was born ten months and two weeks after Ruth Ann. Now, fifteen months later, it was Joanna, our Indian miniature. There would be only 26 months between the birthday of our oldest and our youngest. Lots of diapers, a third child required the hiring an additional ayah to our household.

The economics of our personal finances were good. Our housing was provided. There was a hardship allowance in addition to our regular salary. And things were cheap. It was not possible for us to spend as much money in India as I was earning. Travel was easy. Air service, India's marvelous rail system and our personal automobile made it very convenient to see as much of India as desired. And there was so much to see.

Business and Family Travel in India

We traveled to Agra, Kasauli in the foothills of the Himalayas and then, wherever else we wanted. Some travel was required by my work. AID projects were located throughout India. We were so heavily involved with India's development efforts that it was important to understand what was being done by them, not only our own inputs to those efforts. The United

States had consulates in Madras, Calcutta and Bombay and the consuls wanted to stay informed about U.S. activities in their areas of responsibility.

Our family took vacation trips in southern India (Bangalore, Cochin, Madurai) and also to the Ganges Plain (Lucknow, Benares, Putna) as well as Nepal.

We needed to travel each summer to escape the debilitating heat of Delhi. During the winter months, Delhi weather is ideal. But in March, the temperature begins to climb. It becomes intolerable in May and June until the monsoon begins to cool things down in early July. During those sixty days, most Westerners find cooler places for their families to "hibernate."

The foothills of the Himalayas are not too distant from Delhi and allow the working member to join up with the family on most weekends. Kashmir was a most luxurious escape spot during our tours. The trout fishing is world renowned. We took advantage of places like Gulmarg and Pahalgam for extended stays. We even rented a houseboat, sometimes referred to as a little piece of England, on Dal Lake.

I travelled a good deal, sometimes with the entire family and servants, sometimes without servants (a tour through south India, including Goa, Cochin, Periyar Wildlife Sanctuary, Utacamund and the tea estates, Madurai and Madras). Many trips were made by just Joan and me. There were touristic visits to Rajasthan, including the cities of Udaipur and Jaipur as we traveled by rail or air or car. Transport and hotels were inexpensive and we never experienced any cost constraints for travel in India. Joan and I even hosted a New Year's party in 1968 by renting the entire palace formerly belonging to the maharajah at Silisar in Rajasthan, about 100 miles from Delhi and invited thirty of our friends to celebrate. The palace was located on the shores of a small lake. Servants prepared the meals. When the moon rose, the setting was spectacular and the party a hoot.

When there was work to be done, we combined business and personal travel. I was working with people all over the sub-continent: Ahmedabad and Baroda with Indian Institute of Management and Sarabhai; Poona with

Institute for Economic Research; Bombay with Tata consulting; Madras with Central Leather Research Institute; Calcutta with Dastur and the other Indian Institute of Management; Cochin with the Marine Products Export Promotion Council. I felt productive even though "the winds were never at my back."

VISIT TO THE SOVIET UNION

I also travelled to Europe, primarily to develop and maintain relationships with other UN development agencies like the International Trade Center in Geneva, or with other aid donors that were active in India and had bilateral assistance activities that could complement ours. But there was one bit of travel that makes for an interesting story. I was scheduled to travel to Washington for consultation and decided to make a stopover in Moscow and Leningrad (now called St. Petersburg) at my own expense.

Air India had a flight from Delhi to London that made a stop in Moscow. I requested permission from the front office to make a visit. To my surprise, I got lots of cautionary warnings suggesting it would be unwise. Nobody actually told me I could not do it, leaving it up to my discretion, but these trepidations and concern for my safety caused me to worry. I consulted with the spooks.

The senior officer who was designated liaison with the embassy staff listened to my tale, smiled wisely and asked me if I traveled on a diplomatic passport. Yes indeed, was my reply. He then told me that there was little risk to undertaking the visit, so long as I avoided being ensnared in any honey-traps. He told me, if I were in some way to be detained by the Soviets when I wished to leave, that would be the first time they would do that to someone with a diplomatic passport since the Revolution of 1917. Of course, I decided to go. To make it easy for the Soviets to keep tabs on me, I booked my visit, including hotels, a car and driver and a full-time guide, through the Soviet Intourist travel agency. That way I would be paying the cost of their minders.

It was a great visit. The car met me at the airport. I assumed the driver and the guide had their instructions and would report my every move. I'm sure the hotel room was bugged. I had no subversive intentions; I just wanted to see the sights without being hassled. After a couple of days in Moscow, I flew to Leningrad where another car and driver met me with yet another tour guide. We toured the city with visits to the Hermitage, to Pushkintown and to the former tsar's recently renovated palace.

The only conversation of interest I had was with one of the tour guides. I think she provoked me by telling me how silly it was for Americans to have such a fetish about private ownership and the territorial control that goes with it. "So, you want to own the land. Why don't you also want to own the sky, the air? Or the sea?" I did not wish to argue with her. But eventually, I asked her if her apartment was privately owned. No, she said, it was owned by the state. But, there was some talk then that she may be allowed to buy it in the near future. That would be nice. Then she could maintain it better. She had no idea that this was a contradiction in her thinking. Several people approached me to convert dollars into rubles at very favorable exchange rates but I maintained a strict law-abiding position.

I departed as scheduled without incident, after giving substantial tips to all of my minders. It was a very interesting exposure to life behind the iron curtain.

THE AMERICAN THEATER ASSOCIATION

I had been introduced to amateur theater in Ankara, found I loved it and wanted to continue to perform during our tour of duty in Delhi. There were a couple of Indian groups that had been performing plays in English, such as Yatrik and Delhi Players, and I quickly signed up to act in their productions. But then we learned that the new Embassy office building under construction, the West Building, had a small theater in its basement, primarily intended to show films. The AID mission was slated to move its offices from Faridkot House to the West Building so I explored the feasibility of using that space for live theater. It needed only a few structural changes for live theater productions. The embassy agreed and, a few months later, when we moved our offices, we began to think seriously about setting up our own theater group. The British high commission had its own theater group. We intended to name ours the American Theater Group. But then, one of my Indian staff called his friend in the AID Comptrollers office and, after making some discrete inquiries, informed me that there had been an American theater group some years earlier and they had disbanded due to low interest. There still remained a bank account in their name, The American Theater Association (ATA). We adopted that name and, lo and behold, found that we had sufficient funds to put on our first show.

I became ATA's president. During our five years of service in India, ATA put on four shows each year. We normally scheduled four performances for each production. ATA gave me a wonderful creative outlet. I was happy to manage the group and also to perform. We did productions of *A Hat Full of Rain, Tender Trap, View from the Bridge*, and similar shows of that level of popularity. The West Building auditorium held 340 seats. If the show received particularly good reviews in Delhi's English press, we would add a couple of performances to meet the demand for tickets. I managed to wangle a part in just about every production. My circle of friends widened to include the "artsy" crowd in Delhi, including those working in the English language press.

THE FOURTH ESTATE

India has a well-regarded English language daily press. Newspapers such as Hindustan Times and Times of India are published in Delhi; The Hindu is published in Madras (now Chennai). The Patriot was the daily Communist newspaper, published in Calcutta. It seemed to be the leader of the left-wing press and had a large following in the vernacular press.

The availability of "the Nagpur Mail" made it possible for the latest news to be circulated daily throughout India. The Nagpur Mail was an innovation by the Indian postal service. It was a nightly flight of four DC-3 aircraft, each leaving one of India's four major cities at 10 p.m., flying for three hours to Nagpur, a city located in the dead center of the Indian sub-continent. The flights would exchange sacks of mail with each other at the airport in Nagpur, and then return to their home city by 5 a.m., thereby providing overnight air mail service between India's four major cities— Delhi, Calcutta, Madras and Bombay.

The U.S. press had a superb collection of highly professional and well-respected correspondents stationed in Delhi. During my tour, the *New York Times* correspondent was Joe Lelyveld. He eventually became the *Times'* executive editor in the late 1990s. *Time* magazine had Marvin Zim; the Associated Press had Myron Belkind; the *Washington Post* had Bernie Nossiter.

A component of the export industries project that, unfortunately, did not succeed at the time was to set up a business and economic informa-tion service, something like *Bloomberg* business news, to provide trade news both to exporters and government policy staff. I hoped it would be self-sustaining and operate on a subscription basis. Regrettably, I could not generate any interest in the idea at that time. Each major exporter told me he phoned his contact in the market each morning and learned what was happening from him. They were averse to sharing any information with the competition and thought that there was no point to a service that not only gave them the latest market information, but also allowed their competitors access as well. The "information age" had not yet begun.

I found myself drawn to the managers and reporters of the "Fourth Estate," in part because of my effort to promote the establishment of an economic news service. I gained much respect for their professionalism. The Indian editors of these newspapers, people like Mirchandani, Drieberg, had all been trained in Europe or the States.

The work of the U.S. reporters in reporting the Bihar famine during 1966 contributed to Bowles and Lewis' efforts to persuade the White

House to relent on the "short tether" policy. I saw their work then to be highly professional; much more so than the "fourth estate's" performance today, what with its daily shouting by "talking heads" and the "breaking news" frenzy. The advent of the Internet, the likes of WikiLeaks and the frenzied desire to expose something new instantly and over a 24-hour non-stop time frame may be the cause. Perhaps I looked upon the work of the press at that time with youthful naïveté while I see their work today through a more jaundiced eye. But my sense is that the quality of work and the standard of performance have sharply deteriorated.

Delhi Flying Club

In the middle of Delhi, just a short distance from the diplomatic enclave where our Embassy stood, was a small airport. Safdarjung airport had no commercial flights but it was home to the Delhi Flying Club. The Indian government heavily subsidized flying clubs as a means of generating candidates for the Air Force. Young men who were still attending school would be encouraged, or at least given the opportunity to learn to fly. One end of the runway faced the Pakistan Embassy. Each morning, I could see these yellow "Pushpak" Indian-made, two-seat, single-engine trainers taking off and flying directly over the blue dome of the Pakistan Embassy. I was so envious, even though I knew the aircraft was underpowered (it had a 90 hp continental engine) had a canvas-covered wing and fuselage and could barely do 75 mph, even going downhill.

Having just been issued my FAA "private pilot" license before leaving Ann Arbor, I inquired about joining the flying club. I was told to submit an application to the Indian equivalent of our FAA. I did so. These applications were regularly "lost" in the system and I was getting nowhere. One evening, at one of the myriad diplomatic functions, I happened upon the director general of civil aviation, a bright young, U.S.-educated fellow and former air force pilot. We hit it off quite well, shared some flying stories and had a few laughs. I asked him why so many Indian Airlines flights to

Amritsar wound up incomplete— they flew up, found they could not land and then flew back to Delhi. After all, I said, it looked like the valley is more than twenty miles wide. He said, when the weather is bad, the valley shrinks.

I mentioned my desire to join the Flying Club and described my difficulties in getting certified to fly. There was a twinkle in his eye and he told me to come around to his office to see him. Next day, I did that. It took about fifteen minutes and I walked out with an Indian pilot's license and membership in the club. That's how business was done in India.

I put in many hours in those bright yellow Pushpaks, maintaining my flying skills while stationed there. I met some fine young student pilots who gave me many insights into the life of a typical Indian family. Throughout my later service overseas, traveling to places like Nairobi, Cairo, Islamabad, and Dacca for short-term assignments after retiring from AID, I found that I would be well received in any country by going to the flying school or club and showing them a photo of my airplane. It acted as an entry permit to many restricted areas at these airfields, certainly better than a U.S. passport. There is camaraderie among aircraft pilots the world over.

THE ANTIQUE AUTO CLUB OF DELHI

Once a year, in February, the Auto Club would hold a rally in Delhi to display their vintage cars, each of them restored to pristine and better-than-original condition. Rolls Royces from before the First World War as well as some magnificent U.S. makes were shown. Several of our Indian friends were members of this club. Raj Seth, a local businessman, owned a green 1924 Lagonda. These beautiful cars would be proudly presented for public viewing on such occasions.

One day, Raj and his friend Ranjit Shahani were visiting us and began talking about two cars that were on the market, a 1938 Cadillac four door convertible and a 1938 Buick 7 passenger limousine. The maharajah of Jind owned them. He wanted to sell both in a package deal. Ranjit wanted the Cadillac. Would I be interested in buying the Buick? It happened that I loved the 1938 Buick design and quickly agreed to buy it. Soon, on a beautiful morning Raj, Ranjit and I, accompanied by one of Raj's faithful employees, set out for a drive into the Punjab, to the maharajah's palace.

The visit had been arranged by telephone beforehand and we were received by the maharajah's majordomo who showed us into the sitting room. The room was furnished as a circa 1900 European noble's home. There were crystal chandeliers, doilies on the tables, a French settee with needlepoint upholstery and a Persian carpet covering most of the floor. The maharajah rose to welcome us, invited us to sit. Tea was served. Raj's employee excused himself and left the room. The conversation over tea dealt with everything except cars or money. We talked about current events, the dusty roads, international happenings, our recent travels, and of course the weather.

Finally, tea was finished and Raj's employee returned to the room accompanied by the maharajah's majordomo. Both stood there, smiling without saying one word. That meant the deal was concluded, the money had changed hands between Raj's employee and the majordomo, and we were free to go.

Raj then rose to his feet, thanked the maharajah for his kindness and hospitality. We walked to the front door, accompanied by the majordomo. Once the door to the sitting room closed, we were shown the cars, still in the garage and not operational. Raj called for some truckers to help, which had also been pre-arranged. The cars were loaded onto the trucks and we departed for Delhi. Later in the day, I was told the cars had reached the repair shop in Delhi and would be in running shape within a month. Raj was true to his word and I picked up the car, newly registered in my name and brought it to my home.

After this vehicle was completely refurbished and made serviceable, I used it around town for a while and then began thinking of shipping it home upon completion of our tour of service. Imagine my surprise when I learned that Parliament had recently passed a law prohibiting the export of vehicles that were more than thirty years old. It was 1969 and this was a 1938 Buick. I was one year over the limit. I later learned the law was passed at the urging of my good friend Raj Seth, the president of the Delhi Antique Auto club, in order to keep these antiques in India. Thanks a load!

Since I was in the export promotion business I had a lot of friends in the Ministry of Trade. I raised the matter with Brij Raj Bahadur, a deputy secretary. He promised to look into it for me. Every time I met him, he would be full of apologies, explained that he had opened a file on this matter and would soon have a clearance for me. Time after time, Brij Raj apologized but still there was no clearance for the export of my Buick. I finally figured out that I could get the Delhi Auto Club to issue a "Carnet de Passage" which would allow me to pass through the borders if I chose to drive the car out of India.

My drive to Ankara was the highlight of my ownership experience with this vehicle. A few weeks after my return, having delivered and stored the car in Ankara, I ran into Brij Raj again. As he launched into his apology for not having solved my problem, I cut him off and said the problem was solved. He asked how come? I said the car was no longer in India. He said, "We have a loophole?" I replied, "Large enough to drive a Buick through." I expressed my concern that I might have gotten him into difficulties. "No" was the reply. "If there is anything we know how to do, it is how to lose a file!"

THE STORY OF RUBY – GITTI

Another person entered our lives in that last year. We never knew her real name but Joan called her "Ruby." She was a tiny, deformed infant girl abandoned one night at the door of Mother Theresa's orphanage in Delhi. Joan volunteered from time to time at the orphanage, as did another wife of an embassy officer, Margot Born, and both of these women became entranced with the charm of this little tyke. Each would take turns to bring Ruby to their respective homes, first for overnight visits, then gradually longer stays. Ruby had been born with a deformed leg. It was missing the thigh. A deformed orphan girl in India had absolutely no chance at survival without outside help. Our entire family and servant staff became focused on the future of this child. As the Talmud instructs, "He who saves one human life, it is as though he saved the entire world."

The two women set to work trying to find an Indian family that would be willing to adopt Ruby. Eventually they were successful. Hetty and Richard Prim, an Anglo-Indian family living in the foothills of the Himalayas, did adopt the child. Ruby was renamed Gitti and Joan helped settle her after getting medical guidance on minimizing the effects of her deformity. A prosthesis was built to allow her to walk almost normally. Later, on one of our return trips to India, we even saw her dance. We did give some support to the family over the years but it was the Prims who saved this child and gave her a decent home. She graduated from university, is married, has two grown daughters of her own and lives a productive life in Delhi.

THE FINAL MONTHS

Before we departed India for home leave in May 1969, the mission requested my return to continue the export project. Since the family had already lived for four years in India, I asked that my third tour be limited to a single year. I had become concerned about our young children's lack of knowledge of, and lack of identification with their own country. They were now aged four, five and six and had lived their entire cognitive lives in India, surrounded by the trappings that go with diplomatic life.

Frank Thomas, a State Department officer who had been posted in Madras was selected to work with me for that last year and would then stay on to complete the project. Ken Keating, the former senator from New York, had by then replaced Bowles. Lewis had returned to the States to be dean of the Princeton School for Advanced International Studies and had been succeeded by Len

Saccio. I had worked with Saccio in the late 1950s on the Hardy Committee investigation of the Iran program while he was ICA's general counsel. Before coming to India, he had served as our ambassador to Argentina just at the time Jul arrived there to conduct Ginastera's opera Bomarzo, a few days after the government banned its production. Saccio looked after Jul while he was waiting for the Argentine government to reconsider the banning of Bomarzo. That never happened. I liked and respected Saccio very much.

There was one small point that Lewis let slide but Saccio would not; that was India's refusal to sign the export industries project agreement. Saccio insisted that the project be canceled if India did not sign. After a few tense weeks, the Indian government agreed to sign.

After returning from home leave, the family settled back into its routine in our New Delhi home. We decided to hire a young Tibetan refugee woman, a twenty-year old who had actually walked across the Himalayas into India to escape the Chinese. She joined the household staff and would later come with us to the U.S. to help as we readjusted to life here. Yangchen became a wonderful addition to our lives. She lived with us in our house and worked for us for four years in the States, receiving minimum pay. After that, she was free to either return to India or take up U.S. citizenship and live on her own. That worked out wonderfully. Our children adored her. Eventually, she met another Tibetan living in the States, got married and has raised a family in Patterson, New Jersey.

ACCOMPLISHMENTS?

Were there any accomplishments from our export industries efforts? Not many. The project facilitated the public discussion in India, particularly between the government and the private export community. It also enhanced the capabilities of the Indian consultancy firms that we hired. But, government policies continued to focus on import substitution and public sector regulations that strangled any initiative that the private export community might have taken.

I learned a few things about the business of export and investment promotion. One point, which might be useful to others who engage in this work, is that it is easier to develop new higher value added export products that are offshoots of the traditional export products than to try to find a completely new export line for which there is no established industrial base in the country.

THE DEPARTURE

Having purchased the Pennsylvania property during our 1969 home leave, we persuaded a small group of friends to become investors in The Glendale Corporation. That story is more fully described in chapter 11, below.

During the last few months of our fifth year in India, Joan set about having furniture crafted to take back to the States. The cost of designing and building furniture in India was very low and the craftsmanship was quite good. We were able to furnish our home in Washington quite inexpensively since AID paid for shipping the furniture and household effects. Joan also found a *darzi* and kept him busy making clothes for the children.

We, together with Yangchen, departed Delhi in May 1970, flew to Ankara where we picked up the Buick, then drove to Izmir, put the car on a ship and boarded with it, sailed for Brindisi, Italy, and then drove the Buick across the Alps to Paris. I shipped the car from Le Havre and returned to Paris to join the family for the trip home. We flew to Washington to resettle there. India would be my last long-term overseas assignment for AID.

I found the mood in the States to have totally changed from what I had remembered before leaving for India in 1965. The country was in the midst of the Vietnam War, there was a trade deficit, the dollar was weakening, and U.S. bilateral aid was shrinking as the World Bank assumed the central role in providing large-scale economic assistance. Congress was placing greater restrictions on AID's operations. The favorable conditions for John Lewis' "Big Push for India" had disappeared.

What are my perceptions today, more than forty years after my departure from India, about the work I did and the efforts our AID mission made in those critical five years from 1965 to 1970? What was accomplished by our efforts and by the resources provided to India by the U.S. taxpayer?

Some conclusions come easy. Had we not provided eight million tons of food to India during the 1966 famine, there would have been mass starvation. It is, of course, possible that other countries might have come to India's aid. But India did not have the resources to buy its way out of the agricultural hole dug by Mahalanobis as he made India dependent on foreign food supplies.

But the major policy shift that has unleashed the Indian private sector did not happen until 1991, after the breakup of the Soviet Union when Indian policy makers became convinced that capitalism would not crumble and that socialism was not their future economic system. While we were making that case to them in the late 1960s, there was no one listening on the Indian side.

I also believe our aid lessened the urgencies facing India and provided the Indian government some breathing space, a period of time when the political system of democracy could be allowed to function and take root in their society.

There is still serious poverty and malnutrition in India. I blame the caste system for the inequalities that have been allowed to languish, even though the nation as a whole has become far more prosperous than it was during my time there.

In 2010, John Lewis died. His obituary spoke about his many accomplishments, but the "Big Push," something he had spent a good ten years to try to make happen, was not mentioned. How sad.

My work in India on the export promotion project had caught someone's eye in Washington. In 1970, when my tour was up, I was asked to work in AID's Bureau for Policy and Program Coordination (PPC) to see if this activity could be replicated in other countries receiving U.S. assistance. Now it was I who would take on the role of "special pleader" for inclusion of innovative new projects in other mission programs.

6

SECONDED TO PENNSYLVANIA GOVERNMENT SERVICE 1972 TO 1974

How I CAME TO be assigned to the Pennsylvania State government in Harrisburg as director of the Bureau for International Trade and Investment, an initiative of Governor Milton Shapp's administration, is an interesting story.

The family had returned from India. Ernie Stern was now director of AID's Bureau for Policy and Program Coordination (AID/PPC), the "think tank" of AID. He arranged my assignment to his staff with the task of encouraging other AID missions to take advantage of my experience in India and to initiate export development projects. I was teamed up with Mickey Most, an AID officer who had designed and managed a similar project in Korea. We were asked to replicate our experiences for the benefit of additional countries. Mickey and I were now the "special pleaders" trying to sell this export expansion initiative to other aid recipients.

That lasted one year. The effort did not take, primarily because Congress reduced funding for AID. Each AID mission was being asked to cut back, creating a difficult environment in which to persuade missions to expand activities into new areas.

In a conversation with John MacDonald, a State Department colleague from my Iran Desk days, he asked if I would be interested in being detailed to the State Department. I would work for him in the Bureau for International Organizations (State/IO) as the officer responsible for the UN Industrial Development Organization (UNIDO). Ernie agreed to the change and so I was assigned to work in the State Department proper.

That too, lasted about a year. During that time, I learnt of the inherent shortcomings of the UN's development program and grew skeptical of the effectiveness of the UN system (see chapter 8 for more on my experiences with the UN). But I felt disenchanted with the direction of the aid business inside USAID's bilateral assistance effort as well. AID was instituting more and more rigorous procedures to accommodate each and every one of the complaints made by members of Congress in order to continue to receive its appropriations, even when these procedures vitiated its own effectiveness in accomplishing its goals. Also, I found myself more and more skeptical that bilateral annual chronic economic assistance was still justified. I felt that bilateral aid had run its course over the twenty-year period, 1950 to 1970, the exception being the delivery of emergency humanitarian or disaster relief. The assistance to a particular country now became more difficult to coordinate with other aid donors, particularly the multi-national agencies, and also tended to be substitutive for the domestic policy reforms that needed to be undertaken by the aid recipients. It seemed to me, at that time, that bilateral aid could only be justified if it served U.S. political interests.[8]

On the other hand, my dream of private sector achievement, the Glendale project, (chapter 11) was a siren luring me to another life, one free of frustrations. I was cognizant that I had eighteen years of government service and needed only seven more to retire at age fifty.

The Glendale project frequently took me to Harrisburg, the seat of Pennsylvania's government. Our lawyer was based there. Most regulatory

8 See annex 9.

controls, particularly with respect to the water and sewerage companies, were centered there. Our association with the neighboring Prince Gallitzin Park had led me to the director of Pennsylvania's park system in Harrisburg. I had heard that the Federal Personnel Service, in an effort to upgrade the personnel of state government departments, had established a program to allow for federal employees to be "seconded" to state government agencies if specifically requested.

I made inquiries in Harrisburg to find a job that would interest me sufficiently and explored whether someone in the governor's office might find me useful. Governor Shapp's office referred me to Walter Arader, secretary of the Pennsylvania Bureau of Commerce. The meeting was serendipitous. Arader was trying to set up a bureau to attract foreign investment and to help Pennsylvania's exporters expand overseas. He was pleased that I was interested, invited me to come aboard and made a formal request to AID Washington for my services.

The family would have to move for a second time in two years. We had settled into our D.C. home upon return from India two years before. Our three children were attending a good public school and were thriving. We had built Yangchen an extra room in which she was comfortably situated. Joan had settled into a pleasant routine and was enjoying raising the children at their golden age. I was now proposing to uproot them all and move to Harrisburg.

In retrospect, this was a bad move. No one in the family made a single friend in Harrisburg that resulted in a lasting relationship. We found that our neighbors, the children's classmates and my associates at the office all thought on a different wave length, had a different set of values, and embraced political views that were many degrees to the right of anything we thought or felt.

We arrived in Harrisburg in a presidential election year. The Democratic Party candidate was George McGovern. Joan worked at the Democratic Party headquarters with a few brave souls. Ruth Ann, in fifth grade, was the only child who voted for him in the school mock election. A neighbor came over to further complicate our lives by telling us that her evangelical religion was the true religion of God. She "spoke in tongues" and held séances. David came home from school the day before Passover and insisted we hold a Seder. Fortunately, Carol Ridker, the wife of a colleague who had been stationed with us in India and was now living in Washington DC, was sympathetic to our call for help, quickly packed her two children into the car and drove from Washington that afternoon so we could hold a Seder.

At my office in the Commerce Department, the old line staff resented the new "foreign" initiative being funded with monies they thought should go to their bureaus. One of them is reputed to have told a Japanese businessman who asked for the location of an office, "You had no trouble finding Pearl Harbor. You should be able to find what you are looking for!"

On the other hand, I received very positive responses from the Pennsylvania business community, the banks and the press. We actually set up two offices, one in Frankfurt, Germany and one in Tokyo, to feed potential investors into our net and to compete with other U.S. states that were also searching for foreign investors. The position gave me an opportunity to identify certain business conditions, including regulations and other impediments in the investment climate, which needed to be altered to make investment in Pennsylvania more attractive.

The results were disappointing. I argued, without effect, for a high speed passenger rail between Philadelphia and Pittsburgh or, at least an improvement in the existing rail connection. It still took about eight hours for the train to traverse a distance of less than 350 miles. At that time, it involved three crew changes. I got into trouble with the labor unions when I gave a speech criticizing the absence of a "right to work" law. That resulted in an unpleasant exchange with Governor Shapp.

The governor was a rather interesting person. He was a Democrat but selected Walter Arader, a Republican, to be secretary of commerce. Shapp had a business background and understood the problems an entrepreneur faced. He and his partner had started a small business, Jerrold Electronics, the first maker of cable TV boxes and they had made a fortune. There was a story, perhaps apocryphal, about his wife Mildred, a very down-to-earth person. When Jerrold Electronics took off, Shapp invited a Wall Street investment banker to advise them on how to restructure the company's finances. At the time, the company was operating out of Shapp's home. The Wall Street banker made his flip chart presentation in the kitchen. When he was finished, there was silence. Then Shapp said, "Well Mildred, what do you think?" She replied, "Not much!" The banker, speaking condescendingly to Mrs. Shapp, said, "Excuse me for my directness, but what do you understand about corporate finance?" Mildred then is reported to have said in her quiet way, "About corporate finance I don't know much. But I understand money!"

The only lesson I learned from that two year sojourn in Harrisburg was that the personnel system in the Pennsylvania State bureaucracy was steeped in patronage and political deal making. It also became clear that politicians elected to federal office, be they Democrat or Republican, understood their prime responsibility was to "bring home the bacon." They were sent to Washington to collect the state's rightful share of federally funded pork.

As my tour in Harrisburg drew to a close, I received a few warm farewells from some in the business community. I was invited to a farewell dinner, hosted by the senior vice president of Mellon Bank, at the Duquesne Club in Pittsburgh. I had traveled to Pittsburgh for other business with my deputy, Carol Egan. She had to be brought into the club's private dining room through the back entrance and up the staff elevator because, at that time, women were not allowed in the club. The Mellon Bank vice president gave a little speech and then said, tongue-in-cheek, "Well Lu, when you get to Washington D.C., I hope you will not forget us small town bankers!" and laughed heartily at his own joke.

After completing my assignment, I was asked to find my replacement. I persuaded Tom Rogers, former deputy chief of mission at the embassy in Pakistan, who had decided on retirement, to come to Harrisburg.

My family and I returned to Washington in the fall of 1974. We were all happy to leave Harrisburg. We bought a house we could barely afford and took on, what was then, the largest mortgage of our lives. It was located in the best school district in Montgomery County, with the best school system in the area, Joan's absolute, unequivocal benchmark for selection.

But fate was to head me directly into a reduction in force action at AID. Who knew?

7

I Am Fired – AID's Reduction in Force 1975

THIS IS NOT A happy story. Events that put my entire family at risk of severe hardship resulted in a period of deep disappointment and loss of faith in the institutions to which I had pledged myself. The scars that this ten month experience inflicted on my psyche lasted a long time, despite the eventual happy ending.

Earlier stories in this compendium describe my euphoria and pride at having been given an opportunity to join AID and its predecessor agency (ICA) in 1956 and at my successes both in Washington and while serving overseas. I had a growing sense, beginning in the late 1960s, as the Vietnam War sucked away greater national resources and attention, that public enthusiasm for our work was declining.

Each administration showed ever-increasing defensiveness and back-pedaling as Congress pressed to add more "barnacles to our ship" in an effort to serve yet another special domestic interest. We saw the dwarfing of our bilateral aid as the multinational agencies (World Bank, regional development banks, and UN development agencies) grew in size and scope with our own government's encouragement and direct funding contributions.

AID's relationships with its developing nation clients also began to change. What was originally perceived as a temporary and truly cooperative effort to help the newly established nations make the transition from subservient colonial status to political and economic independence, gradually eroded into annual budgeting and allocation exercises. Country programs initially encouraged innovative, new and cooperative ventures to tackle the challenges of economic growth and poverty alleviation. Over time, these substantive program efforts turned into routine annual budgeting exercises to use funds that had been committed to the recipient government, often for political reasons, in a manner that would avoid criticism from special interests at home.

There was also a tendency towards "mission creep." The temporary nature of our assistance began to take on the flavor of a perpetual donor presence that sought to address chronic development problems by transferring resources from rich countries to poor countries. One critic of foreign aid famously defined our work as "… taking money from poor people in rich countries and giving it to rich people in poor countries." Finally, AID's role in the policy formulation process, compared with the political (State) and military (Defense, NSA and CIA) agencies of our government bureaucracy, declined.

Still, I loved the work and threw myself into any assignment that was given to me. It was a growing awareness of the trends described above that, in part, led me to accept the two-year assignment with the Commonwealth of Pennsylvania in Harrisburg. I suppose I deluded myself that the trends would reverse while I was absent and, upon my return, AID would again be allowed to operate with the degree of independence it had enjoyed in the past. But when the Harrisburg assignment ended in August 1974, and I returned to Washington to seek a new position, I found myself in the middle of a Reduction in Force (RIF) exercise.

As a result of budgetary cuts and a reduction in the number of employee positions AID was authorized, the director of personnel was required to carry out the RIF to separate a set number (about 300) of AID's employees in accordance with very rigid Civil Service regulations to "assure fairness" to all its employees. Earlier in the year, I had received a letter from AID's director of personnel that congratulated me for completing twenty years of loyal service to AID (they gave me credit for two years of military service) and for rising to the rank of FSR-2. That rank is the equivalent of brigadier general in our military. The letter was accompanied by the agency's coveted twenty year service pin. It wished me well and expressed hope that I would be willing to continue to serve the agency loyally in the future. I felt confident that a suitable assignment would be found for me.

But rules are rules. The great machinations of the AID personnel system, following the prescribed rules governing the RIF process, ground on and soon produced a letter from the very same director of personnel that I was surplus to AID's needs and would be discharged.

Now, here was my situation. I had just bought a house upon returning from Harrisburg and had used every bit of our savings for the down payment. We had sold our previous house before leaving Washington in 1972. My three children, aged nine, ten, and eleven, had just enrolled in school. My wife had started training for a new career since it was clear that my government salary would be insufficient to pay college tuition for the three children.

I needed to continue my employment with AID a minimum of five more years to qualify for retirement at age fifty. To leave AID then, at 45, would have resulted in my pension being frozen until I turned sixty. I had acquired land in Pennsylvania and formed a company that was not yet earning a profit to pay a salary, while my personal guarantees to the bank on behalf of the company put me at severe financial risk. And, oh yes, where does a 45-year old development economist next look for work? Other than that, everything was great.

I managed to delay the RIF by six months when Ambassador John MacDonald asked that I join the U.S. delegation to the UN Conference on

Industrial Development in Lima, scheduled for March 1975. I was safe until that date (see chapter 8 for more on the conference).

When I returned from Lima, my first task was to file an appeal with the Civil Service Commission to oppose my separation under AID's RIF procedure. To do this, I visited the Office of Personnel to examine the procedures used to select me for separation. I found the staff to be exceedingly sympathetic and helpful. They did not like what had happened to me any more than I did. I also sought help from the American Foreign Service Association (AFSA) and they too guided me through the procedures and data so I could understand the technicalities of the RIF process. Finally, I sent my appeal within the thirty-day window following termination as required by the law. In the interim, I had been awarded a severance package that continued my regular salary payments for another ten months.

I also threw myself into the Pennsylvania project. Glendale Yearound had been a dream for me since purchasing land in Pennsylvania in 1969. Most weekends, I would drive there consumed by an irrational quest to build this oasis, this piece of Heaven on Earth, this symbol of true independence and freedom for myself and for my family (see chapter 11). The problem of the moment, about using my time effectively, was that construction and sales took place in the warm weather. Not much happened during the winter, which was fast approaching

I woke up one morning in 1975, and had no job to go to. How can one change one's behavior so quickly? My morning routine for years had been instilled. First the alarm clock, the shower, coffee, maybe a small glass of juice, a slice of bread, a quick glance at the newspaper, take the garbage out, kiss the kids and Joan, pick up the attaché case and get to the car pool stop in time to get to the office. Now there was all this leisure time. I was alone in the big house. How to organize the time? How could I believe that I was still a person with a purpose for living?

I can't describe my sense of self-loathing during this period. A thought would play through my mind continuously. Maybe I had been ineffectual at my job all these years and, at last, had been found out. I had deservedly, finally, gotten my comeuppance. I had let my family down. Some of my former colleagues added to this feeling by shunning contact, as though I suffered from a communicable disease.

This continued for the rest of 1975. In early 1976, a friend mentioned that AID had begun hiring new staff. I could not believe him but he told me that the Wall Street Journal carried an ad for loan officers for the Near East and South Asia Division. I looked it up, and it was true! After several phone calls, I learned that my former colleague, Ted Lustig, with whom I had worked closely as a loan officer upon returning from Turkey in 1963, was searching for an officer to handle the Afghanistan loan portfolio. I walked into his office and we both had a good laugh about it. He told me the job was classified three grades below my last rank, with a markedly reduced salary. I said I would take it and the deal was made.

Now things got very interesting. When the Office of Personnel learned of this turn of events, it was clear that there would be a lot of egg on many faces if this set of circumstances became public information. How could this impeccable RIF system, designed by the U.S. Civil Service Commission with its exquisite focus on fairness and agency needs, produce this result?

In March 1976, I received my appointment and reported to Ted Lustig's office for work as directed. Ted made things comfortable for me while I tried to mend my self-esteem enough to do a day's work. In reality, my illusions about government employment and its attendant social contract, particularly expectations about loyalty between employer and employee, had been so shattered that I found myself occasionally behaving in the worst possible, petty bureaucratic manner that would have been anathema to me a year earlier.

One month after reporting for work in Lustig's office, I received a letter from the Civil Service Commission finding in favor of my appeal and rejecting AID's action to terminate me. Some obscure technicality that AID had not observed was cited. I was reinstated at my previous rank and salary and a new position was found for me as deputy director of AID's

Office of Nutrition. I said my farewells to Ted Lustig. No efforts were made by AID management to set things right, not even some counseling to deal with my feelings of abandonment. I no longer felt a part of the AID family.

I must admit that over the next four years, until my retirement in 1980, I felt that I never again performed an honest full day of work for AID. Gone were my enthusiasm, my spirit and dedication for the work that I had previously thrown myself into and so enjoyed. A hole had been drilled into my heart and my spirit was broken. All I wanted from AID after the RIF was to be retained until my fiftieth birthday when I could retire.

I became more aware of how the real world had changed, and of how AID's mission had been gradually redefined over the last twenty years. We were no longer talking about being a temporary agency and "working ourselves out of a job" by giving external assistance to the former colonies to help them achieve self-sustaining economic independence. Rather, the task of poverty alleviation had taken on a missionary aspect within the international economic aid community. There was more rhetoric about "resource transfers" to the world's poor, a continuing and perpetual program to equalize disparities in living conditions, "eliminate global poverty" by some ridiculously soon-to-come date. Those in charge seemed to have no appreciation for the limitations of external assistance, and how ineffective it can be without the recipient country taking responsibility for its part.

My enthusiasm for this alternate role and function for AID diminished sharply. I came to believe that program decisions were made increasingly by the political establishment within the State Department. It was my impression that there was increasing acceptance of the concept that annual aid allocation to all poor countries was their due, irrespective of the results achieved. It also provided "walking around money" for U.S. ambassadors (see annex 9).

I gave the Pennsylvania project more and more of my time and attention as a way of preserving joy and meaning in work. For me, the private sector now represented independence just as a government salary represented disillusionment and dependence.

8

THE UN'S CONFERENCE CIRCUIT IN THE 1970s

THE PHRASE, "INTERNATIONAL CONFERENCE" exudes an air of profundity and importance. It conjures up a vision of the best-trained, finest minds on the planet, bringing together their collective wisdom in pursuit of the truth to address a particular global problem. That occasionally does happen, as was the case with the Montreal Protocol concerning the prohibition of chlorofluorocarbons (CFCs). Regrettably, my experience has led me to conclude that UN conferences deal mostly with bureaucratic turf wars among international agencies. Participants endlessly debate arcane political positions and point fingers at the alleged culprits behind the world's ills. The meetings are attended, in large part, by the same set of representatives each time. And it is they who then choose the venue for future conferences from a small list of the world's most expensive fleshpots.

BY WAY OF BACKGROUND

As World War II was coming to an end, the victorious Allied Powers made new arrangements to carry on international relations in the post-war era. The ineffectiveness of the League of Nations in resolving international disputes and coordinating collective responses after the First World War offered some lessons to guide the world's leaders in designing the new international institutional structure. Thus on October 24, 1945, the United Nations (UN), with fifty-one original member states was established with headquarters in New York City. The League of Nations was dissolved and some of the international organizations that had been affiliated with it (i.e., International Labor Organization, the International Telecommunications Union and the Universal Postal Union) were taken over by the UN.

Since these modest beginnings, the UN has become a vast international bureaucracy. It now refers to itself as "The United Nations System." In 2012, the Secretariat and its related entities (but excluding the specialized agencies) employed more than 75,000 persons, more than 42,000 in the Secretariat itself with more than half of those for "peacekeeping."[9] I was never involved with the UN's political or peacekeeping activities. Nothing I describe here deals with these very worthy and important political–military functions. My comments focus exclusively on the UN's efforts in the field of economic development assistance.

The UN Charter stipulates that each of its primary organs, such as the General Assembly, can establish various specialized agencies to fulfill its duties.

Each of these fourteen "specialized agencies" has its own payroll. Total employment by the UN system is now estimated to run in the neighborhood of 100,000. The World Bank Group alone claims to have "...more than 9,000 employees from 168 countries." In 2013, the Rome-based Food and Agriculture Organization (FAO) employed about 3400 permanent staff. The UN Industrial Development Organization, (UNIDO), based in Vienna, Austria is the organization for which I had responsibility in the State Department during various periods in the 1970s. In 2012, it had a permanent staff of about 700 and uses an additional 2500 experts on short-term assignments each year.[10]

---

9   General Assembly document A/67/329 dated 28 August 2012 page 16 (seen at http://www.un.org/en/ga/search/view_doc.asp?symbol=A/67/329

10   See http://www.fao.org/about/who-we-are/en/ as of May 18, 2014

BRIEF HISTORY OF THE GROWTH OF THE UN SYSTEM

With the fighting over, and Europe lying in ruins, everyone was in love with the United States. Our intervention in the war in Europe had led to the destruction of the Axis powers and "saved the free world." We could do no wrong. The dollar was almighty. By and large, the mistakes made by the Treaty of Versailles, following the end of the First World War, were avoided. The Marshall Plan, funded by the United States, focused on rebuilding the war-torn nations of Europe, both the victors and the vanquished. The International Bank for Reconstruction and Development (IBRD), now known as the World Bank, was created in 1945 to facilitate and supplement the Marshall Plan in Europe's "reconstruction." Someone tacked the "and development" phrase on to the name, but there really was no expectation at that time that this institution would take on a major role to aid the poorer nations. India was one of the original 51 members of the UN. Pakistan became a member in 1947, Burma in 1948, Israel in 1949 and Indonesia in 1950. By 1960, the UN's membership had reached 99 countries.

The vision for the future, prevalent amongst the victorious Allies, held unlimited promise. Wendell Willkie, the Republican Party candidate who ran against FDR in 1940, wrote *One World* in which he describes his uplifting vision of a wonderfully cooperating world. Norman Cousins in his essay, "Modern War is Obsolete," explained that there could no longer be armed conflict in light of the existence of the atom bomb. The unification of the 48 states comprising the United States of America was extrapolated by some to conclude that "world federalism" would not be too distant in our future. Even though there was some apprehension about the actions of the Soviet Union and the expansion of communism, the underlying belief was that the horrors of the previous twelve years would never again be repeated on this planet, that colonialism and imperialism had died and that a new world was dawning. The UN would be the instrument to lead humankind towards federal, democratic world government. Some even believed the UN soon might be funded by a global tax instead of assessments on its member states.

The UN's total budget for 1948 amounted to $43 million. Today, the membership has increased to 193 nations and the budget, excluding the peacekeeping operations, runs in excess of $2 billion. The ten richest countries are assessed more than sixty percent of these costs. The U.S. share now is 27 percent of the UN's peacekeeping budget and 22 percent for all other funding requirements.

The "development" focus of U.S. foreign policy grew out of the needs of newly independent states along with the inability of their former imperial rulers to provide assistance. The United States recognized these needs early on, as both our competition with the Soviet Union and our fear that these new nations might fall into the Soviet orbit mounted. Truman's Point Four program (1949) was formal acceptance that the United States had some responsibility to assist these newly independent countries. The UN was expanded by creating specialized agencies, each focused on specific areas of needed assistance: health, agriculture, trade, and industry.

During the early years, U.S. delegations called the shots at international conferences. The relationship between aid donor and aid recipient might have been one of mutual respect; yet the donors still set the terms of aid and the recipients generally responded with gratitude.

By the end of the 1950s, the Marshall Plan had succeeded in reconstructing most of Western Europe. U.S. bilateral aid to the newly independent nations had grown well beyond the scope originally envisioned by Truman's Point Four initiative, conceived initially as a temporary five to ten-year effort. Since IBRD's work in Europe was nearly over, U.S. policy shifted to encourage expansion of multilateral aid. The States sent Douglas Dillon, President Eisenhower's treasury secretary, to persuade the Europeans to take on their share of this responsibility. The Europeans would now step up to the plate and accept their obligation to provide economic assistance to their former colonies. Other UN development agencies, such as FAO, the World Health Organization (WHO) and UNIDO were also positioned to assist. The UN Secretariat created special departments to provide economic assistance and eventually established the UN Development Program (UNDP). Our aid focused more on halting the spread of communism in these politically unstable, newly independent nations, to balance the efforts financed by the Soviets through Comintern, the Communist International network.

Gradually, over the following thirty years, there was a darkening in the mood between both donor and recipient nations with respect to their roles in the "development game." What had begun with euphoria and overt appreciation for the role the United States had taken on seemed, to me at least, to have turned into a sense of entitlement on the part of poorer nations: "We are poor. You are rich. You owe us!"

Soon, aid recipient nations began to coalesce and to act in unison. They formed the "Group of 77" (G-77), sometimes called the Third World or Non-Aligned Movement. The leaders of this group were Yugoslavia, Egypt and India. Algeria and Cuba, both known for their anti-West bias, also participated. Ostensibly, the G-77 claimed the role of Cold War mediator between NATO and the Warsaw Pact. In fact, they quickly evolved into a voting bloc in the General Assembly with intent to establish a "New International Economic Order" (NIEO) to enhance their bargaining power with respect to international resource allocation.

The G-77 argued that each UN member nation was entitled to an equitable share of the world's resources, such as the seabeds, and that the wealthy nations were unjustly using them up. Moreover, it was argued that rich countries owed large and continuous resource flows to poorer states, akin to reparations for past ills done during imperialist days. The UN and its international development conference circuit was exactly the place for the G-77 to apply such pressure.

This new approach to international relations coincided with the growth of anti-Americanism generated by our involvement in the

Vietnam War. The Scandinavians, particularly the Norwegians and the Swedes, who had chosen to adopt the role of the West's "conscience," abetted and encouraged the G-77's demands. Simultaneously, in the late 1960s, U.S. domestic support for foreign aid began to decline. While our aid levels did not decline, the appropriated funding grew more slowly as congressional attitudes hardened and the dollar weakened. Our influence over the UN's international economic assistance program gradually eroded.

STATE'S BUREAU FOR INTERNATIONAL ORGANIZATION AFFAIRS (IO)

It was exactly during that period that I found myself working on UN affairs. I was assigned to the State Department's Bureau for International Organization Affairs (IO) and designated desk officer for UNIDO. It was headquartered in, of all places, the city of my birth, Vienna. I was posted in Washington. Another officer, also with responsibility for UNIDO, was permanently assigned at the embassy in Vienna. It was our job to represent the interests of the United States on all UNIDO matters.

Early in the life of the UN and its specialized agencies, citizens of industrialized nations staffed the UN's technical and administrative positions. But as more aid recipient nations became UN members, their representatives to General Assembly encouraged candidates from their own countries to compete for these positions. Eventually, these representatives, for personal as well as for chauvinistic reasons, first urged and then demanded that a portion of available positions be reserved for those from the developing world. There can be no better job for a person from a developing, aid recipient nation than to work for the UN Secretariat or one of the UN agencies. Salaries and benefits of these positions are set at international scales and are vastly higher than comparable positions in countries in the developing world. Employees travel on UN passports— the equivalent of diplomatic passports—and are given travel allowances at international business rates. Consequently, these positions are highly coveted by citizens of the developing world.

It was acknowledged that the candidates should be "competent and well trained," which usually meant, "foreign trained." These candidates, not coincidentally, came from upper class families in their respective societies. In light of the benefits that went with these positions, these incumbents found themselves "sleeping in the softest bed of all." Yet ironically, since well-trained personnel were in short supply in most developing countries, the assignments to UN institutions constituted a brain drain for governments still consolidating newly independent states.

Even so, once a person had been employed at a UN agency, his government would then pressure him to identify and report new employment opportunities, and to assist applicants from his native country to apply for those positions. When a specialized agency hired a critical mass of employees from a specific country, there would be a tendency for those from that country and region to form a "clique." For example, the FAO is known to have a strong Indian representation among its staff. Old behavioral patterns adversely affecting productivity were sure to emerge. Soon some of these agencies were found to be operating at a low level of efficiency and with similar levels of productivity to that found in the developing world.

Each specialized agency's governing board (in UNIDO's case, 45 member nations) schedules an annual conference to deal with the agency's work programs and funding requirements. Every second year, the agencies hold a general conference of all agency members to deal more broadly with the direction in which the agency's work is going. Both of these conferences deal with programming, funding, and employment issues for the following year. The United States sends delegations to every one of these conferences.

I attended the UNIDO conferences at the Hofburg Palace in Vienna in 1971 and again in 1972. It was there that I learned how important it was for the agency head to achieve personal status within the UN system. The director would constantly seek to upgrade senior positions and to establish a greater number of positions for his senior staff. Employment decisions were at the top of the agenda at these meetings with constant pressure to authorize greater numbers of senior positions. And U.S. influence, indeed the influence of most Western nations– the B bloc– had dwindled as the Vietnam War ground on and on.

The G-77 had embarked on a strategy to wrest control of these agencies from donor nations. One mechanism to do this was the adoption, at the end of each conference, of a "resolution" to be voted on in the hope of arriving at a consensus. The language proposed by the G-77 sought adoption of the principles espoused by their NIEO. The aid donors reacted by trying to "weasel word" the language and make it less onerous, and then crouched low in their respective "fox holes" waiting for the barrage to lift. It never did. But when it was time to vote, the aid donors were reluctant to vote against the "resolution." Instead, they would either abstain or vote in favor but include reservations, which, in effect, watered down or nullified their agreement.

Delegates representing many of the developing nations had a strong cultural bias. They were usually drawn from the upper class, the better-educated, wealthy segment of their societies. Often, they were part of the ruling clique, particularly when representing counties controlled by oligarchies and dictatorships. Drawn from their respective foreign diplomatic services, they often had little technical knowledge of the subjects on the conference agenda. They would travel the world, going from one conference to the next, and make the same speech—changing only the relevant word say, from "agricultural growth" to "industrial expansion" — while continually working their political agendas. To borrow a phrase from *Guys and Dolls*, the meetings had become "the oldest established permanent floating crap game in the world."

These annual meetings should not be confused with the UN's "special" conferences. The UN also holds major substantive special or global conferences on specific economic development subjects that require global consensus. For example, in 1995, a global conference was held in China on "The Role of Women in Development." Conferences have been held on global warming, population growth, malnutrition, industrial development, trade and export growth and many other issues of concern. Some of these subjects involve the work of several different UN agencies. In 2002, these broad conferences culminated in the General Assembly's adoption of the Millennium Development Goals (MDGs). I will discuss those international conferences and the MDGs below.

THE LIMA CONFERENCE OF 1975

Perhaps the most interesting conference I attended was the Second General Conference on Industrial Development, held in Lima, Peru, in March 1975. I was a member of the U.S. delegation, headed by Ambassador William T. Bennett of "Dominican Republic fame." He was the one who had asked the president to send the U.S. Marines to land there in 1964. Here is how Wikipedia currently describes the Lima conference:

UNIDO's second General Conference, held in 1975 in Lima, Peru, adopted the *Declaration and Programme of Action on the Establishment of a New International Economic Order and of the Charter of Economic Rights and Duties of States*, For the first time, industrial development objectives were quantified internationally — the Lima Target anticipated the developing countries to attain a twenty-five per cent share of world industrial production by the year of 2000. As part of the institutional arrangements of the Lima Plan of Action, and with a view to assisting in the establishment of a *New International Economic Order*, it was recommended to the General Assembly that UNIDO be converted into a specialized agency.

The foregoing paragraph correctly describes the mix of substance and bureaucratic self-service that drove this conference. It highlights the conference's two overarching outcomes: (1) the establishment of UNIDO as a specialized agency and (2) the adoption of the declaration espousing the NIEO. And there was quite a dramatic story behind this result.

For a number of years, UNIDO had been lobbying delegates at the UN General Assembly to be upgraded from a section of the UN Secretariat to a fully accredited specialized agency. The benefits of specialized agency status include elevated pay grades for senior staff, greater independence from the Secretariat in New York, and greater control over budgeted resources and staffing. For obvious reasons, aid donor members opposed this turf aggrandizement effort while aid recipient members favored such a move.

The language of the draft "declaration" submitted by the G-77 was so onerous to our delegation as well as to those of other Group B countries that some of us could not imagine how we could vote for it. The Group B delegates adopted their usual tactic of attempting to water down the language but found stronger resistance to their efforts than in previous conferences. We were in constant communication with the State Department to see how to head off this push without giving offense. On the weekend, I decided to write a memo to the head of our delegation, Ambassador Bennett, arguing that, this time, we needed to vote against the resolution in its entirety and try to persuade other aid donors to do the same. I slipped the memo under the hotel room doors of all members of our delegation and waited.

When my colleagues assembled at the Monday morning meeting, it looked as though I had come down with a case of leprosy. Everyone was very polite. The ambassador even gave me a chance to orally present my argument. But then, one by one, the ambassador and each of my fellow delegates said it simply was not possible to take such a hard line. I was crestfallen but accepted the verdict.

On Wednesday however, we received a cable from State instructing us to vote against the resolution. At this point, everyone looked at me as though I had a back channel to Washington and had set up the instruction. After calling Washington and learning that the instruction came directly from Kissinger himself, we agreed it was the right thing to do. Suddenly, the logic of this position was made clear in everyone's mind. I was restored into the good graces of the U.S. delegation. We then attempted to bring other Group B members on board. But our success was limited to getting several of them to abstain with reservations on the final vote. We were the only delegation to vote against the resolution.

Upon returning to Washington, I learned that Patrick Moynihan, then our ambassador to the UN, had met with Kissinger the previous week, before the instruction to vote "No" was issued. In an article published in *Commentary Magazine* (Volume 59 number 3 March 1975), he maintained that we were not properly addressing the unreasonable demands being made by the G-77 at the General Assembly in New York and at other international forums. Moynihan had argued that we should not let these demands stand. Kissinger was persuaded and asked if there might be a meeting going on somewhere and was told about Lima. He then gave the instruction to vote "No" basically to support Moynihan. Serendipity was thus my "back channel."

The G-77 pressed ahead with their demands during the 1980s. This generated increased hostility in the United States towards the UN in general. A paper written by Stefan Halper and published in April 1996 by the Cato Institute (Cato Policy Analysis #253) reads, in part:

> UN budgets are shrouded in secrecy, and the actual performance of the myriad bureaucracies is translucent, if not opaque. There is no reliable way to determine whether the various and often competing specialized agencies (at least two dozen UN agencies are involved in food and agricultural policy) are doing their jobs, and many UN activities, even if they are of some value, can be carried out better and more efficiently by other groups. Other activities should not be undertaken at all.[11]

---

11   See Annex 5 for the full Executive Summary.

I also served on the U.S. delegation to the 1980 UNIDO conference in Vienna but that story was the same as that of the Lima Conference. The G-77 continued to lobby for an NIEO. UNIDO had already achieved full specialized-agency status in the UN system; so that issue was off the table. It was not until the break-up of the Soviet Union in 1989 that the G-77 nations changed their approach. Instead of demanding a "New International Economic Order" they focused on establishing the Millennium Development Goals to "end global poverty."

Furthermore, I served on the U.S. delegation to the 1979 UN Conference on Science and Technology for Development, also held in Vienna. Our delegation was co-chaired by Father Theodore Hesburgh of Notre Dame University and Ambassador Jean Wilkowski. That conference was timely in terms of the breakthrough in information technology. I tried to inject into the discussion the availability of U.S. technology databases that would facilitate the search for technology needed in developing nations through patent records and other public data sources. It was the beginning of the "computer era" and its search engines. We were pushing to facilitate technology transfer. We even delivered a supply of pamphlets, prepared by one of our contractors, which listed a myriad of freely accessible U.S. public sector databases to each delegation. Sadly, few at that conference recognized the opportunities that would soon become available as the age of the computer dawned.[12]

THE UN AND ITS MILLENNIUM DEVELOPMENT GOALS

The Millennium Development Goals (MDGs) adopted by the UN General Assembly in 2002, to be reached by the year 2015, represent a global effort to sharply reduce world poverty and to elicit from the developed world a greater magnitude of resources claimed necessary to achieve them. In 2007, the UN published the following statement to describe these goals:

---

12   Pamphlet titled *Information Resources and Services of the U.S.*, AID/DSA-C-0055, 1979.

The United Nations Development Agenda: Development for All Goals, commitments and strategies agreed at the United Nations world conferences and summits since 1990:

The historic United Nations conferences and summits held in the past two decades generated an unprecedented global consensus on a shared vision of development. These remarkable participatory processes, and the array of development goals that were agreed through them, laid the groundwork for the Millennium Summit, at which a series of challenging time-bound goals and targets were adopted. Many were later collated as the Millennium Development Goals, which have succeeded in galvanizing an exceptional momentum to meet the needs of the world's poorest.

This comprehensive set of development goals, of which the MDGs are an integral part, has come to be called the United Nations Development Agenda. It serves as the internationally shared framework for development–for action at the global, regional, and country levels. The Agenda encompasses inter-linked issues ranging from poverty reduction, gender equality, social integration, health, population, employment and education to human rights, the environment, sustainable development, finance and governance. It includes as well systemic issues, such as the differential impact of globalization, inequalities among and within countries, and greater participation of developing countries in global economic governance.

-- José Antonio Ocampo, Under-Secretary-General for Economic and Social Affairs, June 2007

These Millennium Development Goals are listed in annex 6 of this volume.

ASSESSMENT OF IMPACT

The MDGs have been agreed upon as a set of goals and obligations for all nations to meet. In many respects, they have served to focus attention on the needs of a large segment of the world's population and are an expression of global good intention. The problem with this approach is the difficulty involved in disaggregating MDGs into country-specific targets. I have written in 2005 in my monograph on foreign aid, that these goals "... cannot be defined at the national level where the responsibility for economic development ultimately rests. It is the nation-state that has responsibility for allocation of public resources and promulgation of policies governing the internal distribution of wealth."[13] If specific targets had been set for each country, it would provide some basis to measure individual country performance. But that was not the case.

For example, take the primary MDG, "to halve ... the proportion of people who live on less than $1 a day." UN agencies have recently issued what appears to be a host of self-congratulatory statements claiming that, as of 2013, this goal has already been reached. But an analysis of the data shows that this global target was reached only because two countries, India and China, have achieved such rapid growth in the past fifteen years so as to lift much of their own population above the MDG poverty levels. Moreover, the level of per capita international official development assistance that India and China receive is not significant to these results. What of the other 166 aid recipient nations? Their record of accomplishment varies greatly, with several nations having achieved nothing at all.

Jeffrey Sachs of Columbia University is adviser for the MDGs to the UN's Secretary General. He seems to have become the cheerleader and scold pressing aid donors to increase their ODA contributions and arguing that resource inadequacy is the critical constraint to the achievement of these worthy goals. Many are highly skeptical that this is a valid argument.

---

13 Ludwig Rudel, *Foreign Aid: Will It Ever Reach Its Sunset?* Headline Series, Foreign Policy Association NY, 2005, page 54.

Angus Deaton, professor of economics at Princeton University, puts it this way: "When the 'conditions for development' are present, aid is not required. When local conditions are hostile to development, aid is not useful, and it will do harm if it perpetuates those conditions."[14] This categorical pronouncement needs to be qualified with respect to bilateral economic aid, wherein the donor nation has an overriding interest in pressing for the recipient's economic growth, as is the case with respect to U.S. assistance to our Latin American neighbors (See Chapter 12).

CONCLUSIONS

It seems to me that the MDGs have replaced the G-77's demands for the NIEO in the sense that they help developing nations externalize their problems by focusing on the perceived shortcomings of the aid donors. Are these goals worthy to be pursued? Of course! Can they force developing nations to take meaningful action to adopt the needed domestic reforms? Unlikely. Can the myriad of UN specialized agencies play any meaningful role towards accomplishing these goals? Highly unlikely.

The MDGs provide yet another anvil against which to hammer the aid donors into increasing their contributions to global resource transfer programs for the poorer nations. The focus at the UN continues to be on externalizing development problems rather than persuading and helping aid recipients in taking the politically unpopular complementary reform measures required to make the aid effective (See chapter 10 for a further discussion of the problems with this approach).

It has been a long road from the UN's initial dream to build a mechanism for world federalism to today's partisan dialogue between the haves and the have-nots. The UN's peacekeeping function, despite its many shortcomings, is still better managed than the development work

---

14 Angus Deaton, *The Great Escape* (Princeton and Oxford: Princeton University Press, 2013), page 273.

implemented by an enormous labyrinth of overstaffed and bureaucratic specialized agencies.

How does one fix this dilemma? Regrettably, I can think of no other way to fix this than to start designing the UN system all over again. There are more reasons to move in the direction of world federalism today than ever before. But the present structure of the UN system is fatally flawed. It needs to be insulated against pressure to undertake the myriad of "good things" that liberals and conservatives advocate in the international arena. Instead, it should focus its attention on the few critical global problems that require international consensus i.e. global warming, pollution, international conflict resolution and peacekeeping, international trade and finance flows. These are the issues that require international action. A mechanism is needed to prevent recalcitrant nations from manipulating the system so that the common interests of the majority may be effectively served.

9

A Post-Retirement interlude – Limo Driver

I CELEBRATED MY FIFTIETH birthday on July 5, 1980 and retired six weeks later. Members of the U.S. Foreign Service are allowed to retire at age fifty once they have accumulated 25 years of service. My pension would come to half of my base pay, to be adjusted for a cost-of-living escalator for the rest of my life. While this was insufficient to meet our family's daily expenses, I could now devote more time to Glendale in the hope of reaching the threshold when this project could begin to pay some sort of salary. Also, I was now free to take on short-term international consulting assignments in the field of economic development and foreign aid.

In fact, I had already been offered a consulting assignment, when it became known that I was going to retire. It was with a small firm that worked for the U.S. Department of the Interior, to assist in negotiating the Compact of Free Association with Palau, one of the U.S. Trust Territories in the Pacific. But more about that first consulting assignment later.

There was a sea change in my life's routine. The daily pace of work I had followed for 25 years was now out the window. I no longer had to commute from Bethesda to downtown Washington to get to my office at the State Department on time each morning. There were no meetings to attend. There were no "bosses" to please. There were no lunches to schedule. I did not have to maintain my network of contacts in other parts of the State Department or AID or at international development agencies and embassies. I could have my coffee in bed, read the newspaper and plan my day of leisure or scope out my work at Glendale. And unlike a similar routine during my layoff from USAID in 1975 (see chapter 7), I felt no sense of self-loathing at all. The point that I was fully in control of my own daily schedule had finally registered with me. My pension would continue for the rest of my life. There was no pressure such as had existed for me (and every other wage slave) for, lo, the previous twenty-five years.

But I missed the camaraderie of my colleagues, the daily chatter about current events and the sense of being near the mechanism that everyday decided matters of international import. When some low-level administrative type took my building pass, and my entry into the State Department building was restricted—after having freely walked its halls for 25 years—I felt some sense of betrayal. And although Joan was bringing in a substantial income, I made an effort to market myself with my old contacts at AID and with the "beltway bandits" who had links with the development agencies in order to find assignments in the economic development business.

Soon the summer was over and Ronald Reagan became the president-elect of the United States. Newspaper stories featured the celebrations planned for Inauguration Day (January 20, 1981) with many galas scheduled for that evening. There were reports that every limousine on the east coast was scheduled to descend on the District of Columbia to serve the Republicans in their celebratory efforts and that there was a shortage of drivers. It occurred to me that it might be fun to become one of those drivers for the inaugural parties. I took the Yellow Pages in hand, located a limousine service in southeast Washington and marched down to their offices to apply for a job as a driver.

The limo office was located in a small room that looked similar to what I imagined was a cell in Moscow's Lubyanka jail. The atmosphere, next to the garage, was that of a very busy place. Half a dozen well-attired men reading girlie magazines occupied the driver waiting room adjoining the office. The animated activity, such as the shouting of instructions, was nothing like I had been used to in the staid halls of the State Department.

The supervisor finally acknowledged my presence and asked what I wanted. I said I was looking for work as a limo driver. He looked at me and asked, "Do you have a face?" I must have appeared stupefied at the question, and so he repeated it. "A face; a face. Do you have a face?" And with an expression that showed he was talking to an imbecile, he pointed to his own limo driver's license pinned on the wall—a five-by-twelve-inch laminated card with a big face on it. That was the "face" he was asking for. He explained that I could not drive his cars until I had secured a DC limo driver's license, and told me where to go to apply.

When I learned about all of the things I would have to do to comply with the District's procedures, it became clear that I would not get a license by Inauguration Day, in part because I was currently engaged in a consulting assignment. Nonetheless, I set things in motion to take the test, get a special medical exam, have my fingerprints taken, get a certification from the police that I had not committed a felony in the past 5 years and complete some other miscellaneous tasks. Finally, after covering all bases, I received my limo driver's license at the end of August 1981.

After the Labor Day weekend, I again went down to the limo service. This time there was a lot more action in the garage and office. There were no drivers sitting around and the pace of activity bordered on the frenetic. I got to the supervisor and assured him I now had a "face." He looked at the license, grabbed some car keys from his desk and handed them to me. He gave me a slip of paper with the name and address of the client, pointed to a parked car and said, "GO!" I asked him, "How come the rush?" He explained that the first week of September was the busiest time for them—except for the presidential inauguration—because the annual World Bank/IMF meeting was taking place. Five thousand bankers from around the globe had descended on Washington to discuss the plight of the world's poor, and they all wanted their own limos!

My client for the week was the president of the Andes Bank. He had been stationed in Washington before as the Venezuelan ambassador, knew lots of people here and could also find his way around. He was a pleasant chap, easy to understand and not too demanding. I wore a regular suit. The car was not a long limo but rather a sedan, and so we were not as conspicuous as some of the other luminaries. He always wanted to chat as we were driving and thought he could put his finger on "the pulse of the nation" by interrogating his driver, believing him to be an "average Joe." What did I think of Reagan's first six months in office? How is the job scene? Are food and clothing prices going up? Do I eat in restaurants often? Which restaurants?

I quickly realized that if I let this guy figure out that I was a recently retired Foreign Service officer with plenty of overseas service, there was no way I or anyone else could persuade him that I was not a CIA plant monitoring him. I was careful to answer in the way a typical driver would. "I eat at McDonalds. I don't take the family there too often. My wages are not keeping up with food price increases. Tips are dropping off." On and on.

During the course of that week a number of amusing incidents occurred. One time, I dropped him at the hotel where the meetings took place, parked the car and decided to wait for him in the lobby. Along came Rod Wagner on his way to one of the meetings. When JFK consolidated the various aid agencies into USAID, he brought on some very competent officers from the private sector. William Gaud was recruited to be the head of the Near East and South Asia Bureau, on which I was serving. He, in turn, brought with him a bunch of bright folks like Alex Vagliano and Rod Wagner, both out of JPMorgan bank. I worked with Rod for about a year after returning from Turkey. He had now recycled back to JPM. At the time of this meeting, Rod was probably the "number two" at the bank. We greeted each other warmly. I could tell Rod thought that I too was attending the World Bank/IMF annual meeting. I was too embarrassed to tell him the truth when he asked what I was doing, so I said I was working for the Venezuelans in their "transportation sector."

But the most remarkable event took place towards the end of the week. My client asked to be driven to a very fancy restaurant on K Street NW where he was to meet someone for lunch. I dropped him off, then parked the car and waited. When he finally emerged, he was accompanied by a short, dapperly-dressed elderly gentleman, whom he ushered to the car. He told me to take Ambassador Sevilla-Sacasa to his home at the Chevy Chase Country Club. My client would run some errands on his own and I was to pick him up later.

Guillermo Sevilla-Sacasa was the former Nicaraguan ambassador and former dean of the Diplomatic Corps of Washington DC until the Sandinistas overthrew his brother-in-law General Somoza in 1979. He was now a resident of the United States since he could not return to Nicaragua for fear of losing his life, now that the Sandinista had taken over. He was a gregarious fellow and, as soon as he got himself comfortable in the back seat, began to ask me questions. Where did I grow up? When I told him New York City, he immediately launched into a discourse about this "wonderful city" where he had made so many speeches at the UN. I needed to say nothing further. When he completed his oratory about his times in New York, he fell silent, for about thirty seconds.

Then the next question; had I ever traveled abroad? "Yes," I said, "to India." "Ah, India..." and he spoke at length about his personal relationship with Nehru, his travels to see the Taj Mahal ... on and on. At the end of the oratory, another thirty-second silence. Then, "Where did your wife grow up?" I answered, "Wisconsin." "Ah Wisconsin, a wonderful state. Madison, a wonderful city." He had been there many times to give speeches at the university. Did I know that the University of Wisconsin is the sister school of the University of Nicaragua? Many Nicaraguan students had been on exchange at University of Wisconsin at Madison, and vice versa.

I was getting annoyed with this so-called conversation. We were nearing the Chevy Chase Country Club and I thought I would take a chance. Next time he came up for air, I asked him, "Mr. Ambassador, it has been said that the roots of India's socialism lie in London– at the London School of Economics– because so many of India's leaders had been sent to study there and the Fabian socialism of Sidney and Beatrice Webb rubbed off on them. When they returned to India they practiced what they learned. Do you think the roots of the Sandinista socialists lie in Madison?" There was a long silence after that. Then he said, "Ah yes, Madison. He was a very important president."

I took a few more assignments with that limo service. None were as educational as that first. But some other lessons were driven home to me as a result of this interlude. Things look very different from the front seat of a limo than they do from the back seat. One is forced to see things that are invisible from the luxury compartment such as the pecking order among drivers— the low regard limo drivers have for taxi drivers—and the parking privileges hotel doormen give to beautifully decked-out young women who drive up and are clearly on a business call. Moreover, an unusual number of limo drivers are retired police officers that do this job to supplement their pensions, a good thing to know when you are in traffic and might need help.

10

CONSULTANCIES IN PROGRAM DESIGN AND EVALUATION

My retirement in August of 1980 was a true celebration. Having suffered the RIF five years earlier, I breathed a sigh of relief at gaining a regular monthly pension check that would be deposited directly into my account for the rest of my life. I had no regrets about leaving AID even though I had enjoyed the camaraderie of my colleagues and would continue to miss that forum of intellectual exchange for many years.

Joan completed her coursework at Montgomery College in June 1978. She had finished with a 4.0 average and was the class valedictorian. The entire family assembled on Graduation Day to listen to her witty remarks and then to celebrate the occasion together. I was enormously proud of her for going back to school to qualify in computer science. She immediately landed a job with a firm that worked under contract with the US Army Recruiting Service to manage their computer system. She quickly worked her way up to project manager and continued to work until 1989, by which time our three children had completed their education.

At the time I retired, the Pennsylvania project was still not generating enough extra cash to pay me a salary. But I was sure there would be opportunities for short-term consulting with international development agencies. I registered with several "beltway bandits," as the local consultancy industry was called, to join the teams that bid on service contracts with AID, the World Bank, regional development banks, and the various UN agencies. Soon I was employed to perform several program and project evaluations for AID and for some UN agencies such as the UN Development Program, UNIDO, UNCTAD (now the World Trade Organization) and FAO.

In all, over the next 22 years, I would perform 37 such assignments, each lasting between four weeks to six months. The income from these tasks plus Joan's salary provided the needed supplement to my pension. It kept the family solvent and got our three children through college, although they still needed to avail themselves of the student loan program.

Annex 11 provides an annotated list describing these 37 assignments. The World Bank financed three of these consultancies while another twelve were performed for various UN agencies.

There were a few unusual assignments, such as the one dealing with the U.S. Trust Territory of Palau. Most assignments, however, fell into three categories: (1) Technical Assistance (TA) project design efforts, (2) TA project evaluations and (3) Country Economic Assistance program evaluations.

I specialized in technology transfer, international trade, and domestic and foreign investment. I would be directed to search for ways to build linkages to the local or foreign private sector in these areas. This, of course, often led me to run counter to the socialist-leaning orientation of many policy makers in a number of developing countries.

EVOLUTION OF FOREIGN AID DURING THE LAST HALF OF THE 20ᵀᴴ CENTURY

The world was relatively inexperienced in providing "foreign aid" during my early days with ICA in the 1950s and then with AID. Everyone recognized it was a high-risk activity. Government officials and members of Congress who approved funding were anxious to learn how effectively resources were being utilized. There was also a ferment of intellectual curiosity among those who were responsible for these programs to understand what worked and what did not.

Still, the problems facing the former colonies of the European imperial powers were grossly oversimplified at the beginning of this journey. Some thought a dose of good old American "know how" injected into the mix would solve the problems of these new fledgling nations. U.S. foreign aid programs also had a bit of "economic determinism" built into them. The assumption was that economic aid would help improve citizens' well-being and that, in turn, would improve political stability and buy time for the new government to institute essential reforms. While there is always a political facet to the provision of bilateral aid, some programs, however, were principally politically motivated. In 1946, U.S. programs for Turkey and Greece were intended to mitigate unemployment and strengthen the democratic elements against the influence of their respective communist parties. The primary focus was reconstruction to overcome the effects of the war. But during the course of the following decades, other political crises caused the United States and many other Western nations to apply economic resources to support their political goals.[15]

Furthermore, as discussed in chapter 7, economic aid programs experienced eventual "mission creep." While the initial tenure of the Truman administration's Point Four programs was considered temporary, by 1975, economic aid had become institutionalized with annual aid target levels for virtually every aid recipient nation. The focus was shifting from short-term economic support to chronic resource transfers whose objective was the elimination of global poverty.

Along the course of the last seventy years, besides the attitudinal changes within the aid recipient community discussed in chapter 8, economic assistance has seen frequent changes and shifting emphases and

---

15 For a more detailed history and analysis of the evolution of international economic assistance, please see my monograph *Foreign Aid: Will It Ever Reach Its Sunset?* published in 2005 by the US Foreign Policy Association, New York, N.Y. More recent commentaries about international aid flows may be found in William Easterly, *White Man's Burden*, 2006, and also in Angus Deaton, *The Great Escape* (Princeton University Press, 2013).

priorities within the aid donor community as well. One decade the focus would be on employment generation and industrialization. This shifted to "institutional development," such as education and health systems. Then "basic human needs" became the target. Then it shifted to health and family planning followed by poverty alleviation and malnutrition. Whenever priorities would change, excellent projects that were nearing termination but needed follow-up activities would be abandoned by the aid donor agency to make room for the new "hobby horse." I recall evaluating a superb UNDP project in China that assisted China's efforts to privatize their government enterprises. Retired senior executives of developed nations that had managed large enterprises were brought to China to help prepare their public enterprises for privatization. The project was to end in 1999. The Government of China wanted and needed its continuation. But UNDP had revised its development priorities and would not agree to any follow-up activities, even though the project reaching termination had been hugely successful and needed some follow-on.

More recently, aid recipient countries have been categorized by the severity of poverty levels. ODA pledged by donor countries now focuses more on the nations with lowest per-capita incomes. It was and is hoped that private capital investment will increase in the more stable, middle-income countries.

A BRIEF GLOSSARY OF AID JARGON

Annex 7 provides a description of the common terms that have evolved to depict the operations of economic assistance. Here we simply describe the three kinds of activities I was engaged to perform for many of the 37 short-term consulting assignments.

Project design for an aid donor operating in a foreign cultural setting is more an art than it is a science. It is a search for an intervention, sometimes simple, but often complex because it ideally will bring about a change of behavior, enhance efficiency or yield an output that will improve the well-being of the target beneficiaries over a period of time, say five to ten years. There can be failures and the planned output may only be partially achieved. Investment in the project design exercise is intended to maximize the project's chances of success.

Evaluations. The bottom line for me, with respect to any sort of evaluation effort, is that it needs to take into account Mark Twain's observation: "It ain't what you don't know that gets you into trouble. It's what you know for sure, that just ain't so!"

Project Evaluation assignments measure the effectiveness of the project, either halfway through its life so as to explore the need for some course correction, or at the end to see whether lessons could be learned that would help in the design of future interventions. Legislation authorizing funds for economic aid usually requires that each project be evaluated to determine its effectiveness in meeting its intended objectives and to identify some "lessons learned." Unfortunately, that legislation does not require anyone to actually read these evaluations or to take any remedial actions to resolve the difficulties identified by the evaluators. It has been my experience that operating officials often greet critical evaluations in a defensive manner. The real audience should be the host government or the recipient institution, since it is they who are the intended beneficiaries of the effort. The Chinese government is one of the very few who tend to take evaluations seriously.

Country program evaluations are requested to provide an objective assessment of an aid program for the benefit of senior policy makers. The review team is carefully selected to assure objectivity. I participated in four country program evaluations: Iran 1957, Belgium 1960, The Netherlands 1960, and Pakistan 1988.

Chapter 3 contains a description of the 1957 Iran evaluation. In this chapter I will describe each of the other three country program evaluations I undertook both during and after my career in the U.S. government. They are unique experiences that offer insight into the strengths and weaknesses inherent in the conduct of international aid efforts. The stories behind these evaluations shed light on a few of the subtleties of the business of economic assistance. I certainly learned a lot, especially about our proclivities for self-deception.

But first, let us step back in time to the early phase of my career in government and take a look at my experience with the country program evaluations for Belgium and the Netherlands.

Country Program Evaluations for Belgium and the Netherlands 1960

In 1960, the State Department set up a special evaluation unit to review country assistance programs that had a strategic political focus. Since I had served on the ICA/ evaluation staff in 1957, I was asked to join the new unit to help with their initial evaluations as a way to facilitate the transfer of our earlier experience. Five teams were created; each comprised of a senior State Department official, an economic aid official, and a military official, supported by a staff assistant. Each team would specialize in one geographic area. I was asked to serve as staff assistant for the Europe team. Our first two country evaluations would be Belgium and The Netherlands.

The Europe team comprised a former embassy deputy chief of mission, an Air Force major general and a former aid mission director. We were to spend one month for briefings in Washington to prepare for each trip, then one month at the U.S. Embassy in the capital city of the country, and finally one month writing the report before presenting our findings. The evaluation needed to be thorough and was made available to senior policy makers of the executive branch and Congress.

Teams that evaluated Latin American, Asian, Middle Eastern and African aid programs made recommendations for the future. In our case, the European programs, both the economic assistance from the Marshall Plan and the military assistance resulting from their NATO status were ending.

The NATO alliance had been established in 1949 following the Soviet occupation of Czechoslovakia in 1948 and the Berlin Blockade. In the Treaty's Article 5, the Allies agreed, "an armed attack against one or more of them ... shall be considered an attack against them all." Article 3 laid the foundation for cooperation in military preparedness between the Allies. Our military aid to Belgium and Holland in the 1950s was authorized under this framework.

After extensive briefings by State, ICA (AID's predecessor agency), the Defense Department and CIA, the team left for Brussels in March 1960. Belgium had been in the news on a daily basis because of the controversy surrounding the granting of independence to the Belgian Congo.

I had taken several courses on imperialism and the colonial period with Oscar Janowsky at City College and was particularly dismayed with the record of the Belgians in Congo. After studying the records of the French, the British, the Dutch and the Italians, I had little good to say about any of the European colonial powers. But the Belgian record was truly horrible. For eighty years, the Belgian government exploited the Congo's mineral resources. Nothing was done to educate the population. The colony was run like a prison. When their control eroded, the Belgians engineered a breakaway of Katanga, the province with the most valuable mines. They anticipated maintaining a political link to Katanga and offered freedom to the rest of the territory.

At the U.S. Embassy in Brussels we received briefings, including one from the political counselor who, in my opinion, suffered from a severe case of "clientitis." This is a diplomatic "disease" wherein someone who is sent to a country to represent the States winds up presenting that country's rationales and excuses to his own bureaucracy instead. This fellow described the Belgians as generous and willing to help their former subjects when it was well known that they were not. I got into a bit of trouble with my betters on the team when I wrote the record of his briefing and described his arguments to be thin and hollow.

The U.S. ambassador, William Burden, was a very wealthy political appointee. The team was invited to lunch with him soon after arrival. As we walked into his residence, I noticed the Brancusi sculpture *Bird in Space* standing near the entrance. I had seen it some years earlier at the New York Museum of Modern Art. Unsuspectingly, I whispered to the other team members that here was a copy of that sculpture. I was immediately corrected. William Burden did not have "copies"; this was an original. Properly chastened, I indulged in a lavish lunch, washed down with several glasses of well-aged Chateau Lafitte Rothschild.

The results of the Marshall Plan were clearly evident. Belgium had rebuilt its industry and was thriving economically. But on the military side, there is a very amusing story to tell.

In 1949, NATO allocated defensive roles to each of its members. Belgium had been assigned tasks for its air force and army. But there was no navy. A gentleman named Robin argued that Belgium needed a navy and that NATO should provide one. At first, this idea was resisted since the country had not had a navy for some time. But, since M. Robin was the king's cousin, the request got some "legs." Eventually, it was agreed that the Belgian navy would operate fifty minesweepers and would be responsible for sweeping the Belgian ports and nearby areas in the event of hostilities. The U.S. Navy took fifty minesweepers out of its "mothball fleet," loaded them onto large vessels and shipped them to Belgium. M. Robin became Commodore Robin and a large minesweeper training facility was built at the port of Ostend as part of the package.

But a problem arose when Commodore Robin tried to recruit seamen. Belgium, being a small country, allowed most of its military to leave base and go home on weekends. But if a ship were at sea, that would not be so easy to arrange. As a result, Robin found he could not staff his fifty minesweepers. Some forty of them had to be put back into "mothballs," this time on the European side of the Atlantic. The Ostend training facility was hugely underutilized.

I am embarrassed to report that we depicted this Belgian effort to create a navy for itself as a "success story" in the report and urged that other NATO members make use of the newly built and underutilized training facility.

The ink was barely dry on the Belgium report when we arrived at The Hague to conduct the same kind of review for our program in Holland. The U.S. Military Assistance Advisory Group (MAAG) there was headed by an admiral, in deference to the history of Dutch prominence as a naval power. When the team described our most recent evaluation and its "success story," I could see the stifled smile on the admiral's face. Then our leader asked whether the admiral might send some Dutch sailors for training at the Ostend facility. The admiral lost his smile. "The Belgians teach the Dutch something about the sea? Ridiculous!" was his reply. This seems to be a revealing example to demonstrate how the analysis of national character could have been useful in the decision-making process concerning foreign policy. It would have been helpful if those who had assigned military roles for NATO members understood that Belgium had no naval tradition and capability while Holland did.

The Holland evaluation was straightforward. The aid programs had been very successful. By the time we returned and filed our report, each of the other teams had performed two evaluations as well. That gave the senior staff a critical mass of ten country program evaluations to digest. Later, I was told that these evaluations were used when the Kennedy administration decided to redesign ICA and asked Congress to authorize the establishment of the US Agency for International Development (USAID). That authorizing legislation is still the governing legal basis for U.S. bilateral economic assistance today.

PALAU – ASSIGNMENT IN PARADISE – 1980

Back to my post-retirement years, my first consulting assignment had nothing to do with independent developing countries. Yet, the story is sufficiently revealing and so I offer it as educational amusement for the reader.

The U.S. Department of the Interior had contracted a local consulting firm to perform technical analyses to assist in negotiating the Compact of Free Association with one of the U.S. Pacific Trust Territories, Palau. Palau, with a population in 1980 of 7,000 souls, is a group of small islands in the Polynesian Archipelago that U.S. Marines had fought, bled and died over as they pushed the Japanese back across the Pacific at the end of World War II. Many will recognize the names of Palau's neighboring islands: the islands of Truk, Yap and The Marianas. The flight we took went from Wake Island to Truk to Yap and then to Palau.

At the end of World War II, the UN designated Palau a U.S. Trust Territory. The islands were not part of the United States but were held "in trust" for the rest of the world. The strategically located U.S. Naval base at Palau was part of the grand geopolitical design of the U.S. Pacific defense system. Everyone, including the Palauans themselves, understood that these islands could never maintain their independence. Because of their strategic location, any major power with aspirations for asserting power in the Pacific would seek to control the islands. The Palauans were happy to be under U.S. protection but, of course, they wanted all the financial gains they could get to accept the same status as Puerto Rico. Our job was to help with the negotiations by figuring out a twenty-year development plan and to calculate the funding the United States would provide. Since the Palau investment plan would run well into the future, I could show my smarts by doing discounted cash flow analysis for them.

One fascinating aspect of the Palauans was their acceptance of the weather's vagaries. These islands offered the next best thing to paradise for easy living. There were coconuts to drink from, all manner of fruits and vegetables to eat and a sea full of fish. Clothing was unnecessary since the temperature was a constant eighty degrees all year round. If a typhoon hit, it would sweep away the old huts and the Palauans would just put up new ones. Nothing was built to last. There were hardly any cement buildings. Life was very simple and beautiful.

Palau had the perfect example of the "backward leaning labor supply curve." The higher the wages were set, the less work would be sought because of the very limited need for cash. A major U.S. canning and freezing company had set up a fish processing plant. Labor had to be imported from Korea because the Palauans would not do such hard work and did not need the money. Fifty percent of Palau's labor force was actually on the U.S. government's payroll, doing one good thing or another.

Two weeks before I traveled to Palau, a Palauan delegation had arrived in Washington to sign the Compact. After some photo opportunities with the president, the group departed with the document signed. When their plane landed in Yap, it blew a tire, went off the runway and crashed. No one was hurt but once all had safely exited, the plane went up in flames. The copy of the Compact was destroyed. I was asked to carry another signed copy to deliver to the Palauan government.

Joan accompanied me on this assignment. We stopped at Wake Island and were met by a charming Palauan government employee sent there to accompany us on the next flight so as to ensure a hassle-free landing. She spoke flawless English and the flight was most enjoyable. After landing, I asked her which official should be presented with the Compact. She turned three shades of white and stared at me. "Do you have the Compact in your carry-on?" she asked. "Yes," I told her. She said then that the islanders believed the Compact was cursed and that the Gods caused it to burn in the crash. Had she known I was carrying it, she would never have flown in the aircraft with us. That got us off to a good start.

Compared to working with the Indians ten years earlier, I found working with the Palauans to be easy and stress-free. We put together an investment plan, came up with the financing and got ready to depart. When we returned to Washington DC we presented our product, a signed copy of the staff-level Palauan agreement, to the Departments of the Interior and the Navy. Everyone was happy.

One final bit of joviality came from this assignment. The consultancy firm paid me a lump sum for my work. The check was for $15,000. When I presented the check to my bank, I was told it would take a week to clear. But the check was drawn on a local bank just three blocks down the street. Why not go to that bank and get the check certified? That way the funds would be immediately credited for use. I thought that would be a good idea.

A few minutes later, when I presented the check at the other bank, they told me "it was bank policy" to certify checks only for their customers. That did not sit well with me so I worked my way up the pyramid to the manager. He confirmed that it was indeed their policy to perform such a service only for their customers. "OK," said I. "Then give me the $15,000 in cash." This caused quite a kerfuffle, but I insisted and was finally presented with an envelope full of cash. I did not count it but simply stuffed it into my jacket, quickly looked over my shoulder to see if someone was following me, and ran the three blocks back to my bank. I threw the envelope on my banker's desk, all the while fuming over the stupidity of the other bank manager.

My banker counted the money and—lo and behold—it came to $17,000. What to do? I told her to deposit it into my account. After that I went to see a movie. When I got home, Joan said my company wanted me to contact them right away. As soon as he heard my voice on the phone, my boss asked me if I had robbed a bank. The branch manager wanted to see me right away. "No," said I. "I'll call him in the morning."

Next morning, I phoned the branch manager. He asked if I had noticed some extra money in the envelope. I told him I had and that the amount was $2,000. He told me he would like it returned at once. And then I had my fun. I told him it was "against my policy" to refund money on Tuesdays. He said he understood, and I thought, "You do?" Then I said I charged a fee of $10 on refunds. I would be glad to mail a check for $1,990 to him tomorrow. He gratefully accepted. And so ended the first of 37 assignments.

PROGRAM EVALUATION OF U.S. AID TO PAKISTAN – 1988

The most interesting evaluation in which I participated was that of the USAID program to Pakistan covering the period when the Soviets had occupied Afghanistan. Maurice Williams, USAID's former deputy administrator, by then retired, and I were selected to perform a review of economic assistance to Pakistan for the period 1982 to 1987. We submitted our report in May 1988 after receiving extensive briefings in Washington DC and Islamabad, Pakistan. Maury was the right man to lead this review. Not only was he one of the most senior AID officers, albeit retired, but he had also served as the USAID mission director in Pakistan from 1963 through 1967 and knew the country, as they say, like the palm of his hand.

Our very substantial aid program to Pakistan had been sharply curtailed in the late 1970s after it became clear that Islamabad was pursuing nuclear weapons technology. But when the Soviets invaded Afghanistan in December 1979, everything changed. Anyone who has read George Crile's book *Charlie Wilson's War* (or has seen the film) would have a good grasp of the events that led to the withdrawal of Soviet troops ten years later. Basically, the U.S. government took it upon itself to arm the Afghan Mujahedin to force the Soviets to withdraw. The supply routes ran through Pakistan and so aid to that country was quickly resumed in 1981.

Here is a short extract from the evaluation. It provides the background for our review:

> The economic assistance program during 1982-1987 is unique in several respects. First, a very large level of economic aid, $1.625 billion, was committed for the six-year period, in advance of discussion or agreement on the content of the program. Second, the large-scale assistance at that time represented a sharp reversal of U.S. assistance policy toward Pakistan. For several preceding years, the United States had been scaling down its AID Mission in Pakistan and the level of assistance, so that, in 1981, AID's in-country capability for

program design and implementation was extremely limited. Third, while the rationale for the mounting of a large program in Pakistan was primarily political and strategic, the program that AID launched in 1982 was, in large measure, directed toward longer term economic reform and development objectives.

These unique features may provide special interest for a review of the period, although six years is a relatively short time span to assess the true development impact of the program. The recent experience of aid to Pakistan also may provide grist for the current U.S. Congressional interest in the uses and effectiveness of American assistance programs and how they can be better directed in the decade ahead.

The commitment of $1.625 billion of U.S. assistance to Pakistan in 1981 was part of a broader package of military and economic assistance totaling $3.2 billion, which aimed at strengthening Pakistan at a critical time when Soviet military forces were on its border in Afghanistan. The pressures on Pakistan from this Soviet military intervention were extreme in terms of seeking to undermine Pakistan's basic support for the continuing struggle of the Afghan people and in terms of the almost three million Afghan refugees which found shelter within the borders of Pakistan. Consequently, the U.S. assistance package was of high strategic importance and called for expediency in implementation and maximum political and economic impact. The scope of this evaluation is to review the main features of the 1982-1987 program of economic assistance and to document the strengths.

Maury and I spent more than one month in Pakistan, talking with AID personnel and their Pakistani counterparts and learning about the conduct of the projects over the six-year period. Most importantly, we focused on the dialogue between senior U.S. embassy and mission personnel and those in the Pakistani government responsible for economic policy formulation.

One day, he and I were asked to attend a "brown bag luncheon" with the senior mission staff. The idea was to be totally informal, put our feet on the desks and just chat about our impressions. Everyone was eager to learn what Maury thought about the program. Three important things emerged for me out of that discussion.

1. The mission director explained that he had held some very successful consultations and brainstorming sessions with senior Pakistani government leaders. He said the Pakistanis were open to his ideas for needed reform, listened carefully and took extensive notes during these meetings. Although there had been little concrete action to implement these recommendations to date, he was confident they were seriously considering them.

Maury smiled and responded, "Yeah. They used to jerk me around the same way when I was in your position. The Paks are masters at that game. They know how to make you feel good. I doubt that they are serious. This is a government of inaction." The mission director was crestfallen.

2. Then the program officer asked what Maury thought about the mix of projects that had been selected by the government of Pakistan and the mission for inclusion in the program for funding. Maury responded that the projects selected were "old friends" of his. He too, had focused on the same areas i.e. agriculture, health, and power generation and supply. That said, the development problems had not gone away. He gave the new program credit for identifying the same obstacles to economic development that had existed twenty years earlier.

3. Finally, the mission director asked Maury for his impressions of any major changes he sensed had occurred in Pakistan since his departure. Maury thought about that for a while. Then he offered perhaps the most

prescient observation of the entire review. He said, when he served in Pakistan in the 1960s, he had found that the educated Pakistani visualized himself and his society as being an important part of the South-Asian subcontinent. "Today" he said, "after having lost East Pakistan, they seem to perceive themselves as being the eastern anchor of the Middle-East."

One wonders whether the Indian government understands this significant shift in its neighbor's outlook and how important it is to work to reverse that world view among the Pakistanis for India's own security and well-being.

The most critical findings of the evaluation report are excerpted below:

> The security-development link in U.S. assistance must be balanced and adjusted as conditions change. The level of U.S. economic aid has been closely linked to the cost to Pakistan of financing U.S. military sales. In a real sense, economic aid has been the handmaiden of Pakistan's defense requirements. A balanced and linked assessment of U.S. and Pakistan security interests will continue to be important in the future. Pakistan's military build-up has placed in jeopardy its ability to meet pressing economic and social investments.
>
> In the period following the withdrawal of Soviet forces from Afghanistan, it may be possible to envision that Pakistan's broader security interests would be best served by shifting the balance of U.S. assistance for the 1988~1993 period more in favor of economic objectives, and by the government of Pakistan restraining further increases in its defense budget.
>
> Politically driven aid programs involve trade-offs in economic development performance. The AID Mission is to be commended for its sustained efforts to maximize the possible development impact of the politically justified ESF (economic support fund)

program. A number of highly beneficial development effects were clearly achieved. However, when USAID overstates the development results, it risks blurring the reality of the costs of short term political aid and the resulting weaker performance by the Pakistan economy than might otherwise have been possible. Such distortion tends to hide the adverse effects on Pakistan's economic and political stability over the mid- to longer-term.

When the criteria of performance between ESF and development assistance programs are diluted, the overall standards of economic performance tend to be weakened.

—∞∞—

In early 1989, shortly after completing our work, I took an assignment that sent me to Egypt. While in Cairo, I read an article written by one of my colleagues in the *Foreign Service Journal* that described AID's accomplishments in Pakistan in glowing terms, quite contrary to the findings contained in our recently published report. I felt it necessary to respond to set the record straight. My letter was published in the September 1989 issue of the *Foreign Service Journal*. Here is the text of that letter:

"AID's Barnacles"

It pains me to take issue with Haven North's article, "AID: Development Specialists, Managers, and Diplomats" (May 1989), particularly because I had profound respect for his thoughts over the many years we were colleagues at AID. But the article is symptomatic of AID`s major illness - self-deception - and could mislead those like Congressman Lee Hamilton, at a time when they are attempting to revise AID's legislation to revitalize the agency.

As an example of AID's achievements in policy reform, North cites the $1.6 billion Pakistan program in 1982-87. He states, "The larger U.S. interests in Pakistan were effectively served by the foreign assistance program." In fact, the recent AID evaluation of that very program, which I coauthored with Maurice Williams, makes exactly the opposite point: that the Mission's claims of effectiveness in macro-policy reform were exaggerated, although some successes were reached in the energy sector.

Any program that contributed importantly to dislodging the Soviets in Afghanistan has little for which it need apologize. But the Mission's need to feed material back to Washington to convince the Hill that our aid also achieved important economic policy reforms is an example of AID's unwillingness to own up to its limitations.

The fact is, the collection of barnacles that has been added to AID's legislation these past 20 years has made AID's efforts largely ineffectual, no matter how competent and dedicated its staff. The current legislation contains sops for virtually every domestic constituency and special pleader, at the price of achieving gains in foreign affairs. Since Bill Gaud, there has not been an AID administrator who was powerful enough to shift program direction or to increase or terminate aid to a single country over the objection of the State Department. Nor has AID been willing to stand up to demands of its 435 member "board of` directors" (Congress), no matter how absurd the demand.

There are also too many examples of AID management placing restrictions on itself, beyond those posed in its legislation, in order to forestall threats of imposing even greater congressional constraints on its flexibility. The very projects to which Haven North rightly points as examples of successful institution-building (agricultural universities) have 25-year time horizons; such long-term commitments are not included in the Agency's programs today.

I chose to retire from AID because I was no longer accomplishing enough to justify the effort. Most AID officers are well aware of these limitations and would like to see at least a portion of AID's strength restored, to make it possible to bring about meaningful improvements in the Third World. To admit that Lee Hamilton is right when he suggests that the agency may have become irrelevant does not disparage the integrity of AID's Foreign Service. It simply recognizes the need for radical changes in AID's modus operandi.

-- Ludwig Rudel, Cairo, Egypt

PROJECT DESIGN – EGYPT – AN UNFORTUNATE EXAMPLE –1989

In 1989, shortly after submitting our Pakistan evaluation report to AID, I took an export industries assignment that brought me to Egypt. I was asked by the UNCTAD–GATT International Trade Center (ITC), located in Geneva, to travel to Cairo and design an Export Industries Development Program which would assist the Egyptian Ministry of Commerce in enhancing Egypt's export earnings. The World Bank, which sometimes contracts out project design work when it does not have in-house experts in a particular field, sponsored my work.

The background of this effort is quite interesting. After Egypt signed the peace accord with Israel in 1978, the United States agreed to provide Egypt almost one billion dollars each year in support of that very difficult political act. Thus Egypt found itself less needy with respect to international loans. The World Bank sets stringent conditions to its lending and requires strong political commitment to take reform measures. The Egyptian government fell short in meeting these conditions, even more than usual since it found itself unpressured as a result of the U.S. aid. By 1985, the World Bank decided to withhold further funding, believing that Cairo would come around. But Egypt did not seek World Bank funding if it involved instituting meaningful reform.

Apparently this ever-deepening hole in the World Bank's Egypt loan portfolio put more pressure on the Bank staff than it did on Egypt. By 1989, in an effort to restore relations with the Egyptians, the Bank made an offer to provide grant funding to ITC to design a technical assistance project that would generate a major World Bank loan for expanding Egypt's export industries. In my view, the donor–recipient relationship becomes distorted when a donor finds itself under more pressure to "give" than the recipient does to "receive." I was asked to design this project and given six months to negotiate one that would be acceptable to the Egyptian government.

It was a fascinating six months. I was given every courtesy, was provided an office with staff at the Egyptian Export Promotion Bureau, a government entity attached to the Ministry of Commerce and directed by a professor of economics. The staff was young, bright and eager to accomplish things. The director was somewhat less imaginative and very conscious of his governmental connections and image. I had access to Egypt's private manufacturing sector and was provided with every facility and the freedom to contact anyone that I thought could be of help.

I came up with some ideas and they were presented to a member of President Mubarak's staff for vetting. There was never a rejection, nor was there a commitment of support. Eventually, I began to feel that there was something about this entire exercise that I was not being told.

However, the closer I got to complete the six-month assignment, the more difficult it became to get any agreement on the substance of the design. Finally, I learned what the problem was. It seemed President Mubarak had issued an order allowing my efforts to proceed because they were funded by a grant from the World Bank. However, he had made it clear to his staff that he would not agree to fund the follow-up technical assistance project I was charged to design with repayable loan funds because he believed Egypt did not need technical assistance. Besides, he is reported to have said, "These foreign advisors just come to Egypt to see the Pyramids."

My six-month effort at project design had been a total failure.

Part Three

Development in Appalachia
1970 to 2008

11

DEVELOPMENT VIA PRIVATE SECTOR –
GLENDALE YEAROUND 1970 TO 2008

MY WORKING LIFE CAN be divided into two distinct phases; (a) a 25-year career in the U.S. Foreign Service followed by a 22-year period of part-time consultancies with various international aid organizations (1956 to 2002), and (b) 38 years in the resort land development business (1970 to 2008). I started the Pennsylvania business late during my government career— on a "moonlighting" basis. It was never planned that way. I had no intention of leaving government service to begin another career in the private sector once I became eligible for retirement from the Foreign Service. But events conspired to push me in that direction. Here is the way it happened.

My earlier stories describing life in the Foreign Service during the 1960s, perhaps the most intellectually rewarding and productive period of my career, convey a deep sense of satisfaction with my work and status. Two years in Turkey, five years in India, a year at the University of Michigan sandwiched between, gave me a powerful sense of purpose, a very positive raison d'être. I was working with some of the finest minds of that generation, doing tasks that were clearly of social and political consequence. My abilities were well-recognized and acknowledged by my senior colleagues. My new family—Joan and our three young children—was thriving. Life was good.

But, to my mind, there were two glaring problems impeding this sense of perfection. The first had to do with what might seem to be a minor logistical dilemma for those in the U.S. Foreign Service—where to spend home leave. The second weightier issue was the ability of an officer to freely express his views to his superiors, even when these views ran counter to prevailing government policies. These two issues, hugely different in scope and in their impact on intellectual honesty and integrity, need to be explained. Let's look at them, one at a time.

The issue of "home leave" has to do with the requirement that Foreign Service officers spend about three months in the States between overseas tours so as to become reacquainted with the changes happening in the country they represent. Most in the Foreign Service have homes in the Washington DC area but these tend to be rented out while overseas. It would not pay to evict the tenant for a short-term occupancy. Besides, the furniture is in storage somewhere. Staying with relatives is OK for about three days, no more. Hotels are costly for such extended periods. What to do?

Well, if one had a simple, inexpensive "second home," a cabin in the woods that could serve as a base of operation for the family during home leave, and remain unoccupied the rest of the time … well that would be just perfect. I'm sure that, as a city dweller who grew up on the sidewalks of New York City, the idea of owning a large tract of rural land would have had an additional fascination for me.

My criteria for selecting the site for such a cabin were simple. I bought some maps of the rural areas around Washington DC, drew a circle with a radius of 140 miles around the Capitol, (the distance that a small airplane can fly in one hour) and looked along the edge of that circle for 2000 feet of elevation to escape the damp east coast air, and, finally, a lake for water sports. When our family went on home leave from India in 1967, we explored some of the more desirable areas along that circle, picked

Flinton, Pennsylvania and bought a farm. Well, actually it turned out we bought two adjacent farms of 65 acres each. One of those farms had an old dilapidated farmhouse on it. All we needed to do was to make it habitable. That became the goal to be accomplished before our next home leave, scheduled for the summer of 1969.

The farm met all of our criteria. It was adjacent to the 14,000-acre Prince Gallitzin State Park, which also contained the six thousand-acre Glendale Lake. The geological survey marker on the front step of the farm indicated it was 1543 feet above sea level with much of the farm lying higher. It was inexpensive and there was woodland all around with a rarely–travelled dirt road providing access. We were well pleased. And that was how we came to reside in Flinton, Pennsylvania.

Indeed, during the next two years, we managed to make the farmhouse habitable by remote control—snail mail and a few international phone calls—while we were posted in India. By1969, the family could begin a life in this rural Appalachian community, and we spent our first summer there.

This is where things got complicated. A large tract of woodland adjacent to our newly acquired farm, boasting a long frontage on the dirt road and located just across the road from the state park boundary, had always fascinated me. "The grass is always greener on the other man's lawn," it is said. But in this instance, it really was.

So imagine my surprise when, one bright sunny day, a car drove up to our farmhouse and Dick Rhody, the very neighbor whose family owned that beautiful woodland, stepped onto our porch. "Hey! You guys are buying all this farmland, I see," he said. "Maybe you'd be interested in buying our land as well?" We replied with an unequivocal "Maybe." "How much acreage are we talking about?" He said the parcel measured about eight hundred acres, maybe a little bit more.

I should have said "No thanks!" I should have told him I was a bureaucrat and knew nothing about running a business, especially a real estate land development business. I should have told him that getting involved in such an enterprise would distract me from my primary focus which was to help former European colonies become economically viable, politically independent nations. Instead, I said, "So … how much per acre are you asking?"

The reason I asked that question had to do in large part with my second concern about the Foreign Service i.e. a mid-career officer's need for independent wealth to allow for independence of thought and the ability to accept the consequences of actions that ran counter to prevailing policy.[16]

In years past, the Foreign Service was comprised of those from upper-class families who enjoyed independent wealth. Such officers could speak their minds forcefully and, if need be, tender their resignation and maintain their integrity. But the State Department had become a meritocracy. Recruitment extended well beyond the class elite. I could have been the poster boy for that evolution. I was approaching age forty, had a wife and three small children to care for, and had minimal savings. If I lost my job, the consequences for my family would have been ruinous. Few employment opportunities would have been available to me. My two masters degrees did not equal a Ph.D. and would not qualify me for an appointment in academia.

The Vietnam War was escalating and the general public was losing interest in our many international involvements. Congress reflected these attitudes and heaped unwarranted criticism on our programs. Aid was declining and my agency was becoming more rigid in its work processes. AID's receptivity to new ideas to accomplish our role as change agent in newly established countries, which I had seen in the agency when I joined in 1956, had turned into a defensive posture trying to avoid congressional and press criticism. There were too many instances when I found it necessary to compromise what I loosely term my principles.

Moreover, I had been advocating greater private sector involvement in the economic development process in my work at AID. Here was an

---

16 For an example of this problem see Gary J. Bass, *The Blood Telegram* (Knopf, 2013), the story of the war of independence for Bangladesh, when the US consul general in Dacca reported Pakistan's attacks in 1971 and urged US intervention, causing the ire of Kissinger.

opportunity to put my money where my mouth was. Could I apply some of the lessons I had learned overseas with AID to design a development project in the poverty belt of upper Appalachia?

If some friends and I invested in a sure fire, get-rich-quick scheme, like buying rural land by the acre, parceling it up and then selling it by the inch, we would quickly achieve financial independence. There were thousands of Foreign Service officers who needed cabins in the nearby countryside to provide a place to live during home leave. That beautiful state park, with its magnificent lake, was just across the road. Public facilities were already built and usable. It wouldn't take long to complete this project and risk exposure would be minimal. I could do it part-time. We would get rich and the local community would benefit from the enterprise. What could go wrong?

Self-deception knows no limits.

It was the summer of 1969. We bought the property, formed a corporation, and convinced seven of my colleagues serving with us in India to partner in the enterprise. We raised $110,000 in investment capital and negotiated a loan from a friendly neighborhood bank, which required Joan and me to pledge every personal asset we owned. We did the survey work (which revealed that the newly acquired parcel had 893 acres to be added to the original 130 acres from the two farms), got a landscape architect to design the subdivisions and secured the necessary government approvals. Then we started constructing access roads. We finally began selling building lots in the summer of 1971.

THE BUSINESS OF LAND DEVELOPMENT IN 1970

I write about events that occurred forty-four years ago. It was a remarkable and exciting experience for me. That experience, however, will have no relevance for anyone contemplating a similar project today. Our enterprise started on a shoestring; something you might call a "mom and pop" operation. Amazingly, we were able to bring the project to a successful conclusion. It took us more than thirty years. We had thought it would take five. We did not make our fortunes. But we did not go bankrupt either.

Today, sadly, it is not possible for someone with the limited means we had at our disposal to undertake such a venture. Business conditions in the United States have changed radically during the last four decades, in terms of industry structure, banking practices and governmental regulations, so that a small business cannot complete such a venture successfully. Now only a large, well-financed company with direct access to financial markets can undertake a venture of this scale. Such a company would need in-house legal counsel, civil engineers and accountants. They would probably have their own sales staff. This major change in the United States' business climate is worth further exploration because it has changed the key premises in the debate about promoting small-scale private enterprise in the country.

Today, when one hears arguments in favor of "letting the markets allocate resources," one should be aware that today's markets are not structured the same as yesterday's. Those of yesterday had many buyers and many sellers engaged in competitive trading. Today, most markets are oligopolistic in structure, dominated by a few sellers serving many buyers. The result is that intensive government regulations for consumer protection have become necessary and commonplace. This radical change in the business environment, in the structure of capitalism itself, will be discussed in greater detail in chapter 12, "Conclusions and Implications for the Future."

The business of land development involves many front-end expenses before one can convert vacant woodland into subdivided parcels useable as building lots. Before engaging in the exercise of subdivision, an entire lot plan must be laid out. Sections must be surveyed to establish meets and bounds for the initial development effort to encompass at least a meaningful segment of the property. Some of the planning can be done using existing maps, but eventually, a lot of very expensive survey work is necessary. Then, the subdivision plans prepared by the surveyor must be approved by the local jurisdiction, in our case a township and the county. Our township supervisors had never done anything on such a large scale before, and were fearful of error and criticism. Rights of way are cut and a road network to access these lots is constructed. Finally, the surveyors come back to stake out the lots.

Basic utilities also have to be installed. In the case of electric power and telephone lines, several companies already operated in these service territories. They helped us because they were eager to extend their lines in 1970 and increase their customer base. But what does one do for water and sewerage services in a rural area? We had no choice but to build them ourselves.

To do all of this, we needed to retain, aside from the actual labor force for construction and operation of the facilities, (a) consulting civil and landscape engineers, (b) lawyers and (c) certified public accountants.

A business plan that shows how you will make money must be presented to lenders in order to get the credit needed to meet these basic front-end expenses. The trick was to spend as little money as possible and to build only those things that were absolutely essential to allow us to begin selling lots, and then find a marketing group to sell "the dream" before actual facilities existed. From the time of the first lot sale—a lot covered with trees and certainly not buildable—there was liability. We were committed to deliver a final, fully developed product to the buyer. We were obligated to build the swimming pool complex, the tennis courts, the club house, the children's playgrounds, the fishing ponds, the roads, sewer system, water system, etc. to meet our commitments to each buyer. Once we had sold our first lot, the sales effort drove the entire development process. Revenue from new sales provided the cash to build the salesman's promise of "the dream."

Our company's combined parcels of land contained slightly more than a thousand acres. We designed the resort to be subdivided into about two thousand lots, half of them building lots, the other half to be campsites. We had hoped to sell out in about five years and referred to our resort as "The Promised Land."

SALES AND MARKETING

The sales effort required three key ingredients. The first was a gimmick to bring people to visit the rural property. You cannot bring the mountain to Mohammed; you must get Mohammed to travel long distances -- sometimes for two hours -- to see the mountain. The second was a salesman who could paint a picture to convince the potential buyer in an hour and a half to "buy the dream," The final element was a source of financing for the buyer who normally could put down only about ten percent of the sales price at the time of purchase, just as is commonly done with car sales today.

During the 1960s, there were many horror stories about land developments and the "blue suede shoe" salesmen types who pressured ill-informed widows into buying uninhabitable property at outrageous prices. My colleagues and I had visited some of these operations and swore we would not engage in such sales techniques. "The world will beat a path to the person who builds a better mouse trap," we believed. Besides, we had a market for our lots with our Foreign Service colleagues. They too, had the "where to stay during home leave" problem. We were convinced they were all waiting for an opportunity to buy a lot from us and join us in central Pennsylvania.

It has been said many times that the three most important factors in a real estate project are location, location and location. We did sell ten lots to Foreign Service people but eventually realized that we were located a four-hour drive away from the Washington DC area, about twice the outer travel limit for sales of vacation property. Since we had made a few sales, we were now committed. There was no turning back without losing everything. We had to turn our sales effort in the direction of Pittsburgh.

Some years ago, I went to see David Mamet's play, *Glengarry Glen Ross,* about a group of land salesmen and how they operated. I recognized every one of them. It seemed to me each and every character in the play had worked for me at one time or another. Mamet's characterizations were right on the mark. Over the nearly forty years that we ran the operation,

I have worked with no less than seventy salespersons. Every successful salesperson has a charisma that exudes self-confidence and enables him or her to meet someone and basically seduce them into buying a lot in an hour and a half. The common phrase among salespersons, after the buyer has signed an agreement and left, is "Well, I hope it sticks when the ether wears off!"

Each sales manager has his or her own shtick for their salespersons to convince the buyer that they are fortunate to have arrived when they did because they were then in a situation that gave them a huge price discount if they bought then and there. "How lucky can you get? This lot just came back on the market and has been mispriced! That lot also has some other built-in advantage." Sometimes a short scene is acted out wherein the salesman was not supposed to show a particular lot or has misquoted the price.

However, we were always watchful of the marketing operation and never allowed high pressure selling. It was one of my key tasks to keep this sales crew honest. I resisted pressure from sales groups to engage in "time share" schemes. Besides, Congress enacted the Land Sales Registration Act in 1967 and the U.S. Department of Housing and Urban Development now had the mandate to provide consumer protection. The law mandated a seven-day rescission period for purchasers. And once we redirected our sales focus to the Pittsburgh area, we found that another, much larger land development—Treasure Lake—had engaged in such poor sales practices in the early 1970s that the Pittsburgh market was ruined. It took great effort to get Pittsburgh buyers to even come visit another resort.

Ironically, Treasure Lake was owned by Westinghouse, which also owned TV station KDKA, channel 2 in Pittsburgh. That TV station sent a film crew to our project in 1979 and ran an exposé of our marketing practices on a program called *Two On Your Side*. I wrote a letter to KDKA (see Annex 13) pointing out that the station's parent company had engaged in practices that were far more outrageous than those for which we were being criticized. I inquired into what was behind the attack, why they would pick on us. We were their parent company's closest competition. My other objection had to do with the TV program's fundamental message: "we are making an effort to protect you from predatory sellers." The intended, but never stated message was that KDKA's advertisers were honorable while Glendale Yearound was not. I demanded that my protest letter be placed in the TV station's public file so as to create a public record of this event. But nothing came of my protests. I had been trumped by the first amendment.

The best marketing operation, over the entire life of the project, ran for one year beginning in the summer of 1973. I contracted with a group headed by Dave Major. It was a very slick operation. He established a phone room in Monroeville, a town on the way to Pittsburgh, and had four salesmen. Cora, his wife, ran the phone room. About 25 women would begin telephoning from that phone room every weekday evening beginning at 5 pm. Cora would designate one telephone exchange, which at that time consisted of homes clustered in one section of Pittsburgh. The women would politely inform anyone answering the phone that they were from Glendale Yearound, that a public relations person was in that neighborhood and would like to make a fifteen minute presentation to show them some pictures of our development that evening. If they could set a time, he would come by their home and would like to leave them a little thank-you gift for allowing him to make this presentation. The four salesmen would be waiting in that neighborhood for a reference to any appointment the women could schedule. The women would normally make three to four appointments for each of them every evening.

Each salesman would go to the home, offer a small door opener gift, make his presentation and try to schedule an appointment for a tour that weekend. Hopefully, each would succeed in making one appointment out of the evening's four presentations. The potential buyer would need to give him a deposit of $5 as earnest money and was promised double that amount in return when he or she appeared at the property on the weekend. This exercise was repeated on four weekday evenings (Monday, Tuesday, Wednesday and Thursday).

Each salesman would line up four customers, scheduled two on each weekend day. On Friday, the salesman would confirm his appointments by phone. When the customers arrived at the property, they were already known to the salesman, as were their living situations. Invariably, each salesman would make one sale out of the four tours he set up. There was no hard sell. It was the most successful operation we had in our forty-year history.

Unfortunately, the Majors' sales operation had to close after one year. They were so deeply in debt from an earlier operation at another resort, that they needed every nickel they earned from us to pay those debts, and eventually ran out of money.

For the next twenty-five years, other sales groups came and went. Ellis Goodman from Omaha used mass mailing and offers of prize winnings to bring "Mohammed to the mountain." The LaRue brothers from Minnesota, one of whom was a former U-2 pilot, tried a similar effort. Bert Manchik from Tennessee used four "Treasure Chests," each with different locks holding different prizes, including a new car, to lure potential buyers to the property by mailing an actual key that fit one of the treasure chests. People came to the sales office clutching the key they received in the mail to see which prize they had won. The Patten Corporation, a major NYSE-listed resort marketing company came along in 1987, bought lots wholesale from us and took responsibility for all marketing and sales. They even did their own credit checks and held on to the installment paper generated from their sales. That worked nicely for the two years before they left. Finally, I worked a deal with Bill Barnhart, my deputy manager, for him to take charge of the sales effort. He took over in 1990 and has been running it ever since.

None of the hot shot marketing groups ever made any serious money from their operations at Glendale Yearound. Bill Barnhart did reasonably well, but he had modest expectations and tailored sales efforts to his own capacity to carry them through. Each group took the deal on in light of the low wholesale price I was willing to take for delivery of lot inventory. But they did not reckon on the low market value for real estate in central Pennsylvania. I was lucky to get $20,000 retail for a half-acre home site, while in the Deep Creek, Maryland area similar lots were going in the low six digits.

Overall, we averaged about fifty sales per year. In 1973 -1974 we hit 152 sales with the Major's operation; some other years only 25 lots were sold. It was twenty years before we had made enough sales to build all of the promised facilities. By 1990, we had reached our "threshold." We had constructed every facility we had committed to. Another six years of sales were required to pay back our debts to the bank.

The project was supposed to be a five-year, get-rich-quick scheme. It took nearly forty years. The return on investment was about what we could have earned had we pooled our capital and purchased four single-family residences in the Washington DC area, hired a realtor to manage them as rentals and sold them thirty years later.

The Property Owners Association (POA) – A Microcosm of the Democratic Process

By 1975, four years into the sales operation, about 250 lots had been sold. A water system comprising a well and distribution lines had been installed for section 1 of the home-sites and section 1 of the campsites. A sewerage treatment plant was in place and several sewage collectors were being installed, Penelec, the local power company, had run its lines into those sections. The initial road network for those sections was considered serviceable for cars but not yet brought up to finished grade. A ski lodge had been constructed along the township road and was being used by the sales group to receive customers. At the clubhouse and swimming pool complex site, a huge drawing of the planned facilities stood on four posts.

Another drawing was placed at the site designated for the tennis courts. And yet another was placed at the children's playground location.

It was time to form the property owners association. The Dave and Cora Major operation generated for us more affluent, better-educated buyers, many of whom found the mood of the resort to their liking. They enjoyed being a part of this challenging experiment. Some had paid hard cash for lots when there was nothing to see but the stand of trees on their property. The mood among the property owners was positive. They were ready to participate in the beginnings of their new community.

We set up a board of directors and the property owners met annually to vote for three members to represent them on the seven-member board. Even though everyone knew that our corporation still made all the vital decisions and legally controlled the POA, the owners were happy to have an opportunity to give their input. We held back and let the three owner members make the necessary decisions in all but a very few instances. The POA's annual dues were kept low and we subsidized their operations to keep them so. Their annual financial statements and tax returns were done by professional external auditors to assure members that everything was on the "up and up."

Our POA staff, George Baranik in particular, worked tirelessly to resolve problems that would crop up among members of this close community. He and I also encouraged the more responsible POA members to stand for election to the board. The more reasonable property owners were encouraged to join the various committees and take charge of community affairs. My role was to encourage property owners to take an interest in the POA's operations and participate in community affairs. We established committees for architectural approvals, security, and recreational activities and for managing the clubhouse, swimming pool, tennis courts and other amenities. We informed the membership of the problems the community faced and sought their participation in resolving them.

Here is a story about a petty problem we experienced and the risks I personally, often foolishly, ran. Glendale was a "gated community." The gate was a simple wooden pole that would be automatically raised by a small motor when members drove up to it and punched the correct code into the touch pad. It was not a very sturdy pole and could be easily broken if one wanted to get through but did not have the code. Members who were delinquent in their POA dues would not be given the code until they made some settlement agreement. Often, particularly on Friday nights, when most weekenders would arrive, we found that someone would break the gate.

One particular Friday, I finished my work at the office just as it was getting dark. I thought it might be useful to lie in wait at the gate and perhaps surprise the person who was breaking our gate. One of the property owners who lived near the gate had a very large and vicious dog. Just to feel a bit safer, in case of a possible confrontation, I took along my .22 caliber pistol. I parked my car some distance from the gate and walked back to hide behind some trees. The dog sensed my presence and howled and barked for a while until he heard no further movement.

And there, in the dark, I waited. For a while, the gate operated without any hitches as POA members arrived and used their code to open it. I was getting bored and began to realize this was not a very good use of my time. Suddenly, I heard a car approaching the gate very fast, jam on its brakes and stop. Two teenaged girls hopped out of the car while their boyfriends stayed inside. The girls went into the woods near the gate—barely ten feet from where I was standing—pulled down their pants and proceeded to relieve themselves. One called to her boyfriend and said, "That beer is just running right through me!" At that point, I realized that if either of these girls sensed my presence, they would scream, their boyfriends would come out of the car, wrestle me to the ground and the headline in the papers next morning would be, "Armed land developer attacks two teenaged girls in woods."

I remained very still until the girls finished their business and returned to their car, which sped off down the road. Then I concluded that I was too old for such nonsense and resolved, henceforth, to restrict my work to the office.

POA matters worked well for about ten years. In 1985, a small group of members organized a committee to push me out of my paternalistic role. They hired an attorney and threatened to file suit to force me to give up control. I was incensed and ran to our local attorney, Dino Persio, who over the years had been helping me keep my head above water. I remember our meeting in his office and my bitter, weepy tales in which I sought his sympathy. I railed against the actions of "these ingrates, after all I have done for them." Dino, who was privy to all of my *Perils of Pauline* stories and my constant fear of having the project go belly-up, just heard me out and laughed. He said, "You know Lu, the project must be getting close to reaching the threshold of success. These guys are trying to take it away from you. They must think it's worth the effort."

The committee's efforts eventually atrophied and our role in running the POA continued. But my feelings were wounded and I paid less and less attention to the POA. That was a mistake. By this time, the membership had passed the one thousand mark. Annual meetings were sparsely attended and the "empty barrels" began to sound off and get themselves elected to the board, which drove out the more reasonable members. The only time we had an attendance that exceeded fifteen percent of the membership was when we proposed raising the annual dues so the POA would not need our subsidy and would become self-supporting. Then there was frenzied activity and opposition to the proposed increase. Eventually, I was successful in amending the POA by-laws to provide for an automatic annual three percent yearly rate increase, subject to the decision of the board of directors.

During my last years, I made an effort to convince the membership it was in their interest to buy the water and sewer systems from me. I was not successful in doing so and in 2008 these utility systems were sold to the local municipalities.

BANKING AND CREDIT

I had raised $110,000 in equity from my shareholders (myself included) and had purchased $150,000 worth of land. My deal for the last nine hundred acres was to pay most of the purchase price after two years while having full freedom to start land improvements right away. Now I needed bank financing to meet my front-end costs. I figured I could subdivide the first section of lots and begin sales, thus generating cash to keep going with an additional $40,000. Every town had at least one small neighborhood bank. After getting some introductions from the local lawyers who did the closings on my land purchases, I began to make the rounds to seek financing.

In all, I made about twenty presentations to the boards of local banks in the Blair County-Cambria County-Indiana County areas before one banker made me an offer for a $40,000 loan. That was Bill White, president of what was then known as the Ebensburg National Bank. Joan and I had to pledge all of Glendale Corporation's assets, our personal guarantees and all of our personal assets as collateral for this loan. It was the autumn of 1970. Wow! "Now comes the easy part," I thought. "We will do our construction and begin selling lots in the spring of 1971."

We were able to do that. However, with the buyer paying only fifteen percent as down payment, the rest scheduled over five years, while the marketing costs alone came to thirty percent, I began to notice a small problem. We were holding our own "paper," and our bookkeeper was also handling monthly collections. It became obvious that our cash would not hold out, no matter how efficiently we did the preliminary construction and surveying to provide the sales people with new inventory. Even so, the lots were not developed. These buyers were true pioneers, betting that our company would deliver what it had promised. None of the local banks would consider buying our paper. Finally, I located a bank in Philadelphia (First Pennsylvania Bank) to buy our paper on very onerous terms. The bank would do a credit check on the buyer and would only take those with the best credit. Interest was set at fifteen percent; we were required to guarantee full recourse in case of buyer default and the bank would hold back fifteen percent as a default escrow. It was the best deal we could get and I grabbed it.

We kept looking for "the threshold," the point when we would have completed all of our construction, paid our debts and swept in the profits with the remaining sales. But somehow that day seemed to get further out into the future. Over the next ten years, as we built more and more facilities at the resort, Bill White gradually increased our credit line to $450,000. We needed additional funds for such improvements as a sewerage treatment plant, collectors, water wells, purification systems, distribution lines, club houses, swimming pools, roads, etc.

By the time of Ronald Reagan's election, we were in serious debt. Paul Volker's appointment as chair of the Federal Reserve and the brutal interest rate increases meant to curb inflation caused our variable rate bank loan to climb to 22 percent, with interest payments due every month. The interest rate on the paper we were generating could not reach a level that would be satisfactory to both the buyer and the bank. We returned to holding our own paper. We scaled back on construction plans, building only what was absolutely necessary to produce adequate inventory for the sales group. During the summer, when sales were being made, we were able to handle the cash flow. But when winter came and sales stopped, I could not find enough cash to both meet the company's carrying costs and make interest payments to the bank. I then went to my shareholders and asked those with the means to do so to make some short-term loans to the company. That helped for a while and got us through the 1982-1983 winter.

The following year, I had no choice but to go to the bank and ask for an accommodation. Bill White had retired by then. The executive vice-president, a kind man named Rummel, said he could not do it. I then took the keys to our offices and other facilities out of my pocket and laid them on his desk, telling him that I had to give up. He could just take it over.

There was no need to foreclose; I would just give him the project. That caused a bit of turmoil. The following week, a team from the bank came to the project and we worked out a deal whereby the bank finally agreed to buy our paper and advanced us the funds to get through the winter.

I asked Bill White (he was still chairman of the bank's board and I maintained a personal friendship with him) why had the bank, in the winter of 1983-84, been so strict in dealing with my needs. He told me the auditors from one of the bank's regulatory agencies—the Comptroller of Currency or the Federal Reserve, I no longer recall—had recently classified our loan. I was not sure what that meant. He explained that when bank auditors look over the bank's portfolio of loans, and conclude that one does not meet their idea of a safe risk, they "classify" the loan. That puts the bank's officers on notice that this may be a troubled loan. The bank is required to put aside reserves on its books in case the loan goes into default. I expressed my deep sadness that I might have caused him some difficulties due to his sympathetic dealings with me. He brushed that off, telling me, "Banks like to lend money to those who do not need it. But any bank that has no classified loans on its books is not fulfilling its responsibilities to the community it is supposed to serve. If they only take the safe stuff, and step aside when a marginal project comes along, it does the community no good. Banks must support the entrepreneurs." I will never forget those words and often wonder what today's megabanks' CEOs, sitting in their Wall Street offices, knowing nothing of the communities they are supposedly serving, would think of these comments. It is one of the key reasons I believe that a small businessperson could not undertake this kind of project today.

Another of Bill White's pearls of wisdom was a comment he made about potential borrowers who come into the bank and present their project. Today, when someone presents a business plan, the number crunchers take it apart, enter the data into a computer and grind out the ratios. If it fits the bank's criteria, it is approved. If not, it gets rejected. In Bill's case, when someone would make the pitch, one part of his brain would look at the person and ask, "Is this person going to repay me?" That is what banking should be all about. In fact, banking trends in the United States have moved in another direction entirely. Small banks are merging or being bought up by larger ones. As the decision-making levels are moved up, closer to the headquarters and away from the community being served, the service has become more rigid. Persons that have less knowledge of local conditions are making lending decisions.

Then in 1991, Laurel Bank was merged with the much larger Jonestown Bank and Trust, and it was decided that they would not lend to land developers. It was made clear to me that there would be no further accommodation, should I need it. Fortunately, I was able to persuade another local bank, Central Bank of Altoona, to take over my financing needs.

Things got better after that. Gradually we reduced our debt and, by 1995, we discovered that the water and sewer systems, which had been fully built using our operating cash, could qualify for long-term refinancing from CoBank, a semi-governmental institution designed to support agricultural cooperatives. CoBank had somehow decided to get into funding rural utilities. That was the "threshold" I had been looking for. We negotiated a $1 million loan to refinance the entire utility system. We were now awash with cash and could expand our lot inventory as we wished. Our dependence on the banks had come to an end.

On December 5, 2010 the *New York Times* carried an article by Roger Lowenstein about Jamie Dimon, CEO of JPMorgan Bank, entitled "Jamie Dimon: America's Least Hated Banker." He quoted Dimon extolling the virtues of megabanks. My experience had led me to conclude quite the opposite. I wrote the following letter, which the *New York Times Magazine* published on December 19, 2010.

> Roger Lowenstein portrays Jamie Dimon as believing that economies of scale allow megabanks to give the customer more "so much quicker, better and faster." Yet Dimon recognizes that

borrowers of loans that went bad should have been evaluated one at a time, "the way the bygone corner banks did when a borrower got sick or lost his job." He must be aware that the quality of service has deteriorated as large banks acquired corner banks. The sad fact is that small loans tailored to meet specific business needs are too costly for large banks to administer, despite economies of scale. Loans are now standardized at headquarters and offered in cookie-cutter fashion at their many branches. The business of banking does not lend itself to such an approach. We are now in the era of "competition among the few," where most industries are now dominated by a half-dozen major enterprises.

The enterprise I founded in 1967 — with the help of a corner bank — could be set up today only by a major corporation with easy access to the bond market. If that trend continues, then mega-banks will be happy to deal with these mega-companies. In that case, bankers should not be surprised if they come to be treated like public utilities and are regulated accordingly.

Lu Rudel, Past President, The Glendale Corporation

THE LAWYERS AND THE REGULATORY SYSTEM – 1967 TO 2008

Our first farm purchase in 1967 included a very dilapidated, almost uninhabitable farmhouse. Its claim to fame was a U.S. Geological Survey (USGS) benchmark embedded in its stone front step stating its 1543 feet elevation above sea level. That was our first direct benefit from the work of the federal government. Maps indicated Glendale Lake's elevation to be 1427 feet above sea level and the creek at the bottom of our property flowed into the lake. This gave us some idea of the slope of our sixty-five-acre parcel, with the farmhouse close to the road on top of the gentle slope and the grassy fields used to grow crops below it.

A partially blind recluse, a member of the owner's family, had last occupied the farmhouse. He would sit long by the kitchen window and chew his tobacco. Stains from his spittle adorned the walls and the frame of the kitchen window. There was an outhouse behind the farmhouse with a pipe leading to the indoor toilet. An open, shallow well stood about 25 feet from the outhouse, and a pipe from the well into the house hooked to a pump provided the water supply. An old bathtub sat on the back porch, evidence that the recluse had one day thought of enhancing his very primitive indoor plumbing. Our development plan to make the farmhouse habitable included upgrading the indoor plumbing.

We had a contractor drill a deep well and install a submersible pump. Then we destroyed the outhouse and called another contractor to install a new septic tank and leech bed behind the farmhouse. A fine indoor bathroom was created, using the old bathtub from the back porch. No permits, no government approvals from any public jurisdictions, no inspections were required to accomplish any of these improvements in 1967.

The only contact we were required to maintain with the government was for the renewal of registration for the acreage that had been placed in the U.S. Department of Agriculture's Soil Bank. We purchased the property in 1967, and received government subsidies until we left India in 1970. The attorney who acted as our agent while we were overseas would inquire of us each year, "So...Lu, What is it you are not growing this year? Do we apply for potatoes ... or corn?"

Eventually, we decided to forego this bit of largesse and planted seedlings instead, under the "Pulpwood Reforestation" program. The West Virginia Pulp and Paper Company supplied the seedlings free of charge and the Pennsylvania Department of Forestry paid for the planting. Today, our farm boasts a nearly fifty-year old pine forest of tall trees, located in the once grassy field behind the farmhouse. We were not the only ones taking advantage of these programs. So far as we knew, no one in the community complained about the "big government's" intrusion into their lives.

THE GROWTH OF REGULATION IN PENNSYLVANIA

Before I describe my experience with the changes that have occurred in the scope of government regulation during the past 45 years—many of which both positively and negatively affected the development and operation of the Glendale Yearound Resort—allow me to disclose to you, dear reader, my own attitudes and conclusions on this subject so that you may be wary of my prejudices as you read this.

I have personally seen government wonderfully carry out certain of its assigned tasks. For example, the Marshall Plan, an enormously complex program with many potential pitfalls, was an undisputed success in restoring Europe's economies. The early foreign aid programs, say from 1946 to the beginning of the Vietnam era, also boast outstanding achievements in balancing the efforts of the Soviets' international programs, so as to avoid having the former colonies fall into the Soviet orbit while contributing to the well being of a large number of the world's poor.

During the Great Depression, the New Deal made outstanding accomplishments. For example, the Rural Electrification Administration quickly brought electricity into America's farmlands and made it profitable to do so, over the objections of the U.S. power companies.[17]

The war effort during World War II is another example of impressive governmental performance. I have heard veterans argue as to which branch of the military decisively "won the war." Was it the Marines? The Air Force? The Navy? The Infantry? I believe the credit really goes to the Quartermaster Corps. We out-produced the Axis powers. We built B-17s faster than they could shoot them down. Our greatest achievement lay in organizing the nation's logistics to support our military through the War Production Board and other federal organizations.

Government has been shown to perform well under certain circumstances. Globalization and the evolving oligopolistic structures of industries

---

17 See Robert A. Caro, *The Years of Lyndon Johnson, Means of Assent* (New York: Vintage Books 1990), pages 251 ff, for a well-researched description of that program.

and financial institutions now give us little choice but to continue expanding the government's jurisdiction at different levels and adding to its regulatory power. Powerful government is the only available counterbalance to check on the increasingly concentrated and therefore market-dominant producers. This makes it absolutely essential to reform the U.S. electoral process so that candidates for political office are not beholden to the corporate sector for their campaign contributions. It also makes it of critical importance for the bureaucracy to be efficiently and effectively managed.

The pertinent questions have to do with <u>how</u> to develop a competent and effective government regulatory system. How does government recruit, train and retain staff at the journeyman levels (GS-12 to 14) that are able to figure out the schemes of, and effectively regulate corporate titans like GE's Welch and JP Morgan's Dimon, without smothering their initiative and innovation?

Perhaps we can learn something from an analysis of those government programs that worked well, and then contrast them with those that have been shown to impede the private sector's sound management, to get things right. I do not pretend to be an expert in the fine art of public administration. Still, I hope my experiences will provide those knowledgeable in this field grist for discussion to help them address these questions.

THE REGULATORS

Our experience dealt with federal, state, county and township jurisdictions as follows:

> <u>Pennsylvania Department of Environmental Protection</u> (PADEP): This very powerful state agency had a Cambria County office located in Ebensburg to handle the small stuff and a regional office to do the serious business. Cambria County was initially assigned to the Williamsport regional office but a reorganization in the 1980s reassigned the county to the Pittsburgh office.

The U.S. Department of Housing and Urban Development (HUD) was tasked with implementing the new 1967 legislation dealing with interstate land sales. It created the Office for Interstate Land Sales Registration (OILSR) in 1968. We registered and met the legal requirements of full disclosure for consumer protection in 1971.

The Pennsylvania Department of Parks was an important agency for us since we bordered Prince Gallitzin Park. The department had a strong interest in protecting the watershed that flowed into Glendale Lake, the 1600 acre lake built by Pennsylvania in 1961 and located inside the park.

The two townships—Chest and White—in which we were located had jurisdiction of all land subdivision approvals.

The Cambria County government played an increasing role over time in the regulatory framework affecting our project. The relevant departments include the Planning Commission, the Property Tax Assessment Office, and later in 2000, the on-site sewerage permit unit.

The Pennsylvania Public Utility Commission (PAPUC) regulated all aspects of construction, operation, rate-setting and customer rights dealing with the water and sewerage companies, beginning with their incorporation in 1973.

The USDA Soil Conservation Service managed the subsidy land bank programs in 1967. But, by the 1990s, it had jurisdiction over issuing permits for all construction involving earth disturbances greater than about half an acre.

The Pennsylvania Fish Commission: All waterways in Pennsylvania belong to the state. Any stream crossing requires a permit from them. It also issues fishing licenses and monitors fishing practices.

Environmental Protection Agency (EPA): Most regulatory tasks covering the water and sewerage companies were handled by the

PADEP, but in later years, some jurisdictional issues, mostly about testing drinking water, were handled directly by EPA's office in Philadelphia.

These were the actors. To deal with many of these organizations, we found it necessary to retain either a licensed engineer or an attorney, often both. Indeed, some agencies will not talk directly to the operator without counsel. This adds to the cost of doing business. All such costs are passed on to the consumer.

One particularly egregious practice instituted by several government agencies is the charging of large fees for permits that they are responsible to issue to businesses. This practice was instituted to offset the ever-increasing costs of government operations, but it has created the wrong incentive for bureaucrats responsible for its management. Rather than strengthen the bureaucrat's public service oriented mindset, it encourages them to see themselves as a "profit center" to raise as much revenue as possible for the regulatory agency. Moreover, the permit issuer becomes a monopoly, setting the permit price as high as it chooses. The federal National Pollutants Discharge Elimination System (NPDES) permit, which we required for our sewer system, now has a price tag of $7,500.

Annex 12 to this volume provides a few stories about our dealings with these agencies and how their power, jurisdiction and behavior changed during the forty-year life of this enterprise.

AMERICA'S LAWYERS

Allow me to add to this personal confession my view about lawyers and my experiences with them. Notwithstanding all of the lawyer jokes, we should truly cherish, support and take pride in our legal and judicial system. One cannot survive the regulatory process without them and I was extremely fortunate to have found and retained excellent lawyers. But even the best of them sometimes go off in an unproductive direction, for which the client is charged the same outrageous rate as though they had done the right thing. It would be nice, if it were possible to force one's lawyer to follow their client's guidance but even the best of them will not always do that. A law firm that represented me on a major issue once asked if I could suggest improvements to their operations. My advice was to set up a pillory in the reception area, and place in it, for a set period of time, any lawyer who did not follow his client's instruction.

Furthermore, when I consider my experiences as a development change agent in less developed nations, I find that a reliable, honest judiciary and supporting lawyers operating in a corruption-free system are a prerequisite to effective and rapid economic growth. Many of my colleagues argue that aid donors should not hold recipients to their own high standards or governmental structure. They truly believe that development aid can be effective even in corrupt societies. I do not share that view.

THE LOCAL COMMUNITY

When we purchased our first farm in Cambria County in 1967, I confess to being uncertain about how we would fare in the northern edge of Appalachia, a very poor area of the country. I was a city boy and wondered whether my value system would clash with the community. Still, our travels and exposure to other societies had taught us to be more accepting, less judgmental of other peoples' values and behavior. We realized we had to look at the local culture in a similar way.

I liked a lot of what I saw. First, the landscape was beautiful. Rolling hills, farms and woodland, well manicured with a newly built lake inside a magnificent state park. A lot of pride was evident in the people we met, in what seemed a cohesive community. There was a sense of being at one with nature. While we did not find it easy to get close to any of the locals, there was never a sense of rejection or exclusion. It was only later that we began to understand the deep differences in our respective value systems.

Some of the differences were attractive. There was a strong work ethic. A few locals would try to "game the system" by taking advantage of various government programs, but they were held in low esteem by the others. When I hired personnel and asked them to do a job for me, they worked, whether I was watching them or not. During the forty-years I spent developing Glendale Yearound, employees and locals had all sorts of opportunities to rip me off. But there was only one occasion when this occurred; someone made off with three hundred dollars from company funds.

The area was officially classified as economically depressed. I cannot think of another enterprise of similar magnitude that was started in the area during our forty years there. Large state subsidies supplemented the local property taxes collected to fund the schools. Even so, there was huge local resistance to enhancing their educational system. Much of the school budget was devoted to building sports stadia, and training their teams in football, baseball and basketball. Not much attention was given to academia, and certainly not to the arts. Youth left the area after graduation, ill equipped to fill high paying jobs, looking for low paying jobs elsewhere because none existed for them locally. The elderly would return to retire because of the favorable tax structure. Pennsylvania's corporate income tax rate is still ten percent while the personal rate is just over three percent. That tax structure makes the voters happy on election day but it discourages job creation.

Hunting is an important pastime. The first day of hunting season is looked upon as a holiday. The resort did cause some local upset because we were taking land that had been used by local hunters. I will permit myself to tell only one story about hunting.

After hiring Maurice Lechene, a local farmer, as our first employee in 1970, he became my guide and ambassador as I tried to link up with other local residents. One day, while he and I were walking on the road, another farmer drove by and stopped. Maurice introduced me to him as "the guy who is going to develop these lands." The farmer was very friendly and the first question he asked me was, "Do ya hunt?" Actually I don't shoot, but in India I had accompanied some hunters with a camera. I was worried about answering truthfully for fear that would get me labeled a sissy. So I said I did. His next question was, "So...whaddaya hunt?" The locals would hunt deer, grouse, turkey, etc. and I did not want to get involved in a conversation about how to dress a deer after shooting it. So I replied, in my best Jim Corbett voice, "Well, ...I hunt cats!" "Cats?" he asked. "Yes," I said, "You know, tiger, cheetah, leopard... that sort of thing. I use my 30.06, single-action. Then, if I miss, I've got my machete!" That ended the conversation and he drove off.

During the early years, I would spend a five-day workweek at my air conditioned office at the State Department, often reviewing a message prepared by others, sometimes drafting a memorandum to sort out a problem or review a policy in a far off land. Then, on Friday evening, I would get into my car and drive to the resort to deal with its problems of the past week. I would review the pending sales, check out the lot inventory for sale next week, and look over the progress made by the construction crew. Fortunately, I had a smart, dedicated and energetic head of construction named Bill Barnhart. He lived just a few miles down the road, had worked in Harrisburg at a water authority and was exceptionally skilled operating heavy equipment. I can remember our regular Saturday morning conversations when he would report on the work accomplished or not accomplished. "Well," he would say, "we didn't get done what we had planned this week. The backhoe broke down; we needed a part that had to come from Cleveland. Then we ran into rock and had to blast. I only put in 750 feet of sewer line instead of the 1200 we had planned. But I'll try to make it up next week." I would listen to him and think, "This guy is apologizing to me for not getting that line put in as fast as we planned. Those 750 feet of pipe are going to lie in the ground and do service for a hundred years; I got paid by the tax payer for writing a memo and it took about the same length of time. Maybe I should be apologizing to him."

In the land development industry, it is an article of faith that all resorts will develop friction with the local community. It has much to do with diverging income levels and exclusivity; the fact that a gate keeps non-owners out and that the members are "foreigners" or non-locals and come from big cities. That did not happen with Glendale Yearound until the resort was about twenty years old. There was always an undercurrent that I was an outsider and was getting wealthy by taking away their hunting lands, but only a minority held those thoughts. But then, just around the same time the POA began to feel I was ripping them off and demanded more control over their community operations, we found some open hostility from the locals. It had to do with our water and sewer utility systems, which we had built in the 1970s, and were now serving about 1,200 customers, reaching the system's maximum rated capacity.

THE FINAL BATTLE

Our water system began in 1973 with a single well and a storage tank. It was continually upgraded as needed, to add additional raw water sources and storage capacity as well as treatment facilities. The sewer system, also installed beginning in 1973, comprised of a treatment plant with a rated capacity of forty thousand gallons per day. In 1973, that was considered adequate for the resort's projected future needs. But as new homes and campsites were sold and added to the system, the flows increased. Even though our resort had lots of seasonal occupants, the flow during peak season days was reaching the plant's capacity. I got our engineer to draw up plans for a new treatment plant at about four times the existing plant's rated capacity.

In the meantime, outside our resort, the only small package sewerage plants in the area were serving the state park and the nearby school complex. Everyone else used on-site septic systems. The DEP had been getting increasingly tougher on installation of on-site systems, raising the standards, and thereby the installation costs. Also, some residents who owned larger parcels of land had watched Glendale Yearound grow and decided they too wanted to reap the benefits of subdividing their property. One of them was the local state assemblyman; another was a local evangelical preacher. They decided to form an "Authority" (the Glendale Valley Municipal Authority or GVMA) and seek government financing to build a very expensive and large system for the entire northern portion of the county around the park. It should not be a big surprise if I report that they were able to gain government approval and funding for their project.

Having secured a sizable commitment from the USDA's Rural Utility Service, they tried to force our resort to link its system to theirs by stopping the expansion of our treatment plant. That would put all of the resort's residents into their customer base and would seriously improve the economics of their project. And I would have gladly sold the utilities to the authority. But they seemed to think I should just have given them my systems, together with the customers to whom our system was connected. They were not prepared to buy the collectors.

The utility systems provided the only profit we made from the project. We had paid cash from our lot sales revenues to construct them, and we depended on the eventual sale of these assets to provide our return on the project. From 2000 to 2008, we were at constant war with the local community as they maneuvered to force us to join their planned system on their terms. During the entire period, representatives of the newly created authority never came to seek my advice or engage in a meaningful dialogue to resolve these issues.

Here are some numbers that shed a bit of light on the problem. The sewer system serving our resort had an original construction cost of about a thousand dollars per customer (a little less for camp-sites; a little more for home-sites). The new system, as approved by USDA in 2004, was to cost $18 million of which half would be a grant and the other half a very low interest forty-year loan. It would serve only 850 customers. That came out to more than $21,000 per customer. Our tax dollars at work!

Now, if the locals could add 1200 customers to that system at no cost, … well … that would help a lot. Not only that, but they would be getting those rich people inside the resort to subsidize the operating cost and amortization of those customers who lived outside it.

Every effort I made to meet with GVMA's senior representatives was rebuffed. There was no interest in having a conversation to find a way to settle on mutually satisfactory terms. We spent a great deal of money in legal fees to stop this effort at grand theft in the public interest. Finally, when the scheme's local promoters realized they could not force us to do as they wished, they purchased our sewer system and also our water system at a reasonable price. In 2008, we closed on the sale.

At first, everything went well. Bill Barnhart, who had purchased the Glendale Corporation's land development company from us eight years earlier and had been running it very well, was retained by GVMA on a contract basis to continue to run the Glendale utility systems as he had in previous years. But then, greed took over and the GVMA Board began to increase the rates for our customers. Soon, property owners, especially campsite owners, stopped paying the utility bills, their POA annual dues and their property taxes, pulled their trailers out of the development and let the lots go into default. As revenues declined from delinquent accounts, the GVMA increased user rates yet again. Even worse, they began to charge fees that increased the cost of building line extensions, making it uneconomic to continue to build lot inventory for future sales. Barnhart tried to explain to them that this was the beginning of a cycle that would lead to a death spiral. The townships would be held liable for the huge debt that the Authority had incurred without the revenue stream to meet those obligations. Soon the board tired of his arguments and fired him. USDA approved more loans and kept their project afloat.

In 2013, I made an attempt to intervene with GVMA and proposed some accommodation to solve the problem, but was instantly rebuffed. I turned to the local press, the *Johnstown Tribune-Democrat* and the *Altoona*

Mirror, thinking this situation was ripe for an investigative journalist, and provided them with the basic information to lead them to sources that would let them expose this local folly. Both papers greeted my effort with a resounding silence, a yawn. Neither paper is locally owned. They were in the business of selling advertising and were not about to risk offending the local establishment.

THE MORAL OF THE ENTREPRENEURSHIP STORY

To summarize my conclusions from this venture into the world of small-scale private enterprise, it would seem that the need for widespread government regulation of industry is becoming more obvious with each passing day. Everyone agrees that it is essential to regulate public utilities because each one constitutes a monopoly. Our water company had exclusive rights to supply our customers. The customer had no alternative but to buy from us. In a situation like that it is clear that government regulation is essential.

Industry and agriculture in our country, not quite monopolies, are becoming increasingly oligopolistic; with greater influence than their consumers over their respective markets. There are only a handful of pharmaceutical companies operating on this planet. Patents give them a virtual monopoly in many instances. Banks are, or at least will soon be, enjoying that same status. It has been reported that sixty percent of deposits in the United States are placed in the top ten banks, banks that are "too big to fail." A half dozen agricultural mega-producers control most of the U.S. food supply. The challenge for our society is organizing essential governmental controls and regulations in an efficient and equitable manner so that government can manage these responsibilities well. Instead of debating the need for regulation, one should focus on how best to organize the management structure running regulatory agencies.

As a postscript to this saga, once I had terminated my involvement in the business, I wrote a letter to Governor Edward Rendell, telling him of my forty years of business experience in Pennsylvania, and offering my experiences and thoughts if he were interested in improving the investment climate. I did get an answer from a staff member but the effort came to naught. Later, I tried again with Governor Thomas Corbett. That too, was in vain.

As for the profitability of this forty-year investment, my gain was less than the passively appreciated value of my brother Julius' New York apartment, which he bought in 1974 and has used as his residence for the same period of time.

The entrepreneurial phase of my working life taught me a great deal about the workings of the marketplace and the changes that have occurred during my lifetime in its structure. I regret not one minute of it, even though the level of tension in our household got quite high at certain moments. I would not have been content to spend my entire working life inside government.

The ramifications of these structural changes in our regulatory process for the future of our society are examined in Chapter 12, "Conclusions, Reflections and Implications for the Future."

Part Four

Conclusions

12

CONCLUSIONS, REFLECTIONS AND IMPLICATIONS FOR THE FUTURE

YOU PASS THROUGH JUST once. This vehicle of Life has no reverse gear and I have no complaints! Mine has been a rewarding life. I have enjoyed more freedom, more opportunities, less discrimination and anti-Semitism, more affluence, greater life style choices, fewer threats and dangers than any of my ancestors listed in the family record. There was that moment of danger and high risk in 1938, but once I landed in the United States of America, the opportunities offered by this wonderful new land exceeded anything I had a right to expect. Luck played its part in the most unexpected and unpredictable ways. For example, the ceasefire in Korea occurred on July 27, 1953, while I was in transit to the Far East Command. I saw no combat, for which I am ever so grateful.

The three most fateful decisions of my life were:

1. In 1955 I chose to pursue my career with the federal government even though it entailed taking a significant salary cut from my job in international trade.
2. In 1960 I found my soul mate and married her. Joan is a freethinking Catholic. One of the significant implications of our marriage was that our children are not burdened with the unalterable identity of being

Jewish. Joan's interest in the Old Testament and the Hebrew origins of Catholicism encouraged me to pass on to our children and grandchildren my limited background and understanding of Jewish culture, philosophy, and tradition.

3. In 1970 I embarked on an entrepreneurial venture, laying the groundwork, initially by "moonlighting," to create an enterprise to manage after retirement.

I have no regrets over any of these decisions, nor over their outcomes. My timing was serendipitous. The first decision provided, in addition to an exciting and intellectually stimulating twenty-five year career, a pension that has helped to sustain my family since 1980. The third decision, made in 1970, led me to become possibly the last small-scale entrepreneur to enter the land development business and come out intact, a feat that can no longer be executed today. As I argue in Chapter 11, conditions in our society have changed so much that the project (Glendale Yearound) could not be undertaken today by a small business. It would have to be undertaken by a large corporation with deep pockets and direct access to the financial markets.

SECOND THOUGHTS

Three events compelling me to revise certain decisions resulted in profound changes in the conduct and direction of my life. They are:

1. In 1938, my family's intentions to live in Vienna, Austria, and to forsake the applications, submitted in 1935 to emigrate to the USA (at the behest of my grandfather), were instantly reversed with the German *Anschluss* of March 12, 1938, and Hitler's entry into Vienna.

2. My decision to terminate my first marriage and to marry Joan in 1962 constitutes, perhaps, my most important "second thought."

3. In the 1970s I began to consider embarking on a second career in the private sector rather than remain in government service.

On a conceptual level, I have had to rethink and reevaluate another four key ideas in light of changes in global political and economic forces and to examine how they have played out during the past fifty years. These are:

1. In the 1970s my experiences with international organizations led me to reevaluate my earlier advocacy for world federalism. The anticipated decline of "nationalism" now seems far more distant than I would have liked to believe in my youth.

2. More recently, and much to my regret, I have concluded that the consolidation of the world's economic power among the multinational industrial and financial oligopolies has changed the conduct of the free markets so radically that it will require greater and more powerful governmental controls and regulations together with well-managed supporting bureaucracies, to provide a balance to this growing concentration of economic power.

3. I am now losing confidence in the survival of the prevailing democratic political structure. We are witnessing a clash of technological progress with our social order. Our "Bill of Rights" and the civil liberties as we have come to know them may not survive intact in this ever more dangerous, technology-driven world.

4. My own positive experience as regards immigration to the United States has always encouraged me to view immigration flows as beneficial to our society. Yet, I have begun to rethink this "open border" approach in light of the massive global flows that are likely to materialize in the near future.

OBSERVATIONS AND CONCLUSIONS WITH RESPECT TO FOREIGN ECONOMIC ASSISTANCE

With respect to the business of international aid for economic development, my labors have led me to certain observations and conclusions:

1. Development aid has added significantly to the well-being of the world's poor over the past half century.
2. Humanitarian aid and disaster relief have now become institutionalized within the international community and will continue to save many lives each year.
3. Development aid can be effective in any country where it is accompanied by sensible economic policies. The "development game" in which we are engaged involves trying to change things. We are change agents. We want to change certain practices in the aid recipient's society that we believe is causing that society to remain poor and underdeveloped. If we thought their present system worked fine, we would not have to design elaborate projects. We could just write a check and let the present system allocate these resources (as we do for Israel). Therefore, negotiating a project gets tricky because the aid recipients have to agree to accept behavioral changes for the aid resources to accomplish their intended purposes.
4. External economic assistance buys time for recipient governments to institute needed reforms. But economic development must come from inside the society; it cannot be imposed from outside its own borders. How the recipient uses the "borrowed time" is critical. Egypt under Mubarak is an example of a generation wasted. Turkey under Atatürk, on the other hand, is an example of a successful change brought about, actually imposed by Turkey's own military.
5. The justification for continued international resource transfers, when recipient countries and their governments perform well, lies in our own self-preservation as a society. Throughout history, when inequalities

among societies become too severe, violence erupts. Bilateral ODA can be validly justified on political grounds when the donor nation has an important self-interest in facilitating the recipient's economic growth. But this is not a valid argument to justify continuation of aid when the conditions within the recipient country will make the aid ineffective. This high standard need not apply to humanitarian aid or disaster relief.

6. Bilateral aid should be based on specific political objectives, when the donor nation has an overriding requirement to facilitate economic growth in the aid recipient.

7. With respect to multilateral aid, I am convinced that the UN system of economic aid agencies is ineffectual––with the possible exception of the World Bank. Even the World Bank should not completely "get a pass" on this since, as I described earlier in chapter 10, the World Bank found itself unable to continue to deny loans to Egypt following the period 1985 to 1988. It then sent me to design the export industries loan in an effort to justify resumed lending, irrespective of the recipient's willingness to undertake the needed reform measures.

8. An honest judiciary is essential to unleash entrepreneurship. Without that, no one will take the initiative, because the gains will be taken away by the powerful.

9. "National character" is an important consideration in designing interventions and assessing the adequacy of the reform measures needed to achieve the developmental objectives in a given society. Without resorting to stereotyping, there are embedded in any national psyche certain values and patterns of behavior that must be consistent with the reform measures being advocated. While reforms may be adapted to these values, often the values and behavior patterns themselves will have to change so that needed reforms can be meaningful.

10. Education reform is the true key to achievement of long-term economic development. Fundamental change is more readily introduced into the

minds of children. The Wahabis understand this all too well, as they continue to spread their ideology through an ever-widening network of madrassas.

11. Private donations and aid flows to and through nongovernmental organizations and charitable foundations constitute a growing source of funding to support international economic development efforts by recipient nations that are sincerely trying to solve vexing problems of economic reform.

12. Evaluations of projects and programs are generally accepted as a necessary component of economic aid to add to our fund of knowledge about this work. Unfortunately, one often finds defensiveness among project or program functionaries with respect to criticism contained in such evaluations. However, the most important audience for evaluations is the aid managers of the recipient country. In my experience, only China has shown a serious interest in examining evaluations with a view to gaining the greatest benefit from the resources and effort made to implement aid projects and programs.

THE QUANTUM OF AID DEBATE

Is the amount of international aid provided by donor nations the key constraint, or even a major constraint to achieving the MDGs?

There is a growing body of literature on economic assistance that is highly critical of the current approaches to multilateral and bilateral aid and of the management of resources channeled through various aid agencies.[18] This growing criticism directed at the work of the "well intentioned" may seem harsh, but it does not come from isolationists who, over the past half-century, have opposed the very concept that wealthy nations should provide aid to those living in the poorer developing world. How can constructively motivated and knowledgeable people look at the same

---

18 See my 2005 monograph *Foreign Aid: Will It Ever Reach Its Sunset?* published by the Foreign Policy Association.

issues and draw such divergent conclusions with respect to the policies and approaches underlying this vast, annual flow of public resources?

Jeffrey Sachs argues for the donor community to increase the quantum of resources being fed into the aid system so as to bring about *The End of Poverty*. Others like Angus Deaton (see chapter 8 above) and William Easterly disagree.[19] Easterly and Deaton take the position that the present approach is not working and additional resources alone will not do the trick. The different approaches proposed by Easterly and others are not matters of mere academic debates; they have profound implications for the way aid donors might respond to requests for aid.

Easterly posits some basic assumptions that go to the very heart of the way those charged with managing aid resources (the fiduciaries) program and deliver these funds. For example, he points out that the vast preponderance of successful economic development experience lies with those societies that drive that development effort from within. It has been shown not to work when economic development is imposed from outside that society. Easterly refers to this as "homegrown development."

There are lots of desperately poor people out there. If Easterly and others who have played the role of change agents in foreign lands sometimes seem intemperate in their criticism of the aid establishment, it is because they are trying to call attention to a broken system. One has a sense of exasperation that no one is listening. It seems to be as difficult to change the practices of the change agents as those of the aid recipients.

In my view, the decision to provide aid should be based on a rigorous assessment of what the aid can accomplish. There needs to be a quid pro quo requiring aid recipients to adopt reform measures to achieve the intended goals. Absent these actions, the correct response by donors should be to terminate resource transfers. Annex 9 and 10 provide additional material on this issue.

---

19 William Easterly, *White Man's Burden* (New York: Oxford University Press, 2006); Jeffrey Sachs, *The End of Poverty* (New York: Penguin Press, 2005).

Reflections on Our Changing Times

I have been witness to an amazingly productive period of exceptionally rapid change on this planet. My family and I have enjoyed a multitude of lifestyle benefits that could not possibly have been imagined by my parents, or grandparents as they lived their lives in eastern Austria (now the Ukraine) prior to the First World War. I have a sense of foreboding that the affluence and freedom of our present society will not continue to benefit my children and grandchildren.

I recall a toast once offered by a friend who said, "Here's to the world as it should be!" The allure of that toast was that it allowed all participants to fantasize their wishes for the future according to each one's priorities and values, ignoring all internal conflicts and contradictions. But the powerful forces driving today's global events have no conscience. Thus, it may be more relevant to ask, "How *will* it be?"

The Introduction and Overview of this autobiography identifies four overarching conditions of Western civilization that have undergone unprecedented change during my lifetime. These are:

1. **Population growth**
2. **Scientific discovery and technological innovation**
3. **Changing economic (market) systems**
4. **Changing geopolitical national and international structures**

Understanding the long-term trends in these four critical areas can help us anticipate the shape our society may take in the near future, as continuing enhancements in communications and transport technology shrink the globe. I offer here some observations about the changes that have occurred during my lifetime in these four areas, and attempt to extrapolate some implications for the future.

1. The **population** of this planet during my lifetime has increased almost fourfold, from slightly over two billion souls in 1930 to almost eight billion today, and is still growing. The earth has never before been so densely populated.

   The implications of this near quadrupling involve the amount of daily waste generated, the amount of food consumed daily, the rate at which non-renewable natural resources will be depleted, the discovery or development of substitutes and the changes in behavior of the human species. Food demand will grow as populations increase and larger segments escape poverty. Some factors of production, like land or potable water, have very inelastic supply constraints. At a minimum, these pressures will have consequences for the balance of nature and climatic conditions of the planet. Most importantly, these pressures will affect population movements and migrations.

   The table below shows world population data by continent for the years 1900, 1950, and 2000 and projects the same data for 2050.[20]

POPULATION GROWTH BY CONTINENT
(M=million)

Year	Africa	Asia	Europe	Latin America	North America	Oceana	World
1900	133.0M	947.0M	408.0M	74.0M	82.0M	6.0M	1,650.0M
1950	229.9M	1,403.4M	547.3M	167.4M	171.6M	12.7M	2,532.2M
2000	811.1M	3,719.0M	726.8M	521.4M	313.3M	31.1M	6,122.8M
2050 (estimate)	2,393 M	5,164 M	709 M	782 M	446 M	57 M	9,551 M

A thoughtful examination of these data, and their extrapolation with respect to the projections for 2050 suggests that a significant error may have found its way into these numbers. The projections for 2050 cannot

20 UN Department of Economic and Social Affairs – Population Division, Report ESA/P/WP.228, UN New York 2013 World Population Prospects, The 2012 Revision, Page 2

take into account migrations among and between continents that is likely to accelerate during the next decades. People tend to move from overcrowded, poverty-ridden conditions to more prosperous locations in the hope of finding greater opportunities. Estimates of current migration from less developed nations to more developed nations run to 3.7 million persons annually. It is highly unlikely that by 2050 two continents, Africa and Asia, will host more than seven billion persons out of a total world population of 9.5 billion. Almost certainly an increasing level of migration, legal or illegal, will continue to push out of Africa and Asia into the remaining four continents.

Even now, flows of illegal immigrants from Africa are entering Europe at a rate that has alarmed the Italians, who find themselves the unhappy entry point. We only hear about these flows when a ship carrying them breaks apart in the Mediterranean and a couple of hundred people drown.

The United States seems to be slightly better situated than Europe to limit these illegal flows since it has large oceans on two borders. Europe will not be so fortunate and will likely be inundated from the Middle East and Africa. Both the United States and the European Union are likely to find immigrants resistant to integration and assimilation. They may seek to transfer and perhaps impose their cultural values and customs, taking advantage of Western societies' liberal rules of personal freedom to accomplish this. The first priority for the United States should thus be to make serious efforts to assist the countries "south of our border" become as prosperous as we.

Population growth has not affected every society simultaneously or equally. Western nations were at the forefront of scientific and technological innovation and the first to experience significant population growth. These nations have now reached a plateau with some sign of reproductive decline. Their median age is much higher than that of societies that have gained these benefits more recently. In the event of future conflicts among and between these societies, the military advantage to one society from a younger population (more soldiers and fewer non-productive seniors) can only be offset by the destructive power of technologically advanced weapons.[21] Furthermore, the burden of caring for the elderly with a shrinking labor force will exacerbate this problem for the West.

Unfortunately, modern war has not become obsolete. In any possible future conflicts demographics (the median age) may come to play the essential role in determining the victor. The United States has chosen to institute no systems for national service, either for civilian or military purposes. From whence will the United States draw its military recruits? Not from the elderly! Is there any sign of readiness by our citizenry to lay aside their creature comforts and offer to give their energies, perhaps their lives, to defend our society when called to do so? Moreover, throughout history, large populations with cohesive ethnic and cultural ties have always dominated. Is it not likely that India and China will tend to dominate world affairs in the near future?

Ironically, the demographics in China are similar to those of the West. China's one child policy has had some unintended consequences. It has not only changed its family structures – fewer aunts, uncles and cousins – but each child is treated and protected like a prince or princess. China's population median age has also increased, unlike other societies in Africa, India, South America or the Middle East. They will have the same problems as the West.

Human trafficking of women and boys, a despicable form of modern day slavery, will increase in accordance with the laws of supply and demand.

2. **Scientific and technological discoveries (S&T)** Beginning with the early 1800s, S&T brought about the rapid population increase described

---

21   Turkey's President Erdoğan is calling for larger families as a national policy.

above. I once found myself in conversation with a group of medics and jokingly accused them of causing the world's population explosion. One of them said I should not blame the medics. It was the plumbers who were the culprits. The availability of clean water had more to do with the population explosion than did medicine. Of course, x-rays and antibiotics contributed powerfully to improved diagnoses and treatment leading to increased longevity. Recent improvements in food production techniques have, so far, avoided most famines but may well plateau.

S&T discoveries at exponentially accelerating rates have continued to achieve enormous benefits that have improved our standard of living. With productivity gains, an ordinary citizen in our country now enjoys a lifestyle that, in many ways, would be the envy of nineteenth century royalty. A byproduct of these rising levels of wealth is higher consumption levels, thus generating greater levels of waste and pollution.

There now is increasing evidence of a profound clash between technological progress and our social order. Can the soft sciences and our political mechanisms create systems to keep these forces in balance? Recent tests have revealed that carbon dioxide levels in the atmosphere have risen to their highest concentrations in three million years. The environment may not be able to absorb the waste generated by so many humans without disrupting the basic conditions that now sustain life on this planet.

There is growing concern that recent medical advancements may soon plateau or reverse as cells mutate to develop resistance to the new antibiotics. Moreover, some S&T achievements pose great risks to humanity's survival. Never before in the recorded history of this planet has it been within the capability of a few members of the human species to bring about the total destruction of all life.

There is what might be called the double whammy: the threat brought about by population explosion and the affluence resulting from

S&T improved productivity. These two factors may lead us to exhaust the planet's natural resources (water, cultivable land, etc.) beyond the minimum required to sustain the enhanced lifestyles of a projected population of more than nine billion humans. Hopefully future discoveries and innovation will keep up with these challenges but I have my Malthusian doubts. Having witnessed a world gone mad, as I did during the Holocaust and World War II, one may be forgiven for a predilection towards pessimism and a tendency to anticipate dire things to come.

The social sciences seem to be lagging behind the physical sciences in terms of tackling the present and predicted challenges our society faces. Mankind's challenge for the future will be to employ our knowledge of the social sciences to put in place societal infrastructures and governmental mechanisms that ensure that the positive outcomes of technological prowess maintain dominance over its negative effects.

3. The world's major **economic systems** have evolved in a manner that has changed the basic idea of the "marketplace." The socialist experiment in the former Soviet Union has self-destructed and most economies continue to rely on the market mechanism. But the market has completely changed in character. The old market place with many buyers and many sellers has morphed into one that is multinational, with only a small number of sellers. A handful of mega multi-national firms have come to dominate their respective industries and their globalized markets by taking advantage of economies of scale. Their oligopolistic, price-setting behavior tends to exploit the consumer, absent the kinds of government regulation required to oversee the operations of public utilities.

Perhaps equally important, the historic global trends toward urbanization and automation have accelerated. In 1930, the year I was born, 21 percent of the U.S. population was still engaged in agricultural production (down from 40 percent only thirty years earlier) while 44 percent lived in rural areas. Today less than two percent are engaged in agricultural production while almost eighty percent now live in the cities. Urbanization and the creation of the Internet have impacted on employment opportunities for the next generation, particularly in rural areas. The outsourcing of low- skilled jobs has further exacerbated this situation. Also, opportunities for small-scale entrepreneurs are diminishing due to the various changes described in chapter 11 concerning the Glendale enterprise.

Now that Western nations have satisfied themselves that capitalism has triumphed and communism is defeated, there may be greater willingness to adopt some socialist approaches by which government takes on greater and more effective responsibility to protect the consumer. There appears to be a growing awareness that national and international government regulation will need to expand in order to balance the power wielded by global, multinational oligopolies. This is not a new idea. In 1950, William Fellner tackled this subject in his book *Competition Among the Few: Oligopoly and Similar Market Structures.* Even the corner pharmacy has now become a chain. Call it whatever you want. Our economic system has become a hybrid of capitalism and socialism.

In this age of globalization, urbanization, and oligopolistic production structures it is clear that there is no way to return to what has been. Whether we like it or not, bigger government and increased taxes to pay for it are here to stay. However, if we are going to get more government than we want, at a minimum, we should see to it that it is well managed and its functions sensibly implemented. My experience with the Glendale enterprise, and other data --available to anyone who chooses to seek it -- suggest the major challenge for the future is to find a method to enhance the bureaucracy's organizational and managerial capabilities so that its regulatory functions will be performed in an effective manner, with a reasonable balance between government regulation and private initiative.

Indeed, there are numerous examples of programs undertaken by our government that have, in the past, been well executed. Under Roosevelt's "New Deal" a program was created for rural electrification because the power companies would not extend lines to the farmers. The Allies won the Second World War largely because, aside from the "Manhattan Project", the federal government was able to organize our private industrial and agricultural sectors to out-produce the enemy. The Marshall Plan and the first two decades of our foreign aid programs were exceptionally well managed. Somehow, notwithstanding our unwillingness to raise sufficient tax revenues, our government has been able to install a social safety net that seems to protect the most vulnerable of our society. Even during the recent recession with unemployment peeking at almost 8 per cent, few in the United States went to sleep hungry each night. Regrettably, one cannot point to many examples of imaginative and competent management of needed activities within the federal and state bureaucracies during the most recent two decades. The focus seems to have shifted to "pork barrel politics."

Even beyond that, the image of the legitimate role of government seems to be rapidly changing in the mindset of the public. A quest for universal equality, and an awareness of the enormity of our national wealth have translated into a sense of entitlement, as evidenced by the "Occupy Wall Street" movement, to share in the benefits that come from societal affluence and have been channeled to the top one percent. It is argued that government has an important responsibility to correct these societal imbalances. Our laws now provide each societal member, citizen or not, with a social safety net to care for the sick, the unemployed, the elderly, the poor and needy. Rightly so. Governments have a role in mitigating the inequalities among citizens. But our public sector may be taking on more than the country can afford, even if a more progressive tax structure were adopted.

One unintended consequence of these changes is that fewer resources are devoted for the education of the nations youth. The federal and state governments' long standing mandate to provide for universal free primary and secondary education now seems to be taking second place to attending to our society's elderly. Resources are being expended to serve the needs of the aged while our public school systems, for the past thirty years, have been allowed to deteriorate. In 1938, when I entered the New York City elementary school system, I was fortunate to be exposed to excellent teachers. At that time teaching was well regarded as an honorable calling, and teachers were relatively well paid. Today, many schools, particularly in the poorer neighborhoods, provide sub-standard levels of education; many are dangerous places to study. Parents with the means to do so send their children to private schools. The net effect of this diversion of public resources is to exacerbate the very inequalities that have been the focus of the Occupy Wall Street protesters. Children from poorer segments of society do not enjoy equal opportunities in competing for the higher paying jobs within a meritocracy.

4. The **political structures** of many Western nations have undergone major changes in my lifetime. As recently as the beginning of the First World War, all but three European nations (France, Switzerland and Portugal) were ruled by monarchs. And constitutional protection and elected parliaments provided limited checks on their power. Up until 1914, the average person looked up to the tsar, the kaiser, or the king with great awe and respect and was content to leave complicated affairs of state to him and to the nobility. Just listen to Rimsky-Korsakov's *Procession of the Nobles* sometime. The Renaissance occurred under monarchial systems. There was little public clamor at the time to shift to a more democratic system of government. That did not occur until the end of the nineteenth century.

All this changed in 1918 after the end of World War I, only twelve years before I was born. It has been barely hundred years since democratic systems, patterned after the French Republic and the United States, were established in most European nations. Today, authoritarian regimes are no longer in vogue among Western nations and India although still present in China, Africa and Middle East. Participatory, popularly elected government based on universal suffrage have become rooted in the aspirations of most modern societies.

We tend to think of democracy as God-given and eternal. Yet, in all of recorded history, over the last seven thousand years, there have been only two other societies – the Golden Age of Greece lasting about 250 years and the more short-lived Roman Republic – that have come close to resembling our present Western democratic governmental structures.

Humans are one of the very few species on this planet that have established rules to keep predators in check so as to protect the weak and infirm. Only a few species have mastered this amazing exception from the "law of the jungle." In his essay titled "The End of History?" Francis Fukuyama argues that humans have now evolved a system of participatory government that is the ultimate in meeting societal needs and that no further evolution of the political system is required and therefore will not occur. Fukuyama maintains any shortcomings evident today in the operations of democracy merely reflect imperfections in its implementation. He suggests that the human species has now evolved into a yet higher form of life, for which democratic rule has become a feasible and workable governmental structure.

Fukuyama's idea was expounded in 1989, in the midst of our euphoria at the moment Communism and the Soviet Empire were imploding. It is true that Russia has now adopted some semblance of representative government although it continues to show disdain for the rule of law and minority rights. Even China, the last major world society with authoritarian rule, shows signs of moving toward a more representational form.

The Arab Spring is the latest plea or demand by the masses of poor and unemployed for a voice in government. But I suspect we are a long way from the end of history. Our political system has room to evolve further.

Democracy's performance, like that of the monarchical systems it replaced, has been found to be not without its own shortcomings. The ill-informed vote and their votes count equally with that of a qualified elector. The result has been that money raised by candidates to persuade the uninformed has become a determining factor in selecting a nation's ruling class. As G. B. Shaw put it, "If the lesser mind could measure the greater as a foot-rule can measure a pyramid, there would be finality in universal suffrage. As it is, the political problem remains unsolved."

I fear the present trend towards participatory government and the primacy of individual freedoms may not last much longer. In past contests between individual freedom and national security, national security interests have won every time. I cannot imagine a time in the future when personally intrusive air travel security systems established world wide since September 11 will ever be eliminated.

Political structures at the international level also have changed radically during the past eighty years. Principles of government based on national sovereignty had worked well for centuries. But it is now becoming doubtful that these principles can peacefully resolve the multitude of current international problems.[22]

A different, more decisive global governmental mechanism is needed beyond the present capabilities of the UN. The recent strengthening of the Eurozone to meet its periodic crises provides an example that this problem is being recognized. "Failed States" like Somalia and Afghanistan, perhaps soon Pakistan, that are unable to control activities

---

22   See Charles A. Kupchan, *No One's World* (Oxford University Press, 2012). Kupchan believes the world of the 21st century is headed to a turning point, with the liberal Western democracies stumbling and power diffusing. "The emergent international system will be populated by numerous power centers as well as multiple versions of modernity."

within their own borders and allow terrorists to operate, will need to be controlled. The UN with its 193 member states, holding a myriad of international conferences aimed at dealing with pressing global problems, appears to have had little impact on resolving these issues. These threats may force some aspects of national power to be divested to international organizations, while establishing a less-than-egalitarian decision making structure that is more reflective of the de-facto global power structure.

THE FUTURE

The aforesaid global trends pose potentially massive problems for my children and grandchildren. It is as though my life has been timed perfectly to enjoy the benefits of modernization while its consequences will need to be dealt with by the next generation. If God were writing this opera, it would seem that our civilization has now moved into the third act.

I began this treatise with a quote from Abraham Lincoln, in which he expresses the hope for our remarkable nation "… that by the best cultivation of the physical world, beneath and around us, and the best intellectual and moral world within us, we shall secure an individual, social and political prosperity and happiness, whose course shall be onward and upward, and which, while the earth endures, shall not pass away."

It is said that a society, a civilization, goes into decline when it finds itself unable to meet the challenges of the future. These then, in my view, are the big challenges that the future holds.

1. **Participatory Political Structures.** With respect to the pressing political issues faced by the United States today, I can think of none so critical and urgent as reform of the two party electoral system. No serious effort to fix the election process, to ensure that money does not determine outcome, is currently on track. There is something radically wrong with a system that requires those holding political office

to spend two thirds of their waking hours raising campaign funds for the next election. The government's ownership of the radio spectrum might offer some solutions to this dilemma.

Should every living citizen have an equal vote? Some folks take the trouble to search and understand the issues. Others just vote for the candidate whose billboard they were exposed to on the way to the polling booth. Many do not vote at all. Perhaps a weighted vote might prove beneficial, giving those who make an effort to be well informed some additional voting value while also imposing penalties (as is done by the Australians) on those who do not perform their civic duties.

The "gerrymandering" of congressional districts has resulted in ninety percent of the 435 congressional seats being secured as "safe seats" respectively for one of the two political parties, a condition that could never have been anticipated or tolerated by the framers of our Constitution. Congress itself could change this. Of course, that will never happen. Perhaps the Supreme Court will, one day, be persuaded to pass a ruling, requiring states to establish arbitrary boundaries for congressional districts, such as placing a limit of, let us say eight straight courses of varying lengths to demark the periphery of each congressional district. Now that kind of judicial activism would certainly catch the attention of some of our congressmen!

Leadership somehow needs to remind our citizenry of John F. Kennedy's injunction, at the time of his inauguration, to, "… ask not what your country can do for you. Ask what you can do for your country." A form of National Service might help, (with an option for military or civilian service) not only to provide interim employment to youth as they emerge from the school years while they search for their identity, but also to imbue in their minds and hearts the importance of President Kennedy's plea.

Most important, the government's capacity to administer the increasing numbers of public service programs and regulatory functions will have to rise to a level of competence that will allow those functions to be effectively performed.

2. **Communications in an Open Society.** The press, those of the "fourth estate," must bear some responsibility for the breakdown of civility within our political forum. The search for sensationalism has led to an absence of decorum in human discourse and to the demonizing of those who hold opposite opinions. The Internet has, to some extent, made obsolete Mark Twain's cautionary injunction, "Never pick an argument with anyone who buys ink by the barrel." Still that technological wonder comes to us at a price; we have not yet found a way to hold online liars accountable.

The right of the press to ferret out government secrets has not been challenged, but the government's rights to intrude into the privacy of the citizenry has been. It seems odd that citizens' privacy would be considered to be inviolate, yet the government's privacy to hold secrets is not. Is a free and open society capable of engaging in covert operations, shown to have been vital to national defense and political security in the past? If not, how does one deal with the inevitable international conflicts that will arise with societies not so burdened?

Some years ago I raised a related issue in a personal letter to Joe Lelyveld. At that time he was executive editor of the New York Times. The occasion was an article that had appeared in the Magazine section (April 25, 2001) describing an event that allegedly occurred in 1969 during the Vietnam War, and involved former Senator Bob Kerrey. The article described allegations that Kerrey had participated in an action by his unit that resulted in the killing of unarmed civilians. In my view the article, although citing old information that never resulted in any formal charges against Kerrey, destroyed any chance for Kerrey to make a political comeback. I expressed my concern that this was irresponsible journalism in that it had such profound impact on a person that might actually have the capability to be elected to the office of President of the United States.

Lelyveld's personal response, while quite friendly and polite, declared that it was not the job of a journalist to weigh the implications of what might result from a breaking story. I let the matter drop. Several years later, after Joe retired from the NY Times, he published his memoir (*Omaha Blues*). In it he laid out his own family's secrets in exactly the same fashion; a true "believer" in his own journalistic creed. Let the facts take the story wherever they go. The leak to the *New York Times* leading to the Mosaddegh-CIA coup story (see chapter 3) also happened on his watch. James Risen, the lead New York Times reporter on the Mosaddegh story foureen years ago and the one who obtained and published the so called "CIA Coup" history, is now facing jail time for a separate transgression connected with the publication of highly classified material that he allegedly obtained from a confidential CIA source.

While I applaud Lelyveld's constancy, it is my view that this example of journalistic nihilism should be recognized for what it really is, - an extremism in interpreting the First Amendment to the Constitution that parallels the extremism of the Second Amendment "gun nuts" who claim ultimate freedom to bear arms in any circumstance. Any great principle can be reduced to an absurdity when taken too far. A writer's gift with words, combined with a printing press or the Internet, becomes his or her weapon of choice. With respect to the issues of Freedom of the Press, and also the Second Amendment right to bear arms, it seems these worthy principles have been pushed too far by those who can, and do personally benefit from doing so.

This issue goes beyond the traditional press corps. It affects the other mass media as well. As I pointed out in chapter 11, television station KDKA in Pittsburgh used this mantle to enhance its own commercial interests, as well as those of its parent company (see annex 13). The

Federal Communications Commission was totally ineffectual in curbing that abusive behavior.

3. **Immigration**. The population explosion will continue to cause global mass migrations from poor, densely populated regions to more affluent countries. Most Americans will agree that the United States' "Open Border" policies of the late nineteenth century cannot be sustained today. The current debate in the United States is focused on the disposition of the estimated eleven million illegal immigrants that have already entered and are working and living here. That debate should really be about the next hundred and fifty million who will seek entry. We may soon look upon the present rate of illegal migration as a mere trickle compared with what will take place a few years hence. I do not know how to measure the limit of Europe's or the United States' absorptive capacity with respect to immigration flows, but there definitely is one.

International economic assistance to less-developed nations can provide greater opportunities for self-betterment within their societies, thereby reducing migration pressures. For instance, it would be wise for us to assist the other Latin American populations in their quest to become as wealthy as we, so as to forestall such population movements from the south. U.S. bilateral aid to Latin-American nations on a reliable, long-term basis seems to be well justified to support this effort.

4. **Inequality, the One Percent and Government Fiscal Policy.** The current discussion raging among economists with respect to the national debt and Keynesian expansionism has become a dialogue of the deaf. Push Keynes too far and it becomes an absurdity that preaches fiscal alchemy; become austere to the extreme and you will have a depression. The answer lies somewhere in the middle. The *quality* of government spending is at least as important and should receive as much

scrutiny as the *quantity* of the spending. Pork barrel spending is not the answer.

The contrast between helping Wall Street and helping Main Street is artificial. There is no doubt that mortgagees got short shrift while the bankers received generous bailouts in the last housing crisis. However, in my opinion, that result came about, not so much out of malevolence; but because of incompetent government efforts to assist underwater borrowers while the banking community was able to guide the federal government to do what was needed for them. A way could have been found by federal agencies to keep more underwater homeowners in their homes by offering the mortgage holders an alternative to foreclosure; for example, selling the mortgage to the government at a discount, with the government agency refinancing the reduced balance at then prevailing low interest rates. The Left was preoccupied with trying to punish predatory lenders rather than solving homeowners' problems in a timely manner. The focus today continues to be on reducing the power and wealth of the rich rather than helping the poor.

As a result of my own federal retirement benefits, one thing has become very clear to me; both federal and state governments have a huge unfunded liability with respect to their current and retired work force. I began to receive my pension in 1980. The pension contributions I had made into the system over 25 years were paid out to me within the first fifteen months of my retirement. Pension checks funded by the taxpayer have come to me with great regularity every month since then. And the amount has escalated over the past 34 years to keep pace with inflation. The current active federal work force stands at 2.5 million. All will retire, just as I have. And none of this liability for future pension benefits is included in the calculation of our national debt. The same is also true of the pension structure for most of the UN's international bureaucracy, now estimated to number close to 100,000, plus those who have already retired and are currently receiving pensions. The United States is obliged to provide approximately 22 percent of these UN funding obligations.

5. **The West's Relations with Islam.** One may well recall Islam's glory days of the twelfth and thirteenth centuries when it exercised tolerance towards other beliefs and lifestyles. But today's Islamists seem to be of a more virulent nature. The key to curbing the growth of Islamic extremism might be to disrupt the flow of politicized teachings emanating from the network of Wahhabi-funded madrassas. Additionally, if the West wants to stabilize the economic development process of the Middle East, it needs to find a substitute fuel for oil. Drive down the price of oil and I suspect that other things will fall into place. If that does not happen, the West may be in for a severe conflict that will not be peacefully negotiated. Moreover, we will find ourselves financing both sides of that conflict.

—∞∞—

Lastly, I add a word to admonish those who seem to be hardwired to criticize anything and everything done by my adopted country while, at the same time, choose to avail themselves of its comfort and safety. In Patrick Moynihan's words, "Am I embarrassed to speak for a less than perfect democracy? Not one bit. Find me a better one. Do I suppose there are societies that are free of sin? No, I don't. Do I think ours is, on balance, incomparably the most hopeful set of human relations the world has? Yes, I do."

I do, too, although many urgent problems beg for prompt solutions if we are to allow Lincoln's grand hopes to be realized.

ANNEXES ONE TO THIRTEEN

ANNEXES

Annex 1 [Chapter 3] – Letter *to Foreign Affairs* Magazine dated September 4, 2013, commenting on Akbar Ganji's article on Iran's Supreme Ruler, Khamenei

Annex 2 [Chapter 3] –E-mail to *NY Times Book Review* editor dated November 9, 2013, commenting on Adam LeBor's review of S. Kinzer's book, *The Brothers*

Annex 3 [Chapter 5] – Speech describing the USAID Program to India, by Ludwig Rudel, Chief, Program Division, at Indian Institute of Technology, Kanpur, August 30, 1966

Annex 4 [Chapter 5] – Outline for Export Promotion Commodity Surveys

Annex 5 [Chapter 8] – Cato Institute Policy Analysis No. 253, *A Miasma of Corruption: The United Nations at 50*, By Stefan Halper. April 30, 1996, Executive Summary

Annex 6 [Chapter 8] – UN Millennium Development Goals

Annex 7 [Chapter 10] – A Glossary of AID Jargon

Annex 8 [Chapter 10] – Technical Guidance on Investment Promotion Efforts

Annex 9 [Chapter 10] – Letter to the Editor of the *Washington Post* published August 8, 1996, commenting on several *Washington Post* articles on Foreign Aid

Annex 10 [Chapter 10] –Unpublished letter to *Foreign Affairs* Magazine dated March 19, 2006, commenting on Amartya Sen's review of William Easterly's book, *White Man's Burden*

Annex 11 [Chapter 10] – Ludwig Rudel - Consulting Assignments 1980–2002

Annex 12 [Chapter 11] – Appalachia Project – The Growth of Regulation in the US since 1970

Annex 13 [Chapter 11] – Appalachia Project – Letter to Pittsburgh, Pennsylvania, TV station KDKA in response to their program of September 16, 1979 attacking Glendale Yearound

Annex 1

Letter *to* *Foreign* *Affairs* Magazine dated September 4, 2013, commenting on Akbar Ganji's article on Iran's Supreme Ruler, Khamenei

September 4, 2013
The Editor, Foreign Affairs Magazine
New York, NY 10065

Akbar Ganji paints a comprehensive, thoughtful picture for us of Iran's Supreme Leader and the derivation of his political outlook. Without wishing to nit-pick, there are a couple of important omissions that need to be filled in if we are to better understand Khamenei's mindset and how the United States and the Western Nations can best deal with him.

He describes very well how, like many of us, Khamenei chooses to identify and interpret random facts to support his preferred dogma. His list of "favorite reads" follows that same track but we should not let them mislead us. To identify with a selection of world class literature that tends to reinforce one's opinion that Western capitalism is evil does not, by itself, reflect a cosmopolitan outlook.

My exposure to Iran comes from four years of service (1956 to 1960) on the Iran Desk of the U.S. International Cooperation

Administration, the forerunner of today's U.S. Agency for International Development. I had not been employed there during the period of the Mosaddegh regime but got to know many of the key actors from State and CIA who had served there during the preceding period.

It needs to be remembered that Mossadegh's nationalization of Iran's oil fields in 1951 followed Iran's successful negotiation to persuade the Soviets to withdraw from Azerbaijan just five years earlier. When the Soviets pulled out of northern Iran, they left behind a well-financed local Iranian communist party, the Tudeh Party, strongly supported by the Soviet embassy. This is from whence Mosaddegh drew much of his support and to whom he owed homage.

The Soviets continued to be active in Iran after their departure, seeking to bring Iran into the Soviet sphere, i.e., behind the iron curtain, as they had done to other nations in Eastern Europe. Once Mosaddegh nationalized the oil fields in 1951, the British appealed to the United States for support, pointing out that they had acceded to our request to commit British troops to the Korea "Police Action." These troops were, at that moment, engaged in combat under U.S. command in Korea.

After two years of domestic turmoil and Mosaddegh's unwillingness to negotiate with seriousness for settlement of the oil issue, the Shah ultimately (1953) requested our help in asserting his traditional authority when he dismissed Mosaddegh from the Prime Ministership. Mosaddegh made the mistake of arresting and jailing the Shah's personal representative who had delivered the Shah's FIRMAN that dismissed Mosaddegh. That was the trigger that began the Shah's counteraction, with support from Britain and the United States and what is now called the "coup."

By definition, the word "coup" deals with the action of self-appointed persons to overthrow a legitimate government. In my view the Shah's action to dismiss Mosaddegh does not rise to this definition. The Soviets supported Mosaddegh while the British and the United States supported the Shah in this internal conflict. I believe the United States has been wrongly vilified for its actions to support the Shah.

Ganji accuses the Shah of running an authoritarian regime following the "coup." But when has Iran NOT been ruled by an authoritarian regime? This is the piece of history that seems to be missing from Ganji's essay.

Reza Shah Pahlavi, Mohammed's father, ruled with an iron hand even though a Majlis (Parliament) had been established in 1906 under Iran's new constitution. The country has never had a tradition of democracy. For most of the late 1800s and early 1900s Britain and Russia competed for control over Persia until, finally, they cut a deal with each other in 1907 to divide Iran into three parts. The upper half, adjacent to the Russian border would be Russia's area of influence. The lower fifth adjacent to India would be Britain's. The middle section would be available to both foreign powers. (See P.T. Moon, Imperialism and World Politics, 1926, pages 273 to 289). Iran had no say in any of these arrangements because the imperialist powers bribed whomever they thought were needed to have their way.

The importance of these events is that they are Khamenei's history as well. His current mindset is a mix of his Islamic philosophical training but also his Persian heritage. He is justified in blaming the intervention of foreign powers for most of Iran's problems over the past century although we should not overlook the role played by Iran's corrupt leadership. But the principal culprits who exploited Iran were Russia and Britain, not the USA.

Khamenei demonstrates a forgiving nature when it comes to dealing with the Russians. He is allied with them in their adventures in Syria. He shows a disdain for long established diplomatic protocol and defends the take-over of the U.S. Embassy in 1979 to this very day. He also continues to cause mischief by supporting Hezbollah in Lebanon and threatens the destruction of Israel.

There is nothing anyone can say to him that will cause him to see the West as anything other than malevolent. He likes Howard Fast's novels and Victor Hugo's *Les Miserables* because they support his theory that capitalism is an evil system that causes people to act in an evil manner.

Khamenei is called "the Supreme Leader." Is that not another translation for the word "Shah-en-Shah?" Is there not, in his actions, the same pattern of rule Persia has historically experienced under the Shahs?

Ganji is absolutely correct when he identifies "the decline of the West" as the centerpiece of Khamenei outlook. Khamenei believes he and Iran are on the right side of history. He would be pleased to restore the Caliphate that Ataturk abolished in 1926. No negotiator will ever persuade him that his Koranic system of government should co-exist with Western society except on a temporary basis to give capitalism time to crumble.

However, with respect to the U.S. approach to negotiations with Iran, I differ sharply with Ganji's proposals. If you want to negotiate effectively with Khamenei, find a substitute fuel for oil. Drive down the price of oil and everything else will fall into place. If that does not happen, we are in for a severe conflict that cannot be negotiated peacefully. Moreover, we will find ourselves financing both sides of that conflict. In the meantime, I believe economic pressure on Iran and on its allies (Russia) will delay their abilities to cause mischief abroad.

Respectfully, Lu Rudel

ANNEX 2

E-MAIL TO THE *NY TIMES* BOOK REVIEW EDITOR DATED NOVEMBER 9, 2013, COMMENTING ON ADAM LEBOR'S REVIEW OF S. KINZER'S BOOK, *THE BROTHERS*

November 9, 2013
Editor: NY Times Book Review
New York City

It has always been good sport among certain nonfiction writers to attack decisions taken in a completely different context of time. I want to tell them that some of the very decisions they are now attacking have kept them safe.

The author digs deeply into the secrets of America's foreign policy actions and breezily dismisses hostile provocations taken by the Soviets during the same time period without any critical examination. One wonders why both Kinzer and the reviewer give a free pass to the actions of the Moscow-financed Comintern during the six or so years following the end of the Second World War in countries like Greece, Turkey, Iran, Czechoslovakia, Poland, the Baltic States, Bulgaria, and Yugoslavia. If American foreign policy can be called "interventionist" what should one call Soviet policy in those days?

Kinzer seems to be a leader in a cabal of writers with an anti-American bent that enjoy smearing former government officials by taking events out of context. In the late 1940s and early 1950s the Soviets were openly and covertly supporting the Tudeh Party, Iran's communist party. It is they who succeeded in pressing Mossadegh in 1951 to move against the Shah and the British oil interests just when the US and the Brits were heavily engaged in rebuffing aggression in Korea. The Soviets, and Russia before that, had long coveted Iran's oilfields as well as its warm water port on the Persian Gulf. Soviet intentions were assessed as intending to make Iran another vassal Soviet state, just as they had done to the European Iron Curtain countries, once the Brits pulled out. Iran has a one thousand mile common border with what was the Soviet Union at that time.

Shah Pahlavi was as much an autocrat in that period as his father had been before the war and, for that matter, as is Iran's current "supreme Ruler" Khamenei. The Shah's action to dismiss his own Prime Minister does not rise to the definition of a coup. Our support of the Shah as he asserted his authority has been vilified by those in Iran who would gladly do us harm. Why does your reviewer not treat these writings with greater objectivity?

Respectfully submitted, Ludwig Rudel

ANNEX 3

SPEECH DESCRIBING THE USAID PROGRAM TO INDIA, BY LUDWIG RUDEL, CHIEF, PROGRAM DIVISION, AT INDIAN INSTITUTE OF. TECHNOLOGY, KANPUR, AUGUST 30, 1966

GOOD AFTERNOON LADIES AND gentlemen!

I have been asked to speak this afternoon on a subject which is of great interest to me; the subject of Indo-American economic cooperation. It is a vast and complex subject on which much has been said and written and so my opening remarks this hour shall by nature have to be somewhat selective. First, I should like to describe the composition and magnitude of the joint Indo-American economic cooperation program. Then I will treat briefly some of the accomplishments and failures of the program to provide us with a basis for understanding the third aspect of my talk this afternoon, namely the limitations of external assistance. Lastly, I will deal briefly with a subject that has been the source of much discussion in the press of late (and much of that discussion has been factually and conceptually in error), that is, the conditions or so called "strings" on external assistance.

My visit to your city is really part of an extended journey through Eastern India to visit a number of projects through which we are providing assistance and to discuss with various Indian government officials the possibility of developing new projects. It might be well, therefore, if I described my journey briefly to you because I think it will give you some idea of the breadth of our assistance program.

My journey began in Varanasi where I examined our Rural Manpower Program. The purpose of this program is to mobilize unemployed and under-employed rural labor to undertake labor-intensive public works projects such as the construction or improvement of feeder roads, irrigation canals, water tanks and other projects of benefit to their immediate community. The program provides for the payment of such labor partly in food grains and partly in cash directly to the worker. We thereby create additional employment and make available food grains so that the additional expenditure of funds will not have an inflationary impact.

While there we looked into the possibility of establishing educational programs (films, prerecorded lectures and printed material) to the l.5 million pilgrims who visit Varanasi each year so that they may learn something of basic methods of sanitation, family planning, new techniques in farming such as the use of fertilizers and improved seed, etc., and carry this information back to their villages.

We next drove to Patna where we discussed with the Bihar Government's Agricultural Extension Commissioner his needs for technical advisors to assist Bihar's research program to solve some irrigation and drainage problems currently being encountered in North Bihar. We also discussed the possibility of providing a technical expert to assist in implementing their plant protection schemes and another expert for the development of hybrid maize seed so as to provide the farmer with suitable seed to maximize production on the l.5 million acres currently under maize cultivation in that State.

Our next stop was Durgapur, where I visited the thermal power station which USAID financed under one of our development loans. That unit now has a capacity of producing 285 MW for the Damodar Valley grid, which in turn supplies West Bengal with its power.

We also discussed with the officials of the Fertilizer Corporation of India, who will be putting up a fertilizer plant at Durgapur, their plans for production and distribution of fertilizer to provide the cultivator with this vital input to increase his production. Figuring importantly in that discussion was the feasibility of supplying seed and pesticides through the same distribution channel as fertilizer so that the cultivator may go to one source for all his needed inputs, the need for agricultural credit to permit the cultivator to buy the fertilizer, seed and pesticide and the possibility of repaying his loan after the harvest with grain to the Food Corporation of India at a guaranteed price so that we would find it profitable and feasible to invest in these inputs.

In Calcutta, one of India's leading ports, I discussed the problems connected with the off-loading of wheat sold to India for rupees under the Food for Peace Program. I also looked into the allocation of import licenses to importers of raw material, spare parts, and maintenance items under our non-project commodity import loans.

We also discussed the feasibility of providing experts and training scholarships to assist in the development of Kalyani University's Agricultural College to fulfill its potential as a first rate agricultural university and to provide not only an important center of learning but also to meet its obligations as an important com unity service organization. It is all well and good for outstanding centers of learning to do research, but the results of that research must find their way to the cultivator so that he may make use of them.

Tomorrow I shall proceed to Bhubaneswar to evaluate our assistance program at Orissa Agricultural University. While there, I shall also review our assistance program to the Regional College of Education. As you know there are four such colleges throughout the country, each of them receiving assistance under our program to turn them into first-rate centers for the training of teachers for India's secondary schools.

These are but a few of the joint Indo-American projects in which the U.S. Agency for International Development is participating. Perhaps it would aid in our analyses of the program this afternoon if we looked at these projects under the various categories and groupings and examine the magnitude of resources, which are provided in each of these categories.

U.S. economic assistance to India has, since the inception of the program in 1952, amounted to $7.3 billion (or almost 5,500 crores). In this past year alone (the year ending June 1966), the U.S. provided more than $1.1 billion in the form of concessional loans, sale for rupee payment or outright grants. Now let us see how these funds were used.

The largest segment represents the sale of agricultural commodities for rupees and the subsequent lending of these rupees to the Government of India for development programs. The Food for Peace Program was established at a time when the U.S. had ample stocks of agricultural commodities that were surplus to its needs. Our holdings have reached such a low level that we must now undertake to grow additional commodities in order to make them available for sale under this program. Thus the cost to the U.S. taxpayer now, of providing wheat under the Food for Peace program is the same as if we were providing steel or turbines or generators. The terms of and conditions of our Food for Peace program are now being modified to reflect this change. Last year, because of the severe drought conditions prevailing in India, $685 million worth of wheat, maize and other products were made available under this program. After a certain magnitude, large numbers begin to lose their meaning and so it may be more useful if I explain that under this program the U.S. is shipping about 25,000 tons of food grain daily to India. This represents the arrival of 2% ships per day every day of the year.

The next largest category of assistance is capital loans that we make available on concessional terms. As members of the Aid to India Consortium, the U.S. provides the lion's share (about 43%) of financing made available by the free world Consortium, Other members of the Consortium (Canada, Japan, Italy, France, U.K., Belgium, Austria, Netherlands, West Germany, IBRD and the IDA) together with the U.S. have made available approximately $1 billion per year for each year of India's third Five-Year Plan. Last year the U.S. provided $405 million of capital financing in this way.

Our capital lending program is comprised of two types of loans: project loans (or "visible aid") and non-project loans (or "invisible aid"). Project loans provide financing for a particular plant either in the public sector or in the private sector. An example of such a loan is the Durgapur thermal power station, which I mentioned earlier for which we provided $36.5 million to finance the foreign exchange components of the plant. However, the bulk of our capital loans are for non-project imports, we call this "invisible aid" because the funds are not used to build a specific plant. Rather, the loan is made available in the form of import licenses that are allocated by the Government of India to private and public enterprises to import raw materials and spare parts to keep their plants running at optimum capacity. We believe it is essential for India's economic growth to permit existing plant capacity to be fully utilized for productive purposes. While this program does not lend itself to enhancing the U.S. public image as much as project loans (we cannot point with pride at some plant for all to see what we have given) we are willing to forego this advantage because we believe India's long-run development objectives are best served in this way.

All of the foregoing activities are financed either on concessional sales or loans. The PL 480 sales are paid in rupees (and there are a host of restrictions on the use of the rupee proceeds -- a large portion of these proceeds are either granted to the Government of India or loaned for 30 years). Our capital loans are generally for 40 years with a 10-year grace period at about 2% interest. Even in the U.S. where money can be obtained at a lower interest rate than anywhere in the world, these terms are far more favorable than is available domestically. In fact the U.S. Government, probably the most risk-free borrower in the world, is currently issuing securities at 4.5% interest.

The remaining U.S. assistance programs are provided on a grant basis. Approximately $40 million in the form of special nutritional foods such as vegetable oil and milk powder are made available under Title III of the Food for Peace Program. These commodities are used for an extensive school lunch program and for other programs specifically geared at the vulnerable population groups such as pre-school children and pregnant and nursing mothers.

Finally, our entire technical assistance program is provided on a grant basis. While the magnitude of the dollar expenditure is not great (last year's program totaled exactly $10 million), it financed more than 250 American experts who are assigned to various projects and activities in India and paid for the training costs abroad of some 400 Indian specialists sent to the U.S. for training.

U.S. assistance is programmed somewhat differently from assistance provided by some donors (such as the UN). Most other aid donors will set aside a fixed budget and then respond favorably to almost any request for assistance in any field so long as it does not exceed the predetermined budget, USAID on the other hand, will perform an analysis of the development plan, select certain areas or sectors which we believe to enjoy a high priority and in which the U.S. has a special competence to provide assistance, and then shape a comprehensive plan of assistance around those development goals selected. The total budget, rather than being predetermined, is arrived at on the basis of a calculation of requirements. We ask ourselves, "What sorts of projects and activities are necessary to achieve the sector objectives; how much will it cost to achieve those objectives; and how long will it take?" This requires a very close cooperative relationship with the officials of the Government of India who are charged with responsibility to achieve the plan targets so that a joint program can be developed in which the U.S. supplements the Government of India's efforts by providing resources not available in India. Careful agreement must be reached at the time the project is initiated to delineate the respective responsibilities and resources to be supplied by each participant of the joint project.

Another characteristic of this programming technique is that once a decision has been made with respect to the sectors to which U.S. assistance will be provided; other requests for assistance in areas falling outside those sectors will not be included in the program irrespective of their individual merit. This is the principle of concentration to avoid proliferating our efforts over too large a spectrum, which could result in vitiating our effectiveness.

While our capital loans are concentrated in the "power" and transportation sectors, technical assistance is primarily designed to assist in the fields of agriculture, family planning, science education, and rural manpower utilization. You have probably gathered by now from the description of my field trip what the content of our agriculture program is. In the first instance we offer assistance in developing and expanding the production and distribution system for the necessary inputs that are needed to reach the Five-Year Plan targets for agriculture production. These inputs (new varieties and adequate quantities of seed, fertilizer, water, pesticides) must find their way into the cultivators* hands at a time when he can make use of them.

Secondly, we appreciate the complexities of agricultural economics in a country which has many imperfections in the marketplace. Consequently our assistance strives to assist India to overcome or temporarily compensate for these imperfections so that a stable price for food grains will result which is high enough to induce the cultivator to increase his production, yet low enough to permit the city worker to pay for his daily rations.

In Education we recognize that we are unable to provide assistance in every area of this vast field (and indeed that the Government of India does not have the resources to do all this is needed to build up its educational system all at once). Our assessment, therefore, of the requirements of the fourth and fifth Five-Year Plan leads us to believe that it is most urgent to develop a core of persons skilled in the sciences and technology so that they may engineer, operate and maintain the heavy capital investment which will be make during that period. Our efforts are therefore aimed at improving the quality of science education at the university and secondary school level.

Most of you are aware that your sister institution, the IIT-Kanpur, is receiving assistance from us so that it may perform its role as a "center of excellence" in this important field. Now, I am told that IIT-Kharagpur is striving to be "the" institution of excellence in the field of engineering and technology. I am inclined to think IIT-Kanpur will at least give you some very stiff competition. Besides, there is ample need in India for more than one such institution.

But an institution of excellence requires the sound preparation of its students at the secondary school level, we have, therefore developed a program of Summer Science Institutes to upgrade the existing science and mathematics teaching staffs at the secondary school level and the college level. This summer 260 American instructors cane to India for approximately nine weeks to assist in the operation of 100 such Summer Science Institutes. In all almost 5,000 teachers attended these institutes. It is also important to raise the standard of instruction which newly graduating teachers are receiving during their preparatory training and so we are embarked on a program of assistance to the four regional teachers training colleges.

At the lowest level of the manpower scale we are providing assistance to the Industrial Training Institutes (ITI) by developing a course of instruction for the ITI instructors at the Central training institutes. At the same time we are helping to improve the syllabus at the ITI.

It is perhaps not necessary to explain the need for an assistance program in the field of family planning. We are all familiar with the impending threat of India's development efforts that is caused by the population explosion. Every day the population of this country increases by 32,000 people and these people must share in the limited resources available to India. While we are currently discussing with officials of the Ministry of Health and Family Planning the possibility of initiating a U.S. assistance program in this area, none has so far been developed.

THE ACHIEVEMENTS OF AID

The U.S. assistance program to India began in 1952. What can we say has been achieved during the last 14 years? As I indicated earlier, it is much easier to point to specifics in the capital projects field. One out of every two kilowatts of electricity produced in India today is produced by a power station that we have financed. The U.S. has financed the dieselization of India's vast railway system. We have financed a fertilizer plant at Trombay and numerous other industrial plants throughout India. We have effectively assisted in virtually eradicating malaria in India at a cost of nearly $90 million.

Some of our achievements are less subject to quantitative measurement. We have provided large amounts of non-project financing over the past 10 years thereby permitting a far greater inflow of raw materials, spare parts and maintenance imports to permit Indian plants, both in the public and private sector, to produce needed capital goods for the economy thereby speeding up the economic development process.

Under the Food for Peace program mass hunger has been avoided and food crises have been averted. The added supply of food grains has stabilized conditions in the economy and has provided the government with the time needed to launch its agricultural programs to meet India's food needs from its own production. Last year alone the U.S. provided 8 million tons of food grains to India. One kilo of grain out of every ten consumed in India last year was provided by the U.S. under the Food for Peace program.

LIMITATIONS OF AID

But not all of our endeavors have been successful. Some undertakings have proven to have little lasting effect or have been of marginal value in India's economic growth rate. This is, after all, a very new science (or art) and, as every scientist knows, some experiments are bound to end in failure.

Our evaluation has shown that there are indeed some very specific limitations to external economic aid. In some cases too much has been expected of the assistance: in other cases, the interdependence of our assistance efforts with those of the Government of India has not been fully recognized. The failure to properly coordinate our programs has caused some misspent effort.

Some things are clear; the provision of additional supplies of food grains without requiring immediate cash payment buys time for the recipient government to take necessary action to launch its agricultural program and family planning program. But food grains are consumed over time and, if the necessary but painful agricultural reforms are not expeditiously undertaken, the problem reasserts itself. It is too much to expect such aid to resolve the basic problem.

The same limitation is also true of large scale capital assistance, particularly non-project assistance. The aid temporarily meets an urgent demand and provides an opportunity for other economic processes and programs to be carried out. But in the absence of the effective implementation of these other programs, if the institutional framework of the economy has not been adapted to meet these needs, we can expect the problem, in this case inadequate foreign exchange earnings to meet important demands, to reappear. In fact, given the ever increasing population and the resultant increase in demand, the problem may well worsen during the intervening period.

On the Technical assistance side, external assistance has some very significant limitations. In the first place no external donor can successfully induce a change in an existing institution unilaterally. He can merely provide assistance to an effort by the aid recipient country or institution to implement their scheme, For example, almost everyone agrees that there is a need in India to provide agricultural credit to the cultivator so that he may buy fertilizer and improved seed. Yet it is patently impossible for an aid donor to impose such a system in the absence of the full support and cooperation of the recipient government authorities and their willingness to contribute their resources to the scheme,

Conditions of Aid

It has sometimes been alleged that aid donor countries may impose their will on recipient nations to force them to undertake reforms that the recipient government does not believe to be in its own interest. This leads me to the final portion of my talk this afternoon, the conditions or "strings" on aid. I have found that the word "condition" means different things to different people. Let us keep in mind as we discuss the various conditions connected with U.S. assistance precisely what we mean by the term.

There are very definite conditions placed on all financial agreements (including concessional aid) either loan or grant. A loan is provided on the basis that the loan shall be repaid in accordance with a certain schedule and that interest shall be paid on the outstanding balances. The funds can only be used to purchase some specified commodities, and recently it has been required that such commodities be purchased in the U.S. There are other conditions that assure that the purchasing procedure shall conform to certain normal commercial practices and that the commodities shall be put to effective use when received by the borrower. All of these are conditions to the aid being provided. But most people accept such conditions without fear that the recipient country's autonomy has been undermined.

But the fact is that we impose other conditions on our aid as well. As I stated earlier, our projects are, by their nature, joint projects -- that is we assist an Indian Government Agency or institution in implementing their program. At the time we agree to provide resources and support to a project we ask the other parties to the project to agree to the general outlines of the plan, and also to agree to provide their share of the resources required to complete the activity. Let us take our IIT Kanpur project for example. When we agreed to finance the commodities and equipment which must be purchased abroad, We also asked the Government of India to agree to construct the necessary buildings to house the equipment and to purchase complementary equipment which was available on the local market. I think most will agree that such conditions on aid are not objectionable -- indeed they are desirable to avoid operational problems arising from misunderstanding when the project reaches the implementation stage.

More recently some quarters have alleged that there are political strings attached to aid. Others are concerned that, even though political strings may not exist, other conditions, calling for changes in the country' basic economic policies have been attached to aid.

A review of the events over the last three years will, I think, dispel any argument that political strings have been attached to U.S. assistance to India. I note that U.S. aid to India was provided at ever increasing levels throughout 1964 and 1965 even though the U.S. had been engaged during that period in a war in Viet Nam while India saw fit to criticize us for our involvement in the Viet Nam conflict. I might also note that the U.S. confrontation in Viet Nam is with China, India's aggressive enemy of 1962 that has, from time to time, seen fit to harass India, particularly in September 1965 at the height of India's vulnerability.

It is quite clear that India's statements on Viet Nam have not caused any reduction of U.S. support for India's economic development program, although I must candidly confess that some of our taxpayers are wondering aloud about the reason for such behavior.

In September 1965, during the conflict with Pakistan, all new commitments for additional economic aid (except for the Food for Peace program) were suspended to both countries until peace was restored to the subcontinent. This action was directly in response to the expressed desires of our

Congress, which argued that war was not a basis for arriving at a settlement of the Kashmir problem and that international disputes can and must be settled without the use of force. It was contended that the U.S. taxpayers' funds could not justifiably be made available to any country which was using its own resources to finance military action. Most people agree that the position taken was not designed to force either side to capitulate to the other but rather to bring about a rapid cease-fire. I should also point out that during that entire period, all previous aid commitments to India were honored and PL A80 food grain shipments continued without interruption. While new commitments of PL 480 sales were made on a month-to-month basis, these commitments were entered into in sufficient time to assure the uninterrupted flow of grain. Not one shipload of grain was delayed as much as 24 hours during that entire period, newspaper reports to the contrary not withstanding.

Now let us look at the possibility of "economic policy" strings being placed on aid. In the first place, let me assure you that no one likes to make someone else's mistakes. We Americans are aware of our limited understanding of the problems confronting India's development and appreciate the fact that it is the Indian Government that will bear the responsibility for any policy actions that it takes. Since our expressed interest in India (and the basic rationale for the provisions of such large magnitudes of U.S. assistance) is the support and perpetuation of a democratic constitutional form of government, we would hardly impose conditions that would jeopardize the very objectives we are striving to secure.

In the second place any agreement to undertake a policy change which the recipient government does not wish to carry out can easily be subverted. I can assure you that it takes the most attentive administration to coordinate the efforts of two bureaucracies (the recipient and donor nation) to x carry out a joint program even when the objectives and course of action have received full agreement by all concerned. There is little hope of implementing a project that does not enjoy full mutual support.

There is, however, this to be said for conditions of aid. If we are asked to provide financing for a scheme which we do not believe to be technically sound, then we must defer either to other aid donors or ask that the Government of India finance the scheme with its own resources, I think most people will agree that any aid donor has the right to say that he does not wish to pay for a program he believes will fail in its purpose. Even so, such action is rarely taken, as can be shown by the ever-increasing amounts of U.S. assistance provided annually over the last 14 years.

In summary, Indo-U.S. economic cooperation has weathered many a storm over the 14-year history of the aid program in India. While no relationship between two people or two countries is ever free of controversy during such a long period of time (unless one country dominates the other) it seems fair to state that the relationship is healthy and has contributed to the well being of both countries. I look forward to continued cooperation until concessional aid to India will no longer be required and the Indian economy shall be fully viable and self-sufficient.

ANNEX 4

OUTLINE FOR EXPORT PROMOTION COMMODITY SURVEYS

THE FOLLOWING IS AN **attachment** to an article titled "Towards an Export Expansion Capability" by Ludwig Rudel dated April 1970 and contained in *Proceedings of Seminar on Export Research* held in New Delhi on April 16, 17, and 18, 1970. Published by National Council for Applied Economic Research, New Delhi, 1970.

OUTLINE FOR COMMODITY SURVEY

General

The commodity survey should describe the worldwide supply and demand situation for the commodity and pay particular attention to India 's position in the total world trade picture, and conclude with specific proposals for:

a) investment in the industry which would result in making the product more competitive for export, and

b) policy actions which would aid the industry in exporting larger amounts and earning higher returns.

1. Bibliography

As a first step in performing the commodity survey, the survey team must pull together a complete bibliography of all relevant reports and surveys available on this commodity. The bibliography will be reviewed by the Export Promotion Division of USAID during the initial stage of the Study to be sure that important pieces of information are not overlooked and that the survey will not duplicate work already completed.

2. Description of the Commodity

This section should contain a relatively concise statement, understandable to the layman, describing the commodity, how it is grown and processed, what its major uses are, and describe the most recent technological developments and innovations.

3. Supply

We would analyze, for the industry of each major exporting nation, the production cost structure, where appropriate, for the raw material and for the processing. We would analyze the locations of the industry and its suitability, adequacy of the size, age, technology of the production units, availability of spare parts and balancing equipment, adequacy of cost accounting, and mechanized planning (i.e. e., warehousing - computer solution for U.S. reapportionment problems based on computer solution to DuPont's warehousing problems) and analyze the relative advantages enjoyed by each of the major exporting nations. How does the tax structure effect production and marketing costs? We should attempt to explain the basis on which the relative market shares for each supplier have been determined. We would also examine the relative cost of inland transport, ocean shipping and insurance, and analyze the suitability of banking and financing arrangements for the Indian exporter. Where appropriate, we would also discuss such factors as quality control. We would also describe the investment which has taken place during the past five years.

For India, we would describe the foregoing in greater detail, and analyze the production cost structure with respect to price of raw material (World price vs. domestic price of raw material), availability of raw material, and stability of raw material prices.

The survey should examine, the import content (or foreign exchange cost) per unit of product being exported to arrive at some estimate of the range of foreign exchange costs of the product line being surveyed. Such foreign exchange costs should include not only imported raw material but also a reasonable amortization of imported equipment, royalty payments and interest on foreign loans. If an increase in exports or a given item will require a change in the foreign exchange costs (because of limited domestic resources or addition of imported capital equipment) this should also be indicated.

Such an analysis would provide a basis of comparison between the various commodities being surveyed to identify those exports that have the lowest foreign exchange cost to India.

In describing the organization of the Indian industry for the particular commodity in question the survey should also provide a listing of the names and addresses of the leading Indian producers of the commodity and a listing of the names and addresses of the leading exporters of the commodity.

The survey should also provide, if possible, any information concerning manufacturers of equipment for the producing industry.

The survey should also provide a listing of the non-governmental institutions, organizations, and associations dealing with the production/and marketing of the commodity being surveyed.

4. Demand & Prices

This section would include a market analysis of the major importers, examination of the recent trends to determine elasticity of demand and to make projections for anticipated future demand for the commodity. This section should analyze the price relationships among the various users (compare prices in the hard-currency markets vs., the soft-currency markets) and describe import restrictions and tariff walls around the various markets. Where possible, pricing data for the past five years should also be included for each of these categories and a trend analysis undertaken. Describe any linkages between suppliers and consumers. Is there a vertical integration of the Industry? If so, what are the ramifications of such integration? The survey team should pay particular attention to the availability of substitutes and their relative price.

This section should contain a listing of the leading buyers in the foreign markets.

5. New Product Research & Development

Examine the new innovations and product modifications which have materialized during the past five to ten years, make some prognosis of likely product development and project demand for such products. Indicate who is doing the research and what R&D investment is being made. The team should also consider the existence of substitutes and the possibility of new substitutes being developed.

6. Marketing & Promotion

Describe the marketing arrangements currently in use by the various suppliers. Is there a suitable information flow to provide the Indian exporters with market intelligence? Is this better or worse than the information flow existing for the competitive suppliers? Describe the relationship between the producer in India and the seller abroad. What are the communication facilities available to the exporter (adequacy of telex, etc.)? Are Indian exporters able to deliver on commitments? Do they enjoy a reputation for dependability or for sharp trading? Are there adequate standards and testing facilities? Are there adequate credit facilities or is there a need for export credits? What are the marketing costs in relation to the cost of the product? Can some economics of scale be introduced into the marketing so as to lower the marketing and promotion costs per unit sold?

7. Governmental Control & Regulatory Functions

For each major exporting country, indicate area of governmental control and regulation of production and of export trade. For India, this analysis must necessarily be in greater detail. We must know something about the function as it is theoretically applied, as well as its actual administration. This section should contain a step-by-step description of the procedure following re: production, processing and exportation of the commodity and record the degree of government control at each step of the way.

8. New Investment

On the basis of the foregoing analysis, what, if any, investment decisions need be made with respect to:

a) production of raw material;
b) processing facilities;
c) packaging facilities; and
d) marketing arrangements (including, where necessary direct investment by India in distribution facilities in the overseas markets).

If further investment is recommended, what kind of investment should it be? What magnitudes, and where should it be located?

9. Financial Incentives

This may well be covered under paragraph 2, - Supply. In calculating the production costs, however, if any incentives exist either in India or in the other supplier countries, these should be described. The incentives may take the forms of cash payments, import entitlements, preferential credit, guarantees, tax rebates, or preferential tax rates on export earnings.

10. Conclusions

Indicate here the specific recommendations involving governmental policy actions, procedural modifications and investment decisions for any and all aspects of production, distribution and marketing of the commodity.

ANNEX 5

A MIASMA OF CORRUPTION: THE UNITED NATIONS AT 50, BY STEFAN HALPER, APRIL 30, 1996

EXECUTIVE SUMMARY[23]

The United Nations is under increasing attack by critics in the United States and other countries. At the heart of the organization's mounting problems is an almost total lack of accountability, which gives rise to suspicions of wholesale corruption. Existing evidence indicates that corruption and mismanagement go beyond the routine fraud, waste, and abuse of resources that mark all public-sector enterprises.

UN budgets are shrouded in secrecy, and the actual performance of the myriad bureaucracies is translucent, if not opaque. There is no reliable way to determine whether the various and often competing specialized agencies (at least two dozen UN agencies are involved in food and agricultural policy) are doing their jobs, and many UN activities, even if they are of some value, can be carried out better and more efficiently by other groups. Other activities should not be undertaken at all.

Available evidence coupled with the United Nations' unwillingness to undergo a thorough audit raise serious questions about its mission and

23 Cato Institute – Policy Analysis No. 253, Cato Institute, 1000 Massachusetts Avenue NW, Washington, D.C., 20001. This work by the Cato Institute is licensed under a Creative Commons Attribution-NonCommercial-ShareAlike 3.0 Unported License.

the means used to carry it out. Secretary General Boutros Boutros-Ghali's rationale that the world body is accountable to all its 185 member-states is meaningless. Such an amorphous standard of accountability is akin to saying no one is responsible.

The United Nations is in dire need of reform, starting with a comprehensive, independent audit. Even if a complete audit were performed, however, there is no guarantee anything would be done about the problems identified. And radical change may not be possible, no matter how obvious the need. Given all the earlier, failed attempts to put things right, even on a limited basis, optimism about meaningful reform may be an exercise in wishful thinking.

ANNEX 6

UN MILLENNIUM DEVELOPMENT GOALS

Goal 1. Eradicate Extreme Hunger and Poverty

Goal 2. Achieve Universal Primary Education

Goal 3. Promote Gender Equality and Empower Women

Goal 4. Reduce Child Mortality

Goal 5. Improve Maternal Health

Goal 6. Combat HIV/AIDS, Malaria and other diseases

Goal 7. Ensure Environmental Sustainability

Goal 8. Develop a Global Partnership for Development

Annex 7

A Glossary of AID Jargon

First, some terms of use should be clarified. An **audit**, as we know, answers the question: Were the funds spent as legally authorized? **Evaluations** are broader and usually are concerned with the questions: To what extent did the project or program accomplish its intended purpose? If it failed to do so, what lessons can we learn from the experience? If its objectives were reached how effective was it and how efficiently was it done? Was it well designed? What additional follow-on activities seem to be needed? In short, what lessons have been learned in the course of the project that would provide guidance for similar efforts in the future?

Now let us consider the differences between **country programs, sector programs** and **projects**.

Every **country assistance program** submitted to the US Congress for funding offers an explanation of need and explains what it hopes to accomplish. Goals that have been jointly arrived at between that recipient government and our government are described. The program will often be a collection of specific projects grouped by "sectors", such as Public Administration, Agriculture, Health and Family Planning or Export Development. Each sector will have a set of projects, generally complementary in nature, to achieve a set of sector goals.

The host country contribution refers to a cash or in-kind contribution by the recipient institution or the host government to demonstrate that the project is jointly conceived and managed. Unfortunately, it is often politically too controversial to set forth the policy reform measures that are needed to change some fundamental practices make for a successful project. Achievement of project or sector goals can be impeded if the required policy measures are not taken.

"**Projects**" are specific activities that have a beginning, and an end. Projects have very specific objectives or outputs. Building a factory to manufacture "gidjits" is a project. The effort allows for quantification of inputs and actions from both the aid donor agency and the recipient country. A time schedule when these actions are to take place is created. Expected output of the project can be precisely described.

Several different projects designed to increase the production of manufactured goods for export to nearby countries within the region would be considered a **sector program**.

Finally, a set of projects grouped into sector programs, perhaps including agriculture, health, public administration, education, and manufacturing, designed to help the recipient country increase GDP and reduce unemployment to certain levels by a certain date would constitute a **country assistance program**.

ANNEX 8

TECHNICAL GUIDANCE ON INVESTMENT PROMOTION EFFORTS

FROM TIME TO TIME I have been asked to give some guidance for investment promotion efforts. Here are some thoughts I offered in a note to an officer of the World Bank who asked me to provide my comments on the question of how a developing nation can best promote foreign direct investment. I offered the following comments:

Foreign direct investment (DFI) is sought by developing countries because they want the capital, the technology, the managerial know-how and the international marketing skills that foreign investment can bring. At some point well along the road in the development process it is possible for developing countries to attract portfolio investment by establishing special investment funds that raise capital in the world money centers (Korea, Philippines). For most developing countries today DFI must be sought on a project specific case-by-case basis. Often such DFI requires a local partner who will joint venture the project with the foreign investor.

Often DFI does not flow because the policy framework of the developing country is not adequate. Additionally the perceived risks of such investment are too great when compared with the potential return. The World Bank and other multinational and bilateral donor agencies have programs that address these two categories of constraints. Policy dialogue and technical assistance programs offer advice to developing countries on reform actions that would improve the investment climate. Special guarantees for certain investment related risks are offered by MIGA and bilateral aid donors to reduce the investment risks for firms, thereby improving the risk/return ratios of transactions under consideration.

Even with these incentives and improvement in investment climate the market's imperfections continue to impede DFI flows. Both developing countries and developed countries have instituted INVESTMENT PROMOTION PROGRAMS to encourage and facilitate DFI.

There is a prevailing myth in the conventional wisdom that market imperfections prevent investors from finding out about these wonderful investment conditions in developing countries and that, if the opportunities were revealed to them, they would immediately flock to invest. That is true only in the small minority of instances. Investment promotion programs will work only if 1) the policy framework is satisfactory; 2) the risks are not unreasonable or insurance guarantees are available; and 3) there are attractive credit facilities so that the vast amount of the investment funding will come from locally available sources at attractive rates. Absent those conditions the country's marketing efforts will be like "pushing on a string". Often the poor result of the promotion effort will derive from the absence of satisfactory underlying conditions. Investors have a knack for appraising these conditions and mostly the their appraisal is quite accurate.

My primary candidates for the weaknesses of past promotional efforts are:

- Opportunities for investment have been broadcast widely, instead of being pursued quietly in some sequential manner. This shotgun approach (as distinct from a rifle approach) will discourage the best of the legitimate investors who do not wish to compete as part of the pack.

- Often the promotional effort is not specific, but is a public relations campaign to promote a country. I believe that approach does not work until the word is out that you can "find gold on the streets". That is when country specific capital investment funds can be established to handle portfolio investment. In the meantime a narrower focus would be more effective.

- Investors in developed countries rarely look actively for opportunities, but rather will react if they are approached to consider a specific project. Investors in developing countries who are good candidates for a partnership also wait to have opportunity served up to them. This condition bespeaks of the need for a broker to identify the opportunity and put the two together. Investment promotion programs would be more successful if they used the energies of these existing brokers by providing them with low cost support services than to try to put the deals together themselves. That is why I continue to believe that information and search services to support brokers and any other segment of the deal making community are so important.

Lu Rudel

Annex 9

Letter to the Editor of the *Washington Post* published August 8, 1996, commenting on several *Washington Post* articles on Foreign Aid

On several occasions I was moved to write responses to items that appeared in the press, notwithstanding Mark Twain's other poignant injunction, "Never pick a fight with anyone who buys ink by the barrel!"

Picking Our Spots for Foreign Aid

Every so often, the *Post* publishes an opinion piece that bleats about the shortsightedness in cutting funding for international aid. The most recent article, by Casimir A. Yost and Mary Locke "The Raid on Aid," Outlook, July 28, deals with the missed opportunity to help participatory democracy take root in Mongolia. Previous articles by 'Jessica Mathews ["The New isolationism," op-ed, Feb. 5] and U.N. Development Program Administrator James Gustave Speth ["Foreign Aid for the Price of Cat Food," Outlook, Aug. 6, 1995] have made the same point. But there is another side to this issue.

Ever since the Marshall Plan days, U.S. ambassadors have pressed for "walking-around money" to help them advance American interests abroad. Once in a while, a situation is ripe for that sort of intervention. But our bureaucracy never has been able to distinguish among targets. The State Department makes claims for access to the Agency for International Development (AID) appropriation for every developing nation. If our ambassador in Country A requests funds for a justifiable situation, requests for similar funding cannot be resisted from every other ambassador in that region, lest we appear to slight the rulers of those neighboring countries.

Many years ago, the process became annualized as elaborate budgeting mechanisms were put in place for each succeeding year. This system, as evolved, has resulted in public disenchantment with AID appropriations.

The spate of articles in the *Post* criticizing AID cuts implies that all sorts of wonderful opportunities are being lost by cutting AID appropriations. Those who think so are living in a time warp. What was a sensible program in the 1950s and 1960s, when former colonies were making the transition to political independence, now has become a mockery of its former goals. Now AID programs rarely achieve success, mostly because recipient countries lack a sincere desire for fundamental reform.

Economic and political development can succeed only if directed from within a society. It cannot be imposed from the outside, no matter how much money is thrown at the problem with the best of intentions. Aid can be justified today only to countries that demonstrate a true dedication to serious reform and have definable short to medium term funding needs. If the bureaucracies of the Agency for International Development, the State Department and the United Nations could organize themselves to be selective, current appropriations would be more than sufficient.

LUDWIG RUDEL Bethesda

ANNEX 10

UNPUBLISHED LETTER TO *FOREIGN AFFAIRS* MAGAZINE DATED MARCH 19, 2006, COMMENTING ON AMARTYA SEN'S REVIEW OF WILLIAM EASTERLY'S BOOK *WHITE MAN'S BURDEN*

To: Editor, Foreign Affairs Magazine
Council on Foreign Relations
New York NY

Dear Sir or Madam:

Your selection of Dr. Amartya Sen to review William Easterly's new study, "The White Man's Burden" (March/April 2006, Foreign Affairs) was right on the mark. Both the author and the reviewer are superbly credentialed and recognized authorities on the subject of development aid. Dr. Sen's work in the field of moral and political philosophy, social choice, poverty and social justice has earned him the reputation of "conscience keeper" to the economic establishment on ethical questions concerning the issue whether economic growth is reaching the least fortunate. Moreover, Dr. Sen, a Nobel Laureate, has shown himself, particularly with regard to his work on famines, to be willing to criticize traditional analysis when it is misleading in terms of setting policy.

His review of Easterly's work becomes particularly revealing by identifying the huge chasm that now exists between two groups of development theorists on the current state of play with respect to the development aid business. While Jeffrey Sachs argues for increasing the quantum of resources being fed into the aid system so as to bring about "An End to Poverty," others like Easterly take the position that the present approaches are not working and additional resources alone will not do the trick.

There is a growing body of literature on economic assistance that has become highly critical of the current approaches to, and management of the resources provided through multinational and bilateral aid agencies. (For example, see my monograph published by the Foreign Policy Association last year entitled Foreign Aid: Will it Ever Reach Its Sunset?) This growing criticism directed at the work of the "well intentioned" may seem harsh, but it does not come from isolationists who, over the past half-century, have opposed the very concept that wealthy nations have responsibilities to aid people living in the poorer nations. How can well-motivated and knowledgeable people look at the same issues and draw such divergent conclusions with respect to the policies and approaches underlying this annual, vast flow of public resources?

Sen's review of White Man's Burden depicts its author's disenchantment with "planners" (as opposed to "searchers") to be unfair to the planners. He disparages Easterly's "shotgun summary" and "radical oversimplification in the overdrawn contrasts" but acknowledges that it "...offers a line of analysis that could serve as a basis for a reasoned critique of the formulaic thinking and policy triumphalism of some of the literature on economic development." In short, he damns the study with faint praise.

But the crux of Easterly's arguments runs well beyond the issue of planners vs. searchers. Easterly posits some basic assumptions that go to the very heart of the way those who are charged with managing the resources of the aid system (the fiduciaries) program and deliver these funds. (On Wall Street this is referred to as "playing with other people's money"). For example, he points out that the vast preponderance of successful economic development experience lies with those societies that drive that development effort from within; it has been shown not to work when economic development is imposed from outside that society. Easterly refers to this as "homegrown development".

And he argues strongly that aid be made available to individual change agents within a society, the "searchers". Others have made similar arguments by suggesting that it might be better policy to provide humanitarian assistance to small local entities such as non-governmental organizations when the recipient national government is simply not going to do the needful with respect to aid projects. Such assistance might not qualify as development assistance by the definitions currently in vogue, but it might lead to the introduction of changes that will lay the groundwork for later development efforts. In the meantime it would lessen the suffering of vulnerable groups in the society.

Dr. Sen is right, of course, when he assures us that development aid has significantly added to the well being of the poor over the past half century. He quotes John Cassidy that "aid can be effective in any country where it is accompanied by sensible economic policies." The problem arises when the recipient government is highly corrupt and dysfunctional. Should the donors "just say no" to aid requests from these governments?

The differences in approach proposed by Easterly and others, in contrast to the current norms, are not mere academic debates; they have profound implications for the way aid donors might respond to requests from aid recipients. Easterly suggests that aid provided to "searchers" in a society whose government is not functioning in a way that gives confidence that the aid will be reaching its target beneficiaries, will produce greater gains than aid provided to a governmental entity which might substitute such aid contributions in lieu of needed reform measures or otherwise divert the money.

Dr. Sen must be somewhat sympathetic to this argument because he generously donated much of his Nobel Prize Money in 1998 to establish the Pratichi Trust near Calcutta to support elementary education. He could have donated these funds to the Indian Ministry of Finance, or to the Ministry of Education. Instead, he seems to have chosen the role of "searcher".

There are lots of desperately poor people out there. If Easterly and others who had experienced the role of change agents in foreign lands, sometimes seem intemperate in their criticism of the aid establishment, it is because they are trying to call attention to a broken system. One has a sense of exasperation that no one is listening. It seems to be as difficult to change the practices of the change agents as it is the aid recipients.

One final word about Dr. Sen's selection of the poetry he included in his essay. He cites Kipling's poem, "White Man's Burden", and quotes four lines from it:

Take up the White Man's burden,
The savage wars of peace,
Fill full the mouth of famine,
And bid the sickness cease.

However, Kipling wrote eight lines to that stanza. Kipling's full meaning, which could have profound implications for the foregoing discussion, can only be understood by reading the last four lines as well. They are:

And when your goal is nearest
The end for others sought,
Watch Sloth and heathen Folly
Bring all your hope to naught.

Sincerely,
Ludwig (Lu) Rudel

ANNEX 11

LUDWIG RUDEL – CONSULTING ASSIGNMENTS 1980–2002

April 2002–May 2002

Performed "STUDY OF BANGLADESH CONSTRAINTS TO EXPORT GROWTH - PART II"

The Project Appraisal Document for a World Bank / IDA credit to Bangladesh for Export Diversification (May 10, 1999) included funding for a systematic analysis of the various constraints impeding the growth of export earnings, with a view to identifying actions to reduce their impact.

Part I of this study (2001) undertook a comprehensive survey of more than 150 export oriented firms to gain practical insight into the day-to-day problems besetting the exporter.

Part II of this study analyzed the nature and magnitude of those perceived constraints to growth and diversification of exports in Bangladesh and recommended measures to improve the situation.

April 2000–May 2000

Member of five-person Evaluation Team to perform a midterm evaluation of the USAID Cairo funded EXPOLINK - Egyptian Exporters Association institution building effort to support Egypt's export drive. The Evaluation was performed for the PriceWaterhouseCoopers directed GTG Monitoring and Evaluation Unit in Cairo.

November 1998–December 1998

Leader of four-person Evaluation Team to perform two terminal evaluations of UNIDO implemented institution building projects in India (Machine Tool R&D Institute, and Auto Parts R&D Center, both located in the Punjab). The value of UN inputs plus local government inputs for these two projects exceeded $20 million.

February 1998–March 1998

Leader of four-person Evaluation Team to perform terminal evaluation of the $5 million, four and a half year UNDP funded China Large State Owned Enterprise Reform Programme. This programme supported the Chinese Government market reform effort by divesting ownership in its major enterprises through recapitalization and share issuance so as to shift them from central, command management to market response and competition. It also supported reform of the policy framework within which these enterprises operate.

May 1997– June 1997

Leader of four-person Evaluation team to perform terminal evaluation of the $12 million, six year UNDP funded and UNIDO implemented China Machine Tool Sector Modernization Programme.

March 1997–April 1997

Team leader for Annual Appraisal of Ground Nut Research Program for Latin America, based in Brasilia, sponsored by European Common Fund for Commodities and administered by UNFAO

February 1997–March 1997

Team leader for Terminal Evaluation of UNDP Project IND/91/103, "Establishment of Technology Base (R&D Centre) for Power-line Aggregates". UNDP contribution was $4.1 million with matching Indian Government Contribution.

November 1996–December 1996

Team leader of three-person team to conduct annual assessment of UNDP funded India Jute Sector Modernization Program. The review was intended to examine the effect of the changes made to the Jute Sector program as a result of the mid term evaluation performed in December 1995. (See below)

February 1996–April 1996

Leader of three-person team to evaluate the UNDP funded ASYCUDA program for the former British islands of the Caribbean to computerize customs data and facilitate clearance.

November 1995–December 1995

Leader of six-person evaluation team to perform midterm evaluation of the India Jute Sector modernization program. This is the largest UNDP funded project ($23 million plus an equivalent amount from the Government of India) on record.

December 1993– January 1994

Member of team to perform phase two of World Bank funded examination of economic management structure of the Government of Latvia to improve its resource allocation process. (See below for description of phase I.)

June 1993– July 1993

Evaluation of UNDP Project for Asia and the Pacific Region to install the ASYCUDA automated Customs processing systems for procedural simplification and trade data collection, executed by UNCTAD. As team leader I examined the four-year operations of this project and recommended actions intended to improve the management of this $35 million effort.

April 1993– May 1993

Member of a team, funded by the World Bank, to examine the economic management structure of the Government of Latvia and assess the feasibility of technical assistance to improve the government's resource allocation process as the centralized economic structure is changed to a market driven structure.

January 1993–March 1993

Member of an assessment team, organized by Price Waterhouse Consultants, to examine the Government of Morocco's public sector services with a view to privatizing these services, thereby reducing the burden on public funding. My areas of analysis were international trade, tourism, and the services provided by the Health Ministry.

September 1992–December 1992

Evaluation of AID Core Grant support to International Executive Service Corps for the period 1988 to 1992. As team leader of a four person team, I took responsibility for this independent evaluation to determine how the goals of the grant had been served and in what manner it was useful to modify the grant structure for the following five year period to better serve AID objectives to support private sector growth in AID client countries.

March 1992–May 1992

Evaluation of the Trade and Investment Services project funded by AID's Bureau for Private Enterprise - to assess the impact of the activities and of the institutional abilities of the International Executive Service Corps to manage the project. (Louis Berger, International, Washington D.C.)

January 1992–March 1992

Team leader for Assessment of Feasibility to Establish an Endowment to Sustain the Operations of the Community Development Foundation of

Mozambique. The project was funded by USAID Mozambique through an IQC with Development Associates, Arlington, Virginia.

October 1991–December 1991
Team Leader for evaluation of U.S.A.I.D. $4 million project to assist the Moroccan private producers expand their production and marketing of exportable products. (Louis Berger, International, Washington, D.C.)

August 1991–September 1991
Team leader for evaluation of UNDP/UNIDO project for institutional enhancement of the Pakistan Machine Tool Factory. (International Science and Technology Institute, Washington, D.C.)

January 1991–May 1991
Team leader for thematic evaluation of UNDP high technology R&D institution building projects in China and India. The evaluation included 15 case studies of R&D institutions that had, over time, received $64 million in UNDP assistance, for the purpose of identifying lessons learned with applicability to indigenization, adaptation and diffusion of technology into the productive sector. (International Science and Technology Institute, Washington, D.C.)

August 1990– January 1991
Team leader for design of $12 million USAID Sri Lanka financed "Technology Initiative for the Private Sector" project. This five-year activity is intended to build a link between the private Sri Lankan industry/mining sector and U.S. technology sources, reduce the cost and risk for entrepreneurs to access and acquire technology to modernize the Sri Lankan private productive sector. (International Science and Technology Institute, Washington, D.C.)

November 1988–June 1989

Designed the technical assistance component of the World Bank $125 million Export Industries Loan to Egypt. The activity, to be implemented by the GATT International Trade Center, is intended to encourage growth of private sector export production capacity and marketing of higher value added products in the hard currency markets. (International Trade Center, Geneva) This project was not activated.

April 1988

Evaluated, as member of a team with former AID Deputy Administrator Maurice Williams, the $l.6 billion, six year economic aid package to Pakistan (l98l–l987). (Development Resources, Bethesda, Maryland

January 1988

AID Africa Bureau - Evaluated the Private Enterprise Fund ($6 million). The fund had been in operation for 4 years, managed by the Private Enterprise Office of the Africa Bureau to finance experimental activities of their Missions to strengthen private sector growth in their respective countries. The evaluation was to determine its utility and cost-effectiveness.

August 1987

AID Bureau for Asia and Near East - Review of all Trade and Investment activities funded by the Bureau's 17 Missions, to determine which interventions have shown themselves to be cost-effective and under which circumstances. The study was utilized by the Assistant Administrator at the November 1987 Mission Directors Conference to consider the feasibility of undertaking a new program focus in private sector trade and investment promotion by the l7 Missions. (Study performed through contract with Coopers & Lybrand).

October 1986– November 1986

Consulted with IESC Country Directors, IESC Advisory Councils, and USAID Private Enterprise officers in Sri Lanka, Pakistan, Indonesia, Philippines and Thailand on new IESC programs and proposals (ABLE - joint venture feasibility fund, etc.) to determine applicability of these programs to USAID program goals.

April 1986–May 1986

Performed evaluation of AID/LAC experimental-pilot project "Joint Venture Feasibility Fund." (Honduras, Costa Rica, Guatemala, Haiti) managed by IESC to identify operational constraints, management programs and developed procedures and guidelines for IESC.

February 1986–July 1986

Performed feasibility/design study for AID/ANE of a proposed new activity to assist LDC private companies locate US firms with needed technologies or other complementary resources (Investment and Technology Access Center)

November 1984–April 1985

Advised USAID Thailand in designing a $50 million project to enhance Thailand's science and technology capacity, with special emphasis on Research, Development and Engineering problem solving for its private agro-industry production sector.

October 1984–November 1984

Led two evaluation teams for the AID Bureau for Private Enterprise that examined impact of $2.5 million AID loan to Kenya Commercial Bank and $2.0 million AID loan to Siam Commercial Bank.

August 1984– September 1984

Designed new financial mechanism for U.S. AID India to facilitate joint ventures between U.S. and Indian firms in production related Research and Development.

September 1983–March 1984

AID Bureau for Private Enterprise

 (a) Prepared study entitled "The Feasibility of Local Currency Programming for Private Enterprise Development."

 (b) Member of Project Design Team for India/U.S. Bi-National Foundation for Scientific and Technological Collaboration. Other team members were U.S. Assistant Secretary of Commerce, Bruce Merrifield and former Assistant Secretary of Commerce, Jordan Baruch.

May 1983

AID - Prepared study for U.S. Ambassador to India Harry Barnes entitled *Prospects for a U.S./India Bi-National Foundation.*

October 1982–November 1982

AID – Two-month assignment to U.S. AID New Delhi to assist in design of Social Marketing of Contraceptives project.

April 1982–May 1982

U.S. Department of Interior – Bureau for Territorial Affairs. Designed structure for a newly proposed development bank to serve development finance requirements of U.S. possessions (Virgin Islands, Samoa, Guam), and U.S. Trust Territories.

December 1981

Appropriate Technology International – Examination of means by which ATI might increase its focus on the private sector in developing countries.

September 1980–May 1981

Rivkin Associates – Prepared a long-range development plan for the Trust Territories of the U.S. (Palau) as part of the negotiations of the Compact of Free Association.

Annex 12

Appalachia Project –The Growth of Regulation in the US since 1970

OUR EXPERIENCE DEALT WITH Federal, State, County, and Township jurisdictions as follows:

Pennsylvania Department of Environmental Protection (PADEP). This very powerful State agency had a Cambria County office located in Ebensburg to handle the small stuff and a regional office to do the serious business. Cambria County was initially assigned to the Williamsport office but a reorganization in the 1980s reassigned the county to the Pittsburgh office.

The Federal Department of Housing and Urban Development (HUD/OILSR) was tasked to implement new legislation (1967) dealing with interstate land sales. It created the Office for Interstate Land Sales Registration (OILSR) in 1968. We registered and met the legal requirements of full disclosure for consumer protection in 1971.

Pennsylvania Department of Parks was an important agency for us since we bordered Prince Gallitzin Park. The Department had a strong interest in protecting the watershed that flowed into Glendale Lake, the 6000 acre lake built by Pennsylvania in 1961 and located inside the park.

The two Townships (Chest and White) in which we were located had jurisdiction of all land subdivision approvals.

The Cambria County Government played an increasing role over time in the regulatory framework affecting our project. The relevant departments include the Planning Commission, the Property Tax Assessment Office, and later in 2000, the on-site sewage permitting unit.

The Pennsylvania Public Utility Commission (PAPUC) regulated all aspects of our construction, operation, rate setting, and customer rights dealing with the Water and Sewer companies beginning with their incorporation in 1973.

USDA Soil Conservation Service managed the subsidy land bank programs in 1967 but, by the 1990s, was given jurisdiction for permit issuance for earth disturbances greater than about ½ acre.

The Pennsylvania Fish Commission: all waterways in Pennsylvania belong to the State. Any stream crossing requires a permit from them. It also issues fishing licenses and monitor fishing practices.

Environmental Protection Agency (EPA). Most regulatory tasks covering the water and sewer companies were handled by the PADEP but in the later years, some jurisdictional issues, mostly about drinking water testing, were handled directly by EPA's office in Philadelphia

Those were the actors. With many of these organizations we found it necessary to go to the expense of retaining either a licensed engineer or an attorney, often both. Indeed, some agencies will not talk directly to the operator without counsel.

Let's start at the **County** level. When I recorded the deed for the 900 acres of woodland in 1970, the county assessor used the new purchase price to immediately increase the property valuation. I walked into the Assessor's office accompanied by the lawyer who had done the closing, showed the assessor my plans to develop the property, together with a general plan of development on a sheet of paper, told the assessor I could not afford the new carrying costs and promised that, once we subdivide and make a lot sale, there would be no appeal to him when he assessed the subdivided lot we had sold at our sales price. The assessor immediately reversed his reassessment entry and our property tax for unsold land remained at the pre-purchased assessment level. "I had no way of knowing what your plans were" he said, and apologized for the inconvenience to me.

PRINCE GALLITZIN STATE PARK

Being located next to, and also adjoining this magnificent public recreation area with its many facilities, particularly Glendale Lake, was a very large benefit for our enterprise. Traffic flow for sales would be increased. It also reduced the number of recreational facilities we needed to construct on site. We would merely supplement those that existed in the park. I wanted to see whether the park superintendent would have any problems with our venture on his doorstep.

It was like pushing on an open door. The entire park system was in growth mode. It turned out that a professor of forestry at Penn State named Maurice Goddard thought the State should take lands that had been stripped for coal during World War II and subsequently acquired by the Counties due to non-payment of taxes, and convert them into State Parks. His goal was to build a State Park within 25 miles of every resident. Prince Gallitzin Park was such an enterprise. The Governor made him Director of the Park System and gave him considerable support to make that happen.

When he built the lake at PG Park, the locals made a land grab to build a dense 1500-acre resort community at the park's doorstep. Unfortunately, all that land drained into the newly built lake. When Goddard learned of this he blocked their effort. He was heavily criticized by the locals for impeding economic development. Our lands drained below the breast of the dam, no threat to his new lake. Consequently the entire park bureaucracy was happy to support my efforts.

We needed to erect a sign inside the park at the intersection of the park road and our access road so that people could find us. Would he allow us to do that? I went to Harrisburg and Goddard's deputy, Conrad Lickel, received me. I asked for a letter to permit me to place the sign on parkland at the intersection. He told me to just do it. The Park will not object but a letter is something he was not authorized to provide. The lawyers would not let him. He pointed out that the intersection did have Parklands, but also land on the highway right of way that was under the State Highway Administration, and also land on the Township Road right of way that was the access road to our Resort. Who knew where they cornered, or intersected? No one would challenge me, he assured me.

And, true enough, for 30 years we maintained that sign along the rights of way and the park. It served us well. In 2005 a newly appointed park superintendent happened by and raised a question about this very sign. We had some difficulty prevailing but we did prevail.

Pennsylvania Department of Environmental Protection

Things were not always that easy, even in 1970. After having talked things through with the County Planning Commission and both Township's Board of Supervisors, and having secured White Township's subdivision approval for the first section of lots, I marched myself down to the local DEP office, (no lawyers this time) introduced myself and said I planned to start a development, wanted to discuss it with them and get their advice and blessings. The local in charge gave me a cold look and told me to explain. I had told him I needed to build a sales office out of which to operate. Even though we would eventually install a centralized system with a sewage treatment plant, I needed this office now and wanted a septic permit for it. It would be located in Chest Township, a different township from where the first subdivision would be located. When I got done he began raising all sorts of objections, all of them procedural. The phrase "Can't do it!" was very much in play. Design the entire development, apply for approval of the central sewage system and then we'll talk further. After we left, this chap decided to cite us and stopped us from proceeding.

A hearing was scheduled at the State College Court House. I had to be there with our lawyer, who drove from Harrisburg. DEP summoned the Chest Township Supervisors to the Hearing. At the Hearing this public servant declared that "he had come to know about these plans...." never mentioning that I had come to his office to ask his help.

The Hearing turned negative for him when he asked the Chairman of the Chest Township Board of Supervisors whether he had any objection to our proposed action and the reply was, "It don't look like a problem to me!" We got our permit by agreeing to put a meter on the septic system to assure it did not overload. Our lawyer called that clause the face saving device for DEP. Cost for legal services? $500 in 1970 dollars.

But our relations with DEP were not always negative, particularly when we began to deal with the regional offices. They seemed to be staffed with more thoughtful and better skilled personnel and acted more professionally. In 1973, when our engineers submitted permit applications to Williamsport for the central sewer system and the central water system, their responses were prompt and reasonable; their attitude helpful. Only once did a lower level person from Williamsport behave unreasonably at the time when we needed another well to be approved. In this instance, we were lucky. That issue was resolved when jurisdiction for Cambria County shifted to the Pittsburgh office. We developed excellent relations with that office over the years. Somehow, I always had the impression that the DEP regional office staff tried to be professional and constructive to get their job done with minimum disruption to the operators.

Unfortunately, that was not the case with respect to the Cambria County PADEP staff. One truly outrageous incident occurred in 2007, about a year before I sold the water and sewer companies to the local municipal authority. It represented a flagrant abuse of authority vested in that office.

After the World Trade Center attack on 9/11/2001, one of the DEP employees from the Williamsport office encouraged me to apply to DEP for a grant to explore ways in which water could be lifted out of our ground water wells to our storage tank in the event we experienced an electric power outage of long duration. Our water table is only 60 feet below the surface at the well site. It would need a form of power generation, probably wind, to lift the water to the well head and then overcome another 400 feet of head pressure to reach the storage tank from whence it would gravity flow into the system. It was thought that some non-traditional power generation method might work to provide a back-up system for our community. I applied and was approved for a grant of $150,000. It made all the local papers.

We began to explore wind power. My small aircraft flying helped me locate a wind channel that would be adequate to generate the required power but we discovered that the channel was somewhat distant from the well location. If an aquifer could be found near the wind channel, the problem would be solved.

I called a local well driller to begin prospecting for an aquifer that would be close to the wind channel. He informed me that new regulations (the Well Head Protection Program) had been instituted and now required a DEP permit before one could begin to drill. In the past, we were able to do exploratory drilling and then applied for a permit after we found a good water source. Now the system had been turned on its head.

I called the local DEP staff and they came out to meet with me. They explained the program, informed me I would first have to hire a hydrologist to find a suitable drill site, then apply to DEP for a permit to drill based on his report. The DEP application fee plus the hydrologist would cost about $1,200 per site. I pointed out that we are just prospecting to determine if we could find an aquifer but he was adamant; no drilling could take place without a permit. I then asked if every person who wishes to drill a well has to go through this procedure. He replied that these requirements apply only to public water suppliers and not individuals. I suggested that there is a simple solution. I would drill these test wells as an individual, thereby conserving the Pennsylvania grant funds for later needs. When my personally directed drilling efforts yielded a well, then we would apply for a permit and comply with all the new regulations. He got very angry and told me that "if I try a stunt like that" he would see to it that I never get a permit for the well.

After giving the matter some thought, I decided to cancel the grant and returned the unspent funds to DEP. The recent practice instituted by Pennsylvania to charge high fees for permits and also to authorize the local offices to levy fines has turned these offices into "profit centers". This is also true of the Soil Conservation Service. It is a big mistake to do this. Bureaucrats should consider themselves "public servants" and should be problem solvers. They now tend to behave differently because they are incentivized this way.

HUD/OILSR

The history of interstate land sales regulation may also serve to be informative. In the 1960s, many small-scale entrepreneurs engaged in subdividing land. More often than not they were shysters. The newspapers carried many stories reporting outrageous sales practices by fly-by-night outfits that would prey on the ignorance of the public. Around Washington DC there were many such operations and they used high-pressure sales tactics to intimidate potential buyers, giving them no out after signing an agreement. Often they sold off-site, going house to house and making deals without the buyer ever having seen the land. There were reports of land salesmen selling Florida swampland or Arizona desert lots, using false photos. Widows were bilked of their life savings.

In 1968 Congress passed the Interstate Land Sales Disclosure Act, to force these developments to give full disclosure to the buyers and to provide buyers with a seven-day rescission right. Implementation was given to the Department of Housing and Urban Development (HUD-OILSR). When we registered our resort with them, our attorney helped us put together a four-page disclosure statement called a Property Report, which all buyers had to read before signing any purchase contract. The disclosure statement had to be submitted to OILSR as a record. Any complaints after the sale would allow HUD to impose serious penalties on us. It seemed to work well. My information was, that by 1972 most of the land sales abuses had been curbed. Then came the arrival of George K. Bernstein in 1973 to serve as the new Administrator of OILSR.

New regulations were put in place and the Property Report was expanded to 28 pages. Imagine reading such a legalistic and lengthy document on your visit to buy a lot. The filings had to be prepared by an attorney. In addition, a very high filing fee was imposed by OILSR. The document also had to be periodically updated and an annual fee paid to keep the filing alive. Only one property owner has ever filed a complaint against us with OILSR. The father and his daughter had bought two adjoining lots in 1974. They wanted to build immediately but the sewer lines had not been extended to their properties. We had to extend their lines to avoid hearings and more legal fees. It was settled in about 6 months. The daughter became a member of the POA Board and was one of the most active and useful property owners we had during the project's early years.

There was nothing wrong with the objective of the legislation, nor the idea of full disclosure. It seemed to me, though that the result was not only full employment for attorneys but also another blow to the viability of small-scale enterprise in this sector of the economy. At this time, the OILSR has been cut loose from HUD and, as a result of the Dodd-Frank bill is part of the consumer protection office created by that new legislation. Even though Glendale Yearound is still maintaining its registration, my guess is that not many small-scale resort land sales enterprises have survived. The resort industry is now dominated by the Marriotts, the Hiltons, and the Webbs.

PENNSYLVANIA PUBLIC UTILITY COMMISSION

For our purposes the operation of the Public Utility Commission (PAPUC) is the most relevant of the regulatory agencies. They are regulating monopolies. Our experience with them suggests a number of problems.

The Harrisburg lawyers love the PAPUC. The work is highly remunerative if you know what you are doing. Most lawyers who specialize in utility work cut their baby teeth after graduating law school by working on the legal staff of the PUC. That experience gives them the insights they need later in private practice to prepare rate filings and to negotiate effectively for their clients. (This oddity is also true at the Federal level with respect to the SEC, the FCC, and many other regulatory bodies.)

PAPUC procedures are designed to deal with large statewide or multistate utilities like the power companies or the phone companies. Their filings affect more consumers and are more likely to receive attention from the press. For those reasons and, since the PUC's expenses are met by an annual assessment based on the total revenue collected by all utilities, these companies are more important to the PUC. From time to time there is an expose in the Press about golf vacations taken by PUC Commissioners paid for by large utilities. There are a few short cuts that have been set up to apply to smaller utilities, but they are not significant because the law requires all utilities to be treated alike and for all customers to enjoy the same rights and protections.

There is the Office of the Consumer Advocate. This office involves itself in all rate filings and likes to claim in press releases at the end of the utility rate filing process that it saved the consumer from paying what the company had initially requested. Therefore, company rate filings are generally inflated to allow for a cut back and thus provide the basis for this self serving, self congratulatory press release.

Formal hearings are built into the procedures to allow the customers to have input to the deliberations of the PUC and to critique the staff work. These hearings always require that the utility company have legal representation. There is a judge who receives formal testimony. The focus on public disclosure is so stringent that hearings are required even if the number of customers is minimal, and the written objections are only one or two. The procedure to complete the review often runs into years from the date of filing until a decision is handed down.

It is worth noting that Public (Municipal) Authorities that operate utilities in Pennsylvania are exempt from PUC jurisdiction and can set their rates as they will. These authorities are also exempt from paying federal and state taxes on their revenues and earnings. That does not make for a level playing field. In fact, my best moment came when we sold our two utilities to the local Authority in 2008. We had to secure PAPUC approval to make the sale. A few customers objected and we spent about $140,000 in legal fees to gain the needed approval, all of that money paid out of the utility companies assets. Essentially, I was able to pass these costs on to the consumer. The PUC was well aware of this but was constrained by its procedures to impede the actions of the malcontents even though it would have served the interests of the other customers. But once the sale was made, no further protection was afforded to these same customers, including the malcontents, by the PUC or any other entity.

My experience suggests that the PUC regulatory functions are essential to balancing the interests of the customer with the enterprise, but the devil is in the details. In Pennsylvania, there is need to reform the system to bring it back to its original mandate and apply some common sense to implementation of its rules.

ANNEX 13

APPALACHIA PROJECT – LETTER TO PITTSBURGH, PENNSYLVANIA TV STATION KDKA IN RESPONSE TO THEIR PROGRAM OF SEPTEMBER 16, 1979, ATTACKING GLENDALE YEAROUND

September 23, 1979

Mr. Jonathan Hayes, Vice-President and General Manager
KDKA TV
1 Gateway Center
Pittsburgh, PA 15222

Dear Mr. Hayes:

I write to express my concern at the so-called investigative report broadcast on KDKA Channel 2 Pittsburgh at 6:45 p.m. Monday, September 16. The program is called "Two on Your Side." I believe the program was also carried on KDKA radio.

The program unfairly disparaged our vacationland development, Glendale Yearound, which adjoins Prince Gallitzin State Park, by implying that our marketing program misleads the public.

In fact, it was your presentation of the facts which now misleads the public and has caused serious damage to the reputation for honesty and fairness that our company has built over the past ten years. The description of our invitation letters and incentive program to encourage Pittsburgh residents to visit our project was taken totally out of context, was not compared with the normal practices of our industry or the marketing practices of nationally known organizations such as the Readers Digest, the Book of the Month Club, or indeed your own parent company, the Westinghouse Corporation, which coincidentally, also controls and operates Treasure Lake, a vacation land development, located only 35 miles from our property, and is our main competitor.

If your investigative reporter really wanted to help the consumer evaluate our marketing program, she could have explained that the entire industry uses some form of incentive to induce prospective purchasers to visit their property. Land cannot be carried around in display cases by salespersons, from door to door like Fuller Brushes. The proverbial Mountain cannot go to Mohammed. Therefore, the salesperson must persuade MOHAMMED TO VISIT THE MOUNTAIN.

In the case of vacation land located some distance from the prospective buyers, the industry attempts to reduce the cost of his travel by offering incentives or compensation. Sometimes, to add to the fun and to stimulate excitement and enjoyment, an element of chance is injected and a few lucky prospects win even larger prizes than those ordinarily given to all who visit the property.

Everyone is given something for visiting Glendale Yearound and the minimum fair market value of any gifts offered under our program is $10, with most gifts in the $30 to $40 range. To single out our development, disparage the fair market value of the gifts we offer, and to imply that this is a deceptive and misleading practice unique to Glendale Yearound, is grossly unfair when similar incentive programs have been commonly offered by at least a dozen other developments in the Pittsburgh area including our neighboring development, Treasure Lake, controlled and operated by a Westinghouse Corporation subsidiary.

I note that your station broadcasts advertisements for the MacDonalds food chain's "Diamond Hunt" program, which has basically the same concept as our prize award program. May I ask why you react critically to the practice of a company that does not advertise on your station, and are uncritical of similar "gimmicks" by a company that has engaged you to carry their advertising?

On September 17th, the same program carried a highly critical and unbalanced report on our project, alleging that the risk to the buyer was too great to warrant purchase when they visit our project. No effort was made to evaluate the merits of our offering in the context of the available choices to the buyer. If a Pittsburgh consumer wants to acquire a parcel of land in a subdivision, what are his choices? Does our project offer a better or an inferior deal to other projects in the area? Are our prices higher or lower? Since all purchases, including Westinghouse products, entail some risk to the buyer, are the risks we pose to our purchasers greater or smaller compared with his other choices? And how do our 600 property owners evaluate their purchase? None of these questions were examined. Yet, the advice offered to your viewers was to be wary and not to buy when they visit our project.

The most sinister aspect of your report has to do with the selection of Glendale Yearound as the subject for your story. We are the closest competitor to one of the land developments controlled by a Westinghouse subsidiary. Your program has served your parent company by reducing the effectiveness of our competition to Westinghouse's own marketing effort. The Westinghouse Corporation, a mammoth "big business", has dressed itself in the guise of a Sir Galahad, and implied to the public that it is slaying a twenty-five ton dragon. In fact, it appears to have engaged in an unfair business practice by using its dominant position in the Pittsburgh area public information industry to harm a small business that is successfully competing with Treasure Lake by offering the public a valuable product at a fair price.

Unlike Treasure Lake, our development has never faced bankruptcy or foreclosure. No property owner has ever filed suit in court against us and no court action has ever been filed against us by any regulatory agency of the Commonwealth of Pennsylvania or the Federal Government. The same cannot be said about Treasure Lake.

Glendale Yearound is managed by the same people today that began the development in 1970. A professional review of our financial statements will disclose that no dividends have ever been paid to the shareholders and that the funds generated from sales have been used to build the promised facilities. It is particularly disconcerting to those who manage a business in a fair and equitable manner and fulfill their obligations to the buyer to find themselves unjustly maligned in the public media by a person bent on making a reputation for herself at any cost to others.

It would therefore appear that your presentation was biased, not only because your parent company has an interest in a competing development, but also because your program, "Two on Your Side", is designed to enhance KDKA's public image as a protector of the consumers interest, in order to imply added credibility to the paid advertising carried on your station. And you do this by making unwarranted attacks on companies that are not advertisers on your station.

To partially rectify the damage you have caused to us I ask that you immediately take the following action:

(1) Your investigative reporter should read this letter, in its entirety at the earliest moment on the same programs, so that the listening and viewing public has an opportunity to be informed of our views on this matter. In the background the viewer should be able to see the photographs you took of our clubhouse and swimming pool complex.

(2) You should make a public retraction, both on station KDKA TV and in writing to me, for your misleading presentation that implied that Glendale Yearound was perpetrating a unique deceptive marketing practice on the public and that the gifts offered by us, in the words of your reporter, "were practically worthless". In fact, the fair market value of our gifts to the user range from $10 to $5,000.

You should also apologize publicly for having drawn unwarranted conclusions about the advisability of purchasing land at Glendale Yearound from a superficial and biased examination of the facts. I have enclosed, as Attachment A to this letter, a preliminary analysis made by me of the factually erroneous statements made by your reporter to substantiate this demand.

(3) You should provide me with a copy of all unedited filming and recording made of Prince Gallitzin Park and our development by your camera crew, as well as a copy of the edited version of material pertaining to our

development as broadcast on KDKA, so that we may study it to determine what action to take to protect our rights.

Failing your immediate action as requested above, I shall demand that this letter be placed into KDKA's Public File. I shall then raise this matter with the Federal Communication Commission, The Federal Trade Commission and the Anti-Trust Division of the U. S. Department of Justice.

Sincerely yours,

Ludwig Rudel
President
The Glendale Corporation

Enclosure – Attachment A

cc: Mr. Tony Hirsh, V.P. and General Manager KDKA Radio
William Danforth, President, Westinghouse Corporation

Attachment A

September 23, 1979
Mr. Jonathan Hayes

Partial Listing of Erroneous or Misleading Statements Made on KDKA TV Regarding Glendale Yearound

A. Statements made concerning which the reporter was in possession of facts to the contrary.

I. "600 land parcels have been sold in the last eight years but, as of the first of this year, only 50 homes and mobile homes have been built or installed so most of the lots are vacant and uninhabited".

Response – The reporter knew that 243 of the approximately 600 land parcels sold were campsites. The vast majority of these sold campsites have been improved by the owners and are extensively used by them. On September 21, there were II7 campers and/or trailers located on these campsites. Approximately the same number would have been located on campsites at Glendale Yearound on September 14; the date the reporter toured Glendale Yearound.

2. Financing Arrangements – "No local bank would finance the vacant land. One bank board member told me that the deal is so speculative that the bank would not touch it".

Response - Paragraph 5 of the property report indicates that the Laurel National Bank of Ebensburg, Pa. has provided financing for the project. In fact, that bank began financing the project in 1971 with a $40,000 line of credit, which was subsequently increased in succeeding years to the present mortgage level of $300,000 as improvements at Glendale Yearound were completed. First Pa. Bank has provided financing to purchasers of lots at Glendale Yearound. That arrangement was made by us after local banks indicated that they could not accept the volume of business which we would generate. In fact, many local banks and credit unions have provided financing to purchasers of lots at Glendale Yearound at the purchasers individual request when these purchasers were regular bank customers. Examples of this are the Dale National Bank of Johnstown, Pa. and the Laurel National Bank of Ebensburg, Pa.

3. In discussing the sewer and water systems, the reporter stated "... but neither system is complete".

Response - Both water and sewer systems are operational. Homes and mobile homes located on the property are connected to sewage collectors which run to the treatment plant and the treatment plant is operational. The water system enjoys the same status. The wells are complete, and feed into a 200,000-gallon storage tank that supplies the distribution system. Additional water distribution lines and sewer collector extensions must still be constructed. Your camera crew took pictures of recently purchased pipe and manholes which are now being installed by our construction crew to complete the system. Water distribution and sewer collector lines generally are not built until the property has been sold and demand for hookup has materialized. To do otherwise would unfairly penalize the customers of the water and sewer companies who would then experience rate increases to meet the cost of maintaining unutilized lines.

B. Misleading Statements, Negligent Reporting and Erroneous Conclusions

1. "In other words, there are no funds guaranteeing that these facilities will ever be completed. . . So all you have is the developer's promise to finish many of the community's facilities."

 - The reporter knew that the cost of the completed recreational facilities (currently estimated at $350,000.) overwhelmingly exceeds the cost of the tennis court, amphitheatre and pond (currently estimated at $40,000.) which still remains to be completed. This is also true of the sewer and water systems and the road system. Yet, the reporter implied that enormous risks accrued to the purchaser because of incomplete facilities.

2. Resale of Property - the reporter alleged that it would be nearly impossible for a property to be resold at a fair market price by a purchaser in competition with the developer. In fact, at least 17 lots have been resold in competition with the developer by property owners, and in many cases, with the assistance of the developer.

3. Property Report - "Some prospective buyers were told they could not have anything in writing unless they made a deposit. According to the government agency, that practice is illegal."

Response - The property report is given to all prospective buyers when they tour Glendale Yearound before they sign an agreement to purchase. Property reports (which cost approximately $1.00 each to print) are returned to us if visitors to Glendale Yearound choose not to purchase, but the report is made available to them to read before they depart and is explained to them in detail. On those occasions, when visitors who have not purchased property insist that they wish to take the property report with them we have accommodated their request although we are not required to do so. It should be noted that a prospective purchaser who takes a report with him and subsequently returns to make a purchase has waived his right of rescission. On the other hand, anyone who signs a purchase agreement and pays a deposit to us at the time he receives his property report has the right to rescind that agreement during the next three days.

The practice described above is not an illegal practice.

4. Prejudicial Language Concerning Property Report - "If you read this report carefully you will find enough loopholes to raise some questions about the purchase of property."

Response - We know of no "loopholes" in the property report. The report was prepared in accordance with the requirements of OILSR and was reviewed by them. The statements contained therein are considered to be a satisfactory explanation of those conditions at Glendale Yearound that are relevant to a prospective purchaser.

INDEX

Made in the USA
Middletown, DE
29 May 2015